Wander the Rainbow

A true story of a living liver donation, an epic journey around the world, and a gay man's search for himself

David Jedeikin

Holistic Ideas Press
www.wandertherainbow.com
www.holisticideas.com/press

Grateful acknowledgement is made for the use of an excerpt from *The Art of Travel* by Alain de Botton, Copyright © 2002, reprinted by permission from Random House, Inc., and Penguin Books (UK) Ltd.

Published in the United States by Holistic Ideas Press, an imprint of Holistic Ideas, Inc., San Francisco, California
www.wandertherainbow.com
www.holisticideas.com/press
Printed in the United States of America

ISBN-13: 978-0-9827059-0-2
ISBN-10: 0982705905

Author's Note

It's all the same, said Jon Bon Jovi, only the names are changed. So too with this book, which recounts what went on before and during this sprawling journey. Inevitably, though, a few liberties have been taken, names changed and events rearranged. Such are the vagaries of storytelling and privacy protection.

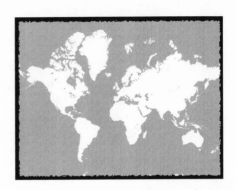

Contents

Origins	*Boston & San Francisco*	**1**
Rocky Mountain High	*Denver*	**8**
Motherland	*Montréal*	**13**
Isle to Isle	*London & Dublin*	**16**
Flanders to Funsterdam	*Bruges & Amsterdam*	**27**
La Belle et le Bad Boy	*Paris & Nice*	**35**
Il Paese Eterno	*Venice, Florence & Rome*	**45**
Habsburgs, Ghosts & Cabarets	*Vienna, Prague & Berlin*	**58**
Legacy of the Kievan Rus	*Moscow & Saint Petersburg*	**73**
Forefathers & Friends	*Riga & Copenhagen*	**82**
The Far Side of the World	*Cape Town*	**92**
Nabatean Kingdom	*Jordan*	**107**
Return to Zion	*Israel*	**116**
Riddle of the Sphinx	*Cairo*	**133**
Emir's Playground	*Dubai*	**144**
The Beach	*Goa*	**153**
Children of Kings	*Jaipur, Udaipur & Delhi*	**163**
Electric City	*Tokyo*	**178**
Empire of Sun & Snow	*Kyoto & Hakuba*	**185**

Yesterday & Tomorrow	*Shanghai*	**191**
Alley, Palace, Wall	*Beijing*	**199**
City on a Hill	*Hong Kong*	**208**
(The Other) City of Angels	*Bangkok*	**213**
Dominion of the Khmer	*Siem Reap & Angkor*	**219**
The Beach, Redux	*Koh Phangan*	**225**
Beyond the Straitjacket	*Singapore*	**233**
Heavenly Isle	*Bali*	**239**
Over the Rainbow	*Nimbin, Byron Bay & Sydney*	**247**
Adventures in Middle Earth	*New Zealand*	**259**
South American Way	*Santiago & Valparaíso*	**274**
Porteños y Cataratas	*Buenos Aires & Iguazú*	**281**
Old Mountain	*Lima, Cusco & Machu Picchu*	**291**
Home	*Miami & Montréal*	**302**

To Jackson, Lola, Sam, Jacob & Layla:
The next generation of world travelers.

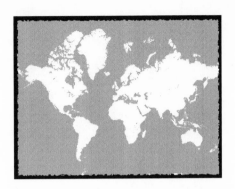

Origins
Boston & San Francisco

*I*t's my very last morning with a liver in one piece.

Bradley, my partner of almost three years, stirs next to me in bed in the predawn darkness. His body is warm—too warm with a mild fever. His normally pinkish, pale skin is jaundiced and sallow, contrasting strangely with his deep brown eyes and dyed black hair. It may be five in the morning but it's time for us to get up—though if all goes well we won't be conscious for too long.

"How you doing, sweetie?" I ask him that a lot. More than most people would deem necessary—but then, Bradley isn't most people.

"Okay, I guess," he replies, kissing me good morning. *Par for the course,* I inwardly sigh. Even on what's probably the biggest day of his life he projects bland neutrality. But I know what lies deeper: a soulful depth, a warm intensity that's entranced me, kept me close, even in moments of conflict or doubt that haunt the best relationships. We're eleven years apart in age and in some respects come from different galaxies, but on a fundamental level we connect. And on another level, too: even in this condition his lanky, broad frame stirs my passions. I know he feels the same about me.

Knock knock. "Boys, we'd better get a move on," I hear my mother's voice through the white hardwood door. My parents have driven the five hours south to Boston specially for this day. In the cozy living room of my South End apartment my father sits in a plushy red-leather armchair watching the Weather Channel.

"It's going to be nice. Almost sixty degrees," he says, though the statement is superfluous: the brightening skies say it all. Besides, none of us plans on spending much time outdoors.

"Come Lee, we have to leave." My mother, ever the organizer. He gets up with a creak—he's recovering from a number of surgeries of his own, on his back and knee. We thunk-thunk down my building's squeaky wooden stairway and emerge into the still morning. Bradley fusses with luggage as my parents pile into his aging plum-colored Infiniti. We hum down a deserted Storrow Drive, the stately brick townhomes of Back Bay glowing orange in the morning sun. To our left the Charles River Basin shimmers, its surface glassy and calm.

At Massachusetts General Hospital we rendezvous with Bradley's parents—graying, heavyset, always primly attired. Appropriate for a boy who used to help pick out his mother's dresses. George and Mary are smiles and friendliness as always, but I sense a bit of nerves. His mother, from whom Bradley gets his square-jawed face and dark hair, talks a mile a minute—though she's an intelligent woman and her observations are apt. She's got a medical background and explains to my slightly befuddled father how it's set to go down.

"They start with David then move on to Bradley," she says. "But Bradley's operation's going to go a lot longer. About seven or eight hours."

We're in the reception area of the transplant surgery room, where a chatty African-American nurse hands us a number. *Like a deli*, I chuckle inwardly, noting the tear-off ticketing roll. I'm not nervous— at least not overtly. I've researched and contemplated and ruminated about this moment for months. Now it all moves forward, full speed ahead.

I'm the first to be seen by the anesthesiologist, a slim, dark-haired woman with a cool, rote demeanor. After a hurried goodbye to everyone I hear the words "I'm going to give you a little sedation." After that, lights out. I don't even make it long enough to hear the countdown.

Biliary atresia is extremely rare. Bradley was born with it, emerging from the womb without a bile duct. Over the years of our relationship I learned a lot about this seemingly mundane yet crucial bit of tubing: it connects the liver to the small intestine, enabling food to be digested. At one month of age Bradley's skin turned brown and he nearly died. Only a then-pioneering emergency procedure, developed in Japan, saved him from becoming an infant-mortality statistic. But jury-rigged plumbing inevitably calls for a permanent fix, and in cases like his that means a liver transplant. He made it longer than anyone imagined without one. When he graduated high school his mother wrote to thank the doctor who'd saved him as a baby—"did a Hail Mary," she termed it. It was only a couple of years into our relationship that his sporadic health problems became acute. He needed a liver soon.

Cadaveric livers are near-impossible to come by these days, but there was hope in a new procedure—living donation. The liver is the only organ in the human body (other than skin) that regenerates, making it possible to chop a healthy liver in two and have it grow to full size in both donor and recipient, like amoeba in biology class. Family members across the country began lining up to be tested…only to discover they didn't match for one reason or another. After months of watching this state of affairs, I agreed to undergo the same testing—and, amazingly, was declared the only match around.

I'll be honest: I didn't want to do it. It's a four-hour operation, a major incision, a big scar. Precisely timed with procedures on the recipient, living liver donation is the moon shoot of surgeries. But in interviewing other donors—including those who endured complications—I came to realize that this was a risk I was ready to take. I wasn't going to let my lover die on me if I could help.

That said, my other niggling worry was our future together. A lifetime of illness breeds caution, rootedness—and endless frustration. Bradley hails from a family who've lived for generations in New England. As a pediatric patient he's been told his whole life the things he could not do—and as the only child of doting, well-to-do Boston-area parents he'd skirted many of the rites of young-adult independence. From the day we met he was a curious creation, a man-child who's had to look death in the face but never finished college.

Sometimes he would get reckless, partying with his youthful peers, occasionally binge drinking and taking days to recover. Up until the surgery my impression of him was of one in limbo. Waiting for an absolution, a life-giving change, a second chance. I hoped this would be it.

I awaken in intensive care, my stomach stiff but in surprisingly little pain. I'm not sure where Bradley is or how he's doing. My only discomfort comes from the tube in my mouth going down my throat; I max out my morphine drip to blur that sensation but my body's not having it: soon my gag reflex kicks in and I puke it up.

"It's okay," the nurse says as she rushes in to clean me up. "That's how some patients tell us they're done with it."

Just then the two mothers walk in. Bradley's doing fine, though his surgery was longer and more complex than they'd anticipated. Recovery for him will be slow. I'm out of the hospital in three days and he follows not too long after. I'm up and walking within a few days, he within a few weeks. His skin is flushed and rosy once more and his liver numbers are stellar. By the end of the summer we're mostly back to normal.

Not so our future together: like a couple thinking a baby will make everything right, I fancied this event papering over the chasms between us. My life lay in a different sort of limbo, a lingering byproduct of the dot-com crash earlier in the decade: a home and boyfriend in Boston, and a software consulting job that tossed me around the American expanse like seeds off a farmer's hand. I wanted out of this craziness once and for all—and Bradley did as well. Our relationship had become de facto long-distance, with endless arrival delays at Logan Airport our typical Friday night ritual.

California offered an answer: although there were tech jobs closer to home, to be sure, all the best work for my subspecialty lay across the continent. San Francisco was one former hometown and a coterie of friends out there worked hard to lure me back. Bradley was at first unsure—he worried about losing his health insurance and about a reprise of his last out-of-town foray: incipient illness saw his schooling in a Midwestern college town abruptly cut short. As the months passed, however, and he grew stronger, he warmed to the idea of life on the other coast. He wanted to return to school and the notion of doing it out there seemed appealing. *Okay, then.* I put my Boston place up for sale and began planning our next steps, a shared life in a new town.

Then it all went up in flames.

A preliminary scouting trip west proved the career possibilities real...but also turned Bradley's mind around. He embroiled himself in a bitter fight with an old friend of mine. *Oh, melodrama.* I didn't think much of it but Bradley did: in a series of ever-degenerating squabbles our own relationship began to founder. When my condo back home finally did sell he panicked, did an about-face, announced he wouldn't be joining me on my move west. Not long after, he jumped into a relationship with someone else.

Four years—the longest I'd ever been coupled. Half my thirties. I packed up my life and headed off alone into the western sky, Elphaba-like from *Wicked,* to start everything anew.

Bradley and I had talked of traveling overseas, but health and timing precluded such ambitions. For me this was nothing new: immigration and limited finances had confined me to North America my entire adult life. I could find my way around airline hubs like Chicago O'Hare airport blindfolded (best burritos: terminal 3 food court), but knew little of the world beyond: the museums of Paris, the traffic in Mumbai, the beaches of Thailand, the ruins of Machu Picchu and Angkor Wat...all little more than abstractions, places other people see and explore.

It wasn't always so, at least not for my forebears: in the early twentieth century two different sets of great-grandparents left their homelands in the Russian Pale of Settlement for the New World. A generation later my father's parents eloped to the Far East where they lived opulent lifestyles in the shadow of a World War. And just one generation ago my mother moved two continents and five thousand miles to marry a man she'd met only once. As a boy, a National

Geographic map hung above my bed; I would sleep and wake beneath the semicolon-shaped islands of New Zealand and the purple-blue depths of Antarctica's Weddell Sea.

I may have suppressed it, but wanderlust runs in my blood.

The old/new hometown, meanwhile, failed to deliver a fresh start. Although the professional side of things went well, the personal grew worse: lingering fallout from the fight between Bradley and my friend Steve continued. Steve grew angry at me too, our own efforts to work through emotional turmoil culminating in a nasty fight. *I want to run away again.* Really away. Right about then I spotted another article about round-the-world journeys, this one in the *New York Times*.

I must admit, I've never been big on "the healing powers of travel." In my youth this often seemed to mean well-off kids slumming it in youth hostels around Europe, mistaking shots of Ouzo in Corfu for an enlarged outlook on life. And I hated squalor: *Generation X* author Douglas Coupland's "Sheraton Enzyme," which supposedly kicks in during the later-twenties, for me kicked in at age five. Dirty bathrooms and crowded dorms were never my thing. Nor was my family, past explorations notwithstanding, all that inclined or financially able to take grand journeys. And we weren't the campervan or trips-to-Africa-to-build-schools sort of clan either.

But now everything's changed. I'm through the looking-glass. Only a very few can claim to have led an extraordinary life; mine feels more like an improbable one. Addressing its turmoil calls for something audacious, something I never would have otherwise considered in ten million zillion years.

Don't just go away. *Go everywhere.*

This first impulse is followed closely by a second.

Come on. That's fucking crazy.

In addition to the obvious reasons—I'm too old, I have practically zero overseas travel experience, I hanker for comfort—there's the deeper question: *what will a journey like this accomplish?*

I'm not sure yet. On one level, maybe it'll help me forget, drown out my angst in a sea of new experiences. More profoundly, maybe it'll help me answer the question: *why does this keep happening?* Oh sure, having your lover break up with you and hop into another relationship after you've donated sixty-five percent of your liver to him might seem unique…but the pattern isn't. In every one of the places I've called home since striking out from my birthplace it's been the same cycle, again and again: anticipation, hope, optimism, a new circle of friends, a new job, sometimes a new mate. And then…disappointment. Discord. Heartbreak. And the cycle begins anew.

Travel may not be the answer, but at least it grants a different approach to the question. Perhaps this ultimate form of nomadism will cure me of this uneasy wanderlust that's plagued me my entire adult life, a rootlessness all too familiar to the American professional class. Up front I decide this will not be a voyage of asceticism, of self-denial. Perhaps that's a reaction to a closeted youth that went on longer than it should, but I've never found I garnered much insight from asceticism—another reason I think purity pledges are bullshit. Instead, my journey will be the opposite. Not the deranged antithesis of restraint, overindulgence. But rather a kaleidoscope, a chromatic dazzle, a Dorothy-stepping into Munchkinland Technicolor adventure.

I sit down and do some math—the genesis of so many things— and discover I can do this not in luxury but with a modicum of style. "Flashpacking," the British call it. I'd just been granted U.S. citizenship, a tether for some but in practical fact a get-out-of-jail-free card for the incipient national—it's easier, as a citizen, to leave the country and return after a long trip. The pile of frequent flyer miles I'd been amassing for Bradley and me to use will now finally be spent. Seven months sounds about right—almost exactly the span of the 1872 Thomas Cook itinerary that once inspired Jules Verne. Though the way I'm feeling now, there's a lingering notion I might not return, become one of those "professional vagabonds" Internetting in from Papua New Guinea or wherever for years on end.

We'll see. For now, I just want—need—to leave.

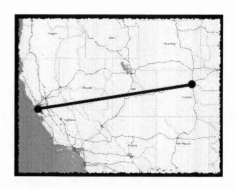

Rocky Mountain High
Denver

We're coming down from an Ecstasy high on an unseasonably warm September morning in San Francisco. Ryan's beat-up Honda Civic pulls out of the Embarcadero Center garage in downtown San Francisco and heads east, across the Bay Bridge to Oakland Airport.

Ryan and I met just after my life went sideways. A twenty-six-year-old wholesome-looking swimming instructor from the eastern reaches of the San Francisco Bay Area, his blue eyes, pug nose, and towhead boy-next-door haircut conceal a wild side. We've managed to sustain a surprisingly solid romance over the past months. In his no-nonsense way he's been a stabilizing force amid all the melodrama. This final weekend together is our send-off, the first push eastward on my globe-circling odyssey.

At this point, though, it doesn't feel so auspicious. Arriving at the long-term lot at Oakland Airport, we haul our bags out of the Civic and await the shuttle bus in the blazing heat. Ryan is uncharacteristically quiet and isn't looking so great. Checked in and at the gate for our flight, he dashes off.

"Be right back."

They're starting to board but hey, business is business: in the bathroom, he throws up. Maybe those pills weren't MDMA after all. Meanwhile, I'm getting antsy as Group One disappears through the jetway onto the canvas-colored Southwest Airlines jet. Finally he reappears and we clamber aboard. The flight is half empty, almost as unusual these days as a hot morning in San Francisco. As we climb skyward and turn east I catch a glimpse of the city's downtown in the hazy distance. Hard to believe I've only been back on the West Coast a year. Events have made it feel like ten.

Arrival. The usual drill for we seasoned domestic travelers: rental car, drive to downtown, check in at hotel. I may be on the holiday of my life but my brain still isn't, as I clumsily and inadvertently cut off a father and young son before hopping on our rental car shuttle. The city's just coming off the Democratic National Convention a couple of weeks before, and sports a freshly scrubbed, slightly weary vibe.

"Nice!" I exclaim as we plop down our bags in our room in one of Denver's more elegant downtown hotels. The room sports a king-sized bed with linens crisply matching walls done up in cream and chocolate brown.

"Yeah, whatever. This isn't even anything special for me," Ryan replies. Okay, *that* was a tad bitchy. I chalk it up to morning-after recovery, though I sense something deeper. Ryan found this deal for us on Priceline—amid my skepticism—and his remark has *I told you so* written all over it.

No time to discuss it now: we pick up Eric, my long-distance friend-with-benefits going back several years. A slender, tall, good-looking mixed-race guy about Ryan's age, he describes himself as the love child of Johnny Depp and Leonardo DiCaprio—if such offspring had become an aspiring gay punk rocker. He points us northwest to the one town in the region I've been long overdue to visit.

I'm a big-city boy, but have always been fascinated by unusually cosmopolitan smaller centers. I call it the *Northern Exposure* effect, after the show and its offbeat center of culture and smarts, Cicely, Alaska. In real-life America it's typically college towns that pull this off—the Ann Arbors; the Madison, Wisconsins; the Burlington, Vermonts. I've been out to Colorado many times—the snowsports enthusiast in me craves big mountains—but this is my first time visiting its entrant into collegiate sophistication: Boulder.

"Dude, we *have* to try the Dushanbe Teahouse," Eric offers. He's right: a small pavilion straight out of Central Asia with elaborate wood-carved ceiling; a dizzying array of infusions black, green, and herbal; and equally diverse range of snacks. We feast on a mélange of scones and chicken curry wraps. Afterward, we stroll the downtown pedestrian mall festooned with post-convention Obama paraphernalia. An Art Deco courthouse façade feels straight out of a 1930s painting. Eric stops in at his favorite anime and comic-book store, which bears an array of works from Japan ranging from the cutesy to the edgy.

Seems that even here, at the base of the Rockies, the rest of the world is calling.

The following day we pick up the partying again. That's the thing about hanging with twentysomethings: there's always another opportunity to get shitfaced. We start things off at a divey gay bar hosting an afternoon beer bust; I'm not much of a drinker—a tendency the liver donation only amplified—so Eric and Ryan leave me in the dust. My substance of choice beckons at our next stop, a house party at one of Eric's friends: Denver, almost as much as San Francisco, is something of a haven for cannabis fans. I get pleasantly stoned and enjoy earnest conversations with the straight female roommate while the boys pound back shot after shot.

Heading down the elevator of the mid-rise apartment building, Eric pulls us in for a three-way kiss. Now *that's* what I was hoping for: that these two fetching lads would hit if off more than socially. Eric breaks the kiss and smiles guiltily at Ryan.

"I'm way too punk-rock for you."

"Oh, you'd be surprised." They start sharing some of their more sordid sexual adventures. *Okay, you've lost me, boys.* Dominance and bondage aren't my thing. Though if there's one thing I've learned to appreciate about the gay lifestyle, it's the receptive attitude toward all kinds of sexual practices. To wit: Eric wants to up the ante even more. He hauls us to a nearby nightspot to see if we'll fancy the couple who'd gang-banged him the night previous.

The couple seem friendly at first, but as they get drunker I get more and more put off: one of them, a pint-sized fellow with beaky nose, starts bossing me around.

"Dance like this," he says, pulling me in. Obviously *he* was a good fit for Eric's submissiveness but it's not flying with me. He tries kissing me but I'm not feeling it.

"Use your *tongue*!" he barks. Okay, that's enough.

"You need to back off," I say. Actually, it's not just him: Eric's gotten too drunk and segued from lively to maudlin. He starts to cry.

"I thought my life would end up like a *Disney movie*," he chokes. He's one of the few adults I know who's got a diorama model of a fairy castle at home. "I'm *always* gonna be single." Like lots of gay guys he vacillates between committed relationships and slutsville, never fully comfortable in either. I turn to Ryan.

"It's time to go home."

He's mad at me again, says I'm being a buzzkill—though he soon relents and comes with me. Back at the hotel, he lets it all out.

"You act like you *always* know everything," he says. "Did you see that father's face when you cut in front of him at the airport?" He reiterates how he's feeling condescended-to about my doubting his Priceline find. He's equally unhappy about how I handled the evening: *he* didn't notice Eric's friend's agro vibe.

I sense what this is really about: our impending parting of the ways. Will we *really* stay in touch for seven months? Will we pick up again after I return—*if* I return? This relationship is in a sense totemic of my headspace as I head off: lots of unfinished business about to go into a deep freeze. We reconcile, however, before falling asleep. The mantra is right-on: never go to bed angry.

Back to the airport the next morning for a hurried check-in on two different flights: for Ryan, it's back to the grind in California; for me, onward to the east. I want to scream at my Air Canada agent, a cranky middle-aged woman with a clipped Franco-Canadian accent.

"You're late," she says, glancing at the time: a mere hour before the flight. "You're gonna have to run," she exclaims, again and again like a schoolmarm. We reach my gate in plenty of time in spite of her panic.

"Let it go," Ryan admonishes, sensing my annoyance. I always have a hard time hearing that statement, though this time it's probably good advice.

"We'll stay in touch?" I say, only half a question. I bought a Skype headset partly for that purpose. He nods.

"I can't get excited. I don't even know if you're coming back."

We agree to set each other free, allow ourselves to remain open to whatever odysseys, romantic or otherwise, might present themselves in the months we're apart. It's an odd quasi-non-breakup, mirroring the equally ambivalent goodbye I bid to the U.S.A., my adopted homeland for more than a dozen years.

Motherland
Montréal

*A*ll nomads have a point of origin, in my case this cold-weather metropolis tucked into Canada's east.

My parents and two out of three sisters still reside here and keep me coming back. Well, not entirely: it's the little ones who do it, my nieces and nephews. Five of them, to be exact, aged one-and-a-half through six. In spite of the continent that divides us I've managed to keep alive a closeness. Practically all the friends of my youth are long gone—a holdover from the bad old days of Quebec secessionism a decade or two back. The upside: my Montréal visits are a concentrated yet enchanting dose of the familial.

To keep things fair to the kids I alternate where I stay on each successive visit and this go-round it's my sister Tamara's turn; her younger son, Jacob, celebrates his third birthday during my time here. Like his athletic father—and unlike klutzy Uncle David—Jacob displays a passion for golf. He takes a fancy to the toy plastic putter I buy him for his birthday—so much that my sister and brother-in-law consign his swinging to the backyard to avoid a lot of shattered glass.

All those platitudes about living vicariously through the eyes of a child truly hit home at this time of year. I still vividly recall when the cycle of seasons was measured from September to September: the welter of anticipation, the smell of new markers and pencils, the fall jackets donned for daily commutes to brick schoolhouses. Montréal's northerly clime is such that even now the chill begins to assert itself. On a rainy, cool morning Jacob's big sister, Lola, age five, starts kindergarten. Her cousin Jackson, meanwhile, oldest of the brood, begins first grade. Some years ago, immediately following Jackson's arrival, I composed a "birth letter" to him. In it I prophesied how, one day, we adults would be engaged in our grown-up activities, attending meetings or fiddling with retirement portfolios (traveling around the world or donating organs hadn't occurred to me yet) while he was trundling home from grade school.

It looks like that day has finally come.

My sisters inhabit lives very different from mine yet it's safe to say we've never been closer. These brief visits serve as concentrated catch-ups on goings-on in our lives: Tamara's job has been an unrelenting misery so she's returning to a previous employer; my other sister Naomi and her husband are in the middle of the high-wire act of selling one home and buying another. All those mortgage complexities leave their nights sleepless. Clearly life in one's thirties, either as a footloose-and-fancy-free American urbanite or as a parent of young children, does not signal the end of change, transition, or uncertainty. This was a conceit of our twenties.

It's good to be surrounded by loved ones right now, as the tumult I've pledged to forget comes lunging back like tentacles in a monster film.

In the middle of a small bon voyage gathering my family throws in my honor, I spot a blinking e-mail notification for me on my mom's computer. It's from Steve, my estranged friend. With he in the midst of some minor foot surgery and I in the middle of prepping for this trip we reached something of an *entente cordial* to leave things for stabler times. Or so I thought.

"What we have is not a friendship," he admonishes in a hostile screed. He's done this before—waited until an impending departure to drop a bomb. Always impersonally, always via e-mail. "Try to be intellectually honest," he adds. He demands closure for the events of this past summer. Now. Immediately. The night before I'm set to fly off.

Why? Why? Last time he did this he was in the throes of drug addiction. But he's been clean now for years. One of my sisters walks in and sees the missive. She puts her arm on my shoulder.

"Don't respond. This isn't the time."

So much for trying to forget. I try to push it all away, but it casts a gloom over what should be a celebratory time—my maiden voyage across the Atlantic as an adult. Bidding the little ones goodbye the following evening, I hoist my eighty-liter backpack over my shoulders and strap on a money belt for the first time. *Weird.* I used to snicker at backpackers in my days of wheelie-bag travel. Off to the airport, down the jetway onto a cavernous British Airways triple-seven. The flight's barely longer than a transcontinental red-eye and as passengers settle in, doesn't feel all that different either. That is, until the effortlessly polite, British-accented voice floats dreamily over the PA.

"Please be suhe to store youh possessions in the ovuhead storage lockuh."

Benadryl makes possible a couple hours of fitful sleep. Awakening somewhere over Galway, I work to stuff the past away in a storage locker in my brain and anticipate the magnitude of what's ahead: over half a year bashing around Planet Earth with a single bag hanging off my back. How will I take to it after a life spent in offices and classrooms, never away from home for more than a week at a time? Will this offer distraction, consolation, perspective, or just seven more months of reminders and angst?

Another announcement over the PA. London calling. We land in less than an hour—my old life, America, Montréal, and the waters of the North Atlantic at our backs.

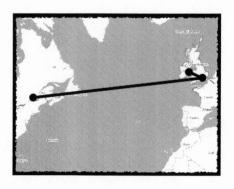

Isle to Isle
London & Dublin

I pour down the jetway into a cloudy London morning filtering through windows of a building under renovation. A mess of exposed ceilings and faded, half-torn-out 1980s décor is my hello to the U.K. Heathrow's Terminal Four is in use beyond its expected lifespan while kinks are ironed out at the flashy yet troubled new Terminal Five.

The building may reflect my unsettled mood, but not to worry: London serves as almost as good a refuge for me as Montréal, filled with close family friends and other chums.

"Seven months? Think you might consider going for longer?" asks Joy, an old family friend who's come to "collect" me from the airport, as the British put it. I'm sitting in what should be the driver's seat of her black Volkswagen Polo as we make our way to northwest London. Over a rolling sea of townhomes I spot the new Wembley Stadium, hulking and colossal.

"Maybe," I reply. *Like forever, even.* I listen up as she plies me with suggestions: like many Brits, Joy's been all over. Once they colonized the world; nowadays they're among the planet's most intrepid travelers. The concepts of Gap Year and flashpacking originated in this island nation. Though Joy, more of an earthy type, tends to do things less princess-fashion than I'm intending.

"I never travel First Class," she says. The expense normally precludes that for me too…but this trip sees me gifted with mileage upgrades. My so-so sleep last night on the plane is already making me salivate over those flat-bed seats.

I'm out walking with Bertie, Joy's soft-spoken husband, to pick up Caribbean food ("take-away") on Willesden's curvy main high street dotted with little eateries. Three-story brick structures press close against the pavement while iconic red double-decker buses roar past at improbable speed. Harry Potter's magical wizard bus wasn't far off the mark.

At last, I'm elsewhere. Mentally and physically alike. I've been waiting for it to hit me—that delightful culture shock sensation when all those elements of the unfamiliar reach critical mass. The feeling helps ease nerves still jangled by recent events.

So too does the food: the jerk chicken's delightful, at once cementing that London's boiled-cabbage days are long past; the city is as aflame with culinary diversity as any other major world center.

"Ooh, trendy," Joy coos when I tell her and some friends where I'm headed for the evening. But the vibe is gentle, as are this crowd of convivial Brits. I sit with Joy, Bertie and some of their friends in the intimate, high-ceilinged living room in their little house off Willesden's high street. Our conversation blends introductions and reminiscences: at fortysomething Joy's the youngest of a clan whose rapport with my family goes back generations. Last time I was here—London's one of a handful of international spots I've visited before—I was a closeted, fretful young teen and she a twentyish party girl.

"I fell asleep in *Cats*," she recounts. My parents had scored us tickets and she used the opportunity to sleep off a big night. This time the tables are turned: she and Bertie are parents of an adorable three-year-old and their sleepless nights, like those of my sibs in Montréal, now revolve around sippy-cups and storytime.

"Bring jetlag, thirst, and dancing shoes," reads the e-mail from a friend of my sister's who's set to be my London nightlife guide. A handsome curly-haired fellow with a silken accent and a name taken from one of the painters of the Renaissance, he meets me at one of the nine entrances to the Old Street tube station. Londoners may grouse about their Underground, but they probably haven't seen the farce of public transit that is San Francisco: halfway across town with two train transfers on a Saturday night takes barely thirty minutes.

Renaissance Man's flat in Shoreditch is trendy indeed: a sliding steel doorway opens onto a quiet courtyard; his two-bedroom is a mess of exposed brick and photography gear belonging to his roommate, a chatty bespectacled gal from the American Midwest. I'm handed a "spliff," cannabis Euro-style, a joint blended with tobacco. Then it's off for the evening.

"See that?" Renaissance Man points to some artfully styled shape graffiti-ed in white paint on a wall outside his place. "He's a well-known artist."

Shoreditch is a cauldron of activity, a once-dangerous stretch of inner-city transformed into a trendy fantasia of bars, fusion restaurants, and flats for office workers who want to live walking distance from the square-mile financial district known as the City. My habitually flawless gaydar pings uselessly—it's near-impossible to tell the hets from the homos here. Renaissance Man, straight himself but with a friend circle that takes all comers, explains.

"We call this district 'post-gay.'"

Indeed, members of all persuasions commingle more freely here than back home. Tippling too spills out onto the street, a phenomenon confined to only two cities I know of Stateside, Vegas and the Big Easy. It's a good thing too, since frequent venue changes are mandatory to keep the buzz going: "pubs" close early, as they did in olden times; "bars" close later; and "clubs" stay open all night long.

There's more than just drink to be had: all manner of substances flow as openly in this town as sexuality. From some known street vendors Renaissance Man scores some cocaine and powdered MDMA—stuff that hasn't been readily available in America for years. I'm not one for snorting, but a dab on the tongue renders my mouth pleasantly numb and my psyche ready for what's next.

Off to Heaven. The club, that is—a huge disco under the Charing Cross train station. Lots of cute boys but I'm not really in pick-up mode. Instead I sit with Renaissance Man in a cave-like chill-out space and compare life stories. His is pretty compelling: one of eleven children of a family of Italian peasant hippie Christians, he grew up all over the world before ending up in the U.K. working in West End London theatre. Now *that's* not a bio you hear every day.

Ecstasy often serves as truth serum, which for me would normally mean retelling my recent melodrama in full. But not now, not this time. I shorthand it some, still trying to push it away. Renaissance Man picks up on that and gives me a brotherly pat.

"Let's see if we can cheer you up."

He puts on his wingman hat, trying to hook me up with a cute Italian boy from Torino sitting on the concrete outside the club: dark hair, pale skin, pupils the size of UFOs. Renaissance Man chats with him in Italian but the guy's too cracked out, gnashing on a stir-stick to a plasticky pulp. No action for me—and Renaissance Man's got a girlfriend—so it's home by five a.m. The taxi ride to Willesden is glorious, passing Marble Arch and the elegantly lit-up buildings of the West End. The price tag is equally rich: for a five-mile trip it's £30, which doing the math comes to…US$50. *Ouch.*

Times have changed since I was here last. The pigeons and their droppings have vanished from Trafalgar Square. Odd-shaped skyrises of steel and glass crowd beside stone façades in the City—the gherkin's my personal favorite, an ovoid sausage some forty stories tall. The once-forlorn Underground trains are a cheery blue, red, and white hurtling through century-old tunnels.

Nevertheless, some things resonate: the bored-looking young woman in the Manet painting at the Courtauld Collection. The chiseled lettering on the Rosetta Stone at the British Museum. *But now I actually give a shit.* As a lad it felt like a chore, a duty, to see Sights of Great Importance. Now appreciation and interest flow effortlessly.

Joy's parents, Sidney and Ray, hold mystical import in my family: my sisters and I owe them our very existence. Decades ago they cajoled my then-hesitant mother to call back the fellow with the unpronounceable name when both were here on a visit from opposite sides of the world. To commemorate the occasion I meet the elder pair at Fortnum & Mason, a three-hundred-year-old department store whose top-floor St. James Restaurant has to be the best place to enjoy afternoon "cream tea": a long, classically done-up chamber in a pastiche of blues and satin-white moldings. A grand piano provides the finishing touch. The tea and melt-in-your-mouth scones deliver the goods—as does the clotted cream, a buttery-looking but impossibly light concoction that lesser establishments try to substitute with the plain old whipped variety.

Sidney and Ray make me reflect on how people age—something I think about more and more as the sun begins to set on my thirties. Fair-skinned Sidney is as chipper, jovial, and sharp as he was two decades ago: he segues from bad puns to discussions of computer software as effortlessly as I spread cream on my scones. His wife, Ray, a heavyset, olive-skinned woman whose jet-black hair has gone gray, is not so fortunate: her once sharp wit has turned hazy; a diagnosis made not long after my visit reveals she's in the earliest stages of Alzheimer's.

Back at Renaissance Man's place, he's cooking up a fabulous pasta. At the table are his roommate Esther, his girlfriend Tanya, and Tanya's tall, slender, long-fingered blonde roommate—a shy, sweet New Zealand gay boy named Sam. Alas, my near-instant crush on him isn't reciprocated. In fact he looks almost uncomfortable in his alluring bit of gay getup: day-glo Converse and lurid-hued denim pants ("trousers, trousers"—"pants" are undergarments this side of the Atlantic).

We chug down more cocaine and weed—this time I get the gang to dig up a bong and smoke it unadulterated, the way the California cannabis gods intended. Then off for more carousing.

Soho, London's gay district, is dizzying even for me who's seen it all Stateside: hordes of people spilling in and out of dozens of bars, discos, and everything in between. We end up at a more gender-blender spot, Circus. Sam gets into dancing like a pro—though later Tanya lets on it's one of a very few times he's been out on the town. His aloof demeanor is really just fear and inexperience. I can relate: that was me once upon a time, though Lord knows I didn't dress nearly as well.

Late that night, back at Renaissance Man's pad, I make a call.

"Hey baby."

"How *are* you?" says Ryan in that polished, courteous tone honed from years of speaking to swimmer-kids' parents. It's our first call using Skype.

He's keeping busy, but I can tell he's a bit down.

"I want to keep a weekly phone date," he says, "but I can't do 'hey baby' for seven months. I don't think I can handle that."

Fair enough. I agree. No terms of endearment. Our conversation feels good, something of a smoothing out after the bumpy, conflicted farewell back in Denver. I'm not sure if we're being unrealistic, trying to keep this pilot light going for all these months, but somehow it feels right: even in my desire to put the recent past in the rearview mirror, I relish the opportunity to glance occasionally back at the good parts. We'll see how long that lasts.

London suburbs give way to iridescent rural green. The train tilts and glides north from Euston Station, up through the spine of England and into northern Wales. Fittingly, I see poxy white dots of grazing sheep in the field, and, farther on, hollowed-out ruins of ancient stone castles. I half-expect a gaggle of Monty Pythoners to turn up, on the run from airborne cows or killer bunnies.

We arrive under slate-gray skies at the ferryport in Holyhead, Wales. It's pretty quiet; my guess is Tuesday in late September isn't exactly peak season to cross the Irish Sea.

The term "ferry"—conjuring up in my memory those modest vessels across Lake Champlain in Vermont—almost seems like an insult to this behemoth. At around 600 feet long and over 20,000 tons displacement, this ship is the size of ocean liners of yore. Much of its space is reserved for vehicles, but there's still ample room in the three or so passenger decks—which include three restaurants, two movie theatres, a deluxe "club lounge," and a currency-exchange office—to spread out. I explore the vessel's nooks and crannies and catch a nap on one of the leather sofas. A couple of hours later and we arrive in Dublin. My first-ever passport stamp in the European Union.

Ireland's done well in the EU. This is immediately apparent on the taxi ride along the riverbank into the central city: gleaming new office towers, upscale shops, gossamer-light metal footbridges traversing the river. The heavy gloss of prosperity.

"Why are you still in the room?"

It's my first stay in a hostel and my abrupt intro to budget accommodation. This one's got private rooms and I book myself into one, but on day two I'm told I need to switch rooms. It's 10:30 and guests need to be out of the rooms by ten—and that's not a suggestion as the burly middle-aged lady sent to tidy my room makes clear.

It's also not the most congenial place. Its mezzanine-level common room is mostly empty; scattered individuals making use of free Wi-Fi sit in plushy armchairs. Looks like I may need to take matters into my own hands if I want to meet people. Not a problem: I long ago outgrew my fear of going out alone, a practice that holds far less stigma in gayland anyway.

As a mid-sized city (population a million-and-a-half or so) in a traditionally Catholic nation, Dublin's reputedly a modest gay center. And it's midweek—not exactly party time. Still, the pub-besotted town has become a drinking destination for Brits—stag and "hen" (as they call bachelorette) parties flit through the city's raft of bars as I chow down on arguably the priciest burger I've ever eaten at a joint in Temple Bar, the city's medieval-core-cum-tourist-mecca.

The gay scene consists of a scattering of pubs nearby...though what's supposed to be the biggest of these isn't promising: The George looks like one of those dumpy gay bars from decades past. Small, dank, mostly empty. But wait—that's just the antechamber. A much larger space hides upstairs, a glitzy multi-level affair replete with a dance-floor, a stage, and—soon after I arrive—a drag show. Not bad for a Wednesday night. Even the, uhm, ladies put out enough garishness and over-the-top humor to pass muster back home.

The crowd, meanwhile, is friendly and cute.

"How old are you?" asks one tallish dark-haired fellow with pale skin, an echo of Ryan the swimmer but for his inky-brown eyes and hair. I tell him and he nearly keels over.

"Christ, I'm twenty!" he says. This city's a big university town and bereft of America's twenty-one-and-over drinking restrictions. The guy doesn't blow me off altogether, amiably tapping me as he passes throughout the night. Meanwhile, on the dance floor, a waifish, fair-featured boy eyes me more eagerly. We dance, closer and closer, moving to embrace and eventually to making out. Then we introduce ourselves.

"I'm Michael," he says. He's even younger than the last one—nineteen—a science student from County Wexford attending Trinity College. *I pegged him for a science geek.* Coyly fetching in size twenty-eight jeans, he's the sort who's too cute to be a nerd in real life but might be cast as one in some romantic comedy.

We walk hand in hand, past the elegantly lit-up shops of Grafton Street, across the banks of the River Liffey to my hostel. Good thing I scored that private room, I consider, as we make for the bed in passionate liplock. He stays the night, and on top of the usual bedroom activities—kudos to youthful libido—we end up chatting till dawn.

"So did you see *Far & Away*?" I ask. I'm always curious to know how locals feel about Hollywood depictions of their homeland.

"Yes," he replies, eyes rolling. Hardly necessary, but he confirms Tom Cruise's Irish brogue is pitiable. He may not know it yet but he's a charmer, this boy—and not just thanks to his near-perpetual, beefy erection that literally lasts all night. I tell him he's cute and he shakes his head, bashful, mouthing, "I'm *not*."

I'm *such* a sucker for modesty.

As I stop for breakfast the small voice in my head returns: *should you really be hooking up now?* It could be called fucking my way into distraction. Or maybe not: at this point the companionship of others, however temporary, feels right. Part of the journey, I guess.

Meanwhile, on to daytime activities: sitting in a bagel joint in Temple Bar begins to rev up my curiosity machine. *How did it get that way?* The neighborhood, not the bagel place. It's the question that nags constantly for the curious, history-minded traveler—this one at least— that is, whenever nightlife and tumescent nineteen-year-olds aren't keeping me otherwise distracted.

A few plaques on buildings reveal that Temple Bar is not named for its present-day use as sousing central (though of course there is a bar *called* the Temple Bar...that turn of phrase was too good to pass up). Wandering its narrow laneways lined with townhomes in the sober light of day, I learn it's named for the riverbank on which it sits. Nearby is an equally misnamed relic, a sprawl of mismatched structures. Dublin Castle.

English, Irish, whatever. I knew about the I.R.A. and Home Rule and all that, but in North America it's a blurry distinction, Celt from Briton. Well, not here: the English controlled Ireland for eight hundred years, and the center of their power was this sprawling complex with an Anglo-Norman tower—okay, *this* part looks like a castle—at its heart.

Another icon looms not far away. *My first church in the Old World,* I muse while ambling into soaring St. Patrick's Cathedral. *Probably not the last* is the thought that immediately follows. Still, this place provokes a tremble: it's *the* St. Patrick's. Built on the spot where the man himself began Christianizing the Irish circa 500 AD.

Confession: religion isn't my thing. Not even my own. Not even the innocuous-seeming Eastern faiths popular back home. All those praying practitioners reciting lurid tales of the fantastical beyond— "fairy tales," cynics like comedian Bill Maher call it; all those rituals that captivate many but feel empty to me...I just don't get it. Sure, I wonder about what's out there and hold an Einsteinian fascination with the grandeur of creation. I'm just left blank at humankind's attempts to express such things through organized faith. "Retail religion," I call it. The events of last summer didn't help: part of my falling out with my friend Steve had to do with his newfound sense of spirituality, the Northern California variant of religious awakening.

But enough of that. Sitting in a pew beneath the tall stone walls and vaulted ceiling it's hard not to be enthralled by the artistry primed by faith. I consider, much like that scene in Richard Linklater's *Before Sunrise*, how inspiring this place must have been to those sad, lonely souls seeking solace and comfort. Never mind the supernatural: for me the edifice itself holds the power to uplift.

Some organ music plays, brooding and rich, for a quarter-hour or so. Walking around, I discover this was the very place where Handel's *Messiah* was first performed in 1742. Around the same time, Jonathan Swift was Dean.

And now for something completely different.

On the taxi ride into town a couple of days earlier I spotted a number of signs advertising adventure-style boating excursions—"Sea Safaris"—heading out on the river into Dublin Bay. At first I'm skeptical. *Too touristy.* But it's a five-minute walk from the hostel. Plus, it's as good an opportunity as any to test out that quick-drying clothing all those backpacking books cajoled me to buy.

"There's a crowd of twenty or so coming," indicates the fellow running the place out of a waterfront booth. Almost as soon as he says it, they materialize: chatty, amiable, all business-casual khakis and button-down shirts. A gang of office workers from one of the glassy waterfront buildings nearby. AIB to be exact, Allied Irish Bank (no relation to the troubled AIG back home) out on a "team-building exercise"—something I've done myself more than once in my career as a corporate grunt. As we head down the Liffey, past derelict industrial buildings and out toward open water, we compare notes on cities and workplace cultures. As I suspected: techie Ireland is a lot like San Francisco.

We pick up speed once out on the Bay. The boats engage in a bit of a splashing and 180-degree spins in the water.

"I'm drenched!" screams a blonde lady sitting at the prow. Glad I plunked myself in the spongy middle of the boat, ensuring my camera will live to photograph another day. We rumble past rocky islands dotted with abandoned stone forts and old lighthouses.

"See that water," our guide says, pointing to the surface. A layer of liquid is peeling back like a bedsheet. "That's the tide going out." I'm told this is the sunniest day in Dublin in weeks, and we're all a bit warm out on the water in musty-smelling orange life preservers.

We return to the dock exhilarated. Valuable Lesson for me, the diligent planner: stick my nose out of the guidebook or Wikitravel page and just go with the flow sometimes.

A final spin through the city schools me in more history: from the National Museum, located in an austere old army barracks just west of the center, I learn about the 1916 Easter Rising that led directly to Irish independence in 1922. A stroll back along the Liffey leads me to broad O'Connell Street, where a new monument—the Dublin Spire—has been erected at its center. The term "erected" is apt for this long, slender needle of skinny brushed metal. Still, it manages to harmonize with the lumbering stone structures around it.

Okay, this worked. My first-ever outing as a solo backpacker. My first fling on European soil. Some success distracting myself from past events. Granted, it was gentle terrain: aside from the Gaelic on street signs Dublin could be any funky mid-sized city back home. But it casts the die for what's to come: discover a new place, find new friends (occasionally with benefits), reconnect with old ones (where they exist). Shake, stir, reflect as needed. The moody, rainy British Isles did the trick: I leave with spirits lifted, new chums acquired, old connections rekindled…not to mention a newfound appreciation for the boys of Dublin.

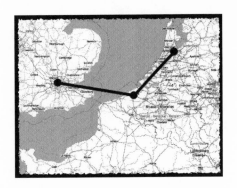

Flanders to Funsterdam
Bruges & Amsterdam

'*T*t's about as exciting as riding BART to Oakland."
That was one friend's take on the Eurostar trip beneath the English Channel. But nay, I refuse, *refuse*, to be so blasé about the engineering triumph of the late-twentieth century. When I heard of the completion of the EuroTunnel—the rail tube running between Britain and mainland Europe—I vowed to make it my first Channel crossing. In spite of cost overruns, initially low ridership, and—only a few weeks before I board—a fire in the tunnel that reduces service, nothing stands in my way of crossing this body of water without leaving terra firma—or, for that matter, my seat.

The escalator offers a slow-motion reveal of the long, sleek, blue-yellow-and-white tube of wheeled steel. Even though I'm in First Class, my plushy gray seat is a bit worn—a reminder that all this is business-as-usual travel in these parts.

The Brits recently—and at long last—completed their high-speed rail link from the tunnel opening near Dover right into the heart of London. To go with it, they remodeled St. Pancras railway station, a soaring masterpiece of red-brick Victorian gothic revival. So grand was this station that it stood in for neighboring Kings Cross in the *Harry Potter* films; before boarding I spot a luggage trolley embedded into a brick wall below a sign for "PLATFORM 9 ¾."

As we glide out of the station on time, a voice comes over the intercom indicating that service will be slower due to the fire. *Uh-oh.* I envision hours-long delays, like those at U.S. airports during thunderstorm season. The conductor, in English and French, obligingly details the delay to profuse apology.

"We'll be arriving in Brussels nine minutes behind schedule."

Tragedy.

High-speed rail lines are purpose built: their solid welded tracks, curved embankments to handle centrifugal forces, and grade-separated construction (no street-level crossings) facilitate speeds in excess of 150 miles an hour. To enable such velocity, these trainsets—using the same TGV technology as those in France—are known as "EMU." Not after the animal, but short for "Electric Multiple Unit." Each train car is a locomotive in and of itself. As we leave suburban London and reach the countryside around Kent, I spot cars on the freeway traveling at half our speed.

Soon after—black. Yes, twenty-some minutes inside a tunnel should be as exciting as watching grass grow, but it's the *idea* of it—the dream of centuries, confounding Napoleon and scores of others with conquest or connectedness on the brain. Now it's the province of bored Euro-commuters who are unwittingly transforming the London-Paris-Brussels-Amsterdam nexus into one West European mega-center. Some may cringe but for me it's a delight.

We emerge on the other side and on the surface, nothing's changed: more rolling green fields, more country roads, a smattering of cars. But look closer: the signage is French, the cars right-hand drive. The Continent awaits!

Brussels is boring. Or so they say. I don't bother finding out as I'm more interested in one of Belgium's smaller centers. Sleepy and forgotten for centuries, nowadays it's hot on the tourist map—at least if the plethora of guidebook sales is to be believed. It was even the star of a recent indie crime thriller: *In Bruges*.

Bruges is perhaps the ideal spot to indulge anyone's "how did it get that way?" fixation. It was, by my estimation, the New York City of the 1200s: a Middle Ages trading powerhouse equivalent to the London of the day. But times and the city's fortune changed: West Flanders declined in power and importance, and the city's river silted in, leaving Bruges cut off from the sea. (A latter-day nearby port, Zeebrugge, retains some importance.)

An early-evening reconnoiter reveals few cars but lots of bicycles speeding along the narrow, curving streets. I'm nearly jingle-belled to death, a fate I suspect the Brugians enjoy inflicting on the hordes of tourists passing through their burg. I reach Markt, the main town square, shrouded in the moody mist. It's adorably lined with upscale touristy eateries and stairstep-gabled roofs. With lights aglow and horses atrot on the cobbles, it's hard not to feel overcome with nostalgia and romance and think…

Wow, it feels just like Disneyland.

There's more to that sentiment than dumb Americana: Walt and his team of "imagineers," in re-enacting medieval town centers with toy-like precision, were actually on to something that town planners of the 1950s utterly failed to appreciate. People *enjoy* spaces like these for their scale, their accessibility, their mix of residence and commerce, church and hearth. It was only decades later when urban gentrification took root that architects and city officials paid heed; nowadays everyplace wants to be Bruges, or Bruges-esque.

That's not English they're speaking. Glottal Flemish carries on the soggy breeze. So what? I grew up in a city where English was the minority, and that's partly why this pricks up my ears. Secessionist-era Quebec wasn't exactly the friendliest to Anglophones. Aside from my hometown, I haven't visited a non-English-speaking place in decades, and perhaps the stale memory of that tense time partly accounts for that. Still, Flemish and English share common roots, as evidenced by looking around: a sign over a local pub bears a polished black wood-carved feline with wording above that reads "DE KAT."

"They're called 'smartshops.'"

So says a hefty Canadian guy. He and five of his friends—two others guys and two girls—are sitting in a circle drinking beer in my hostel's chandelier-draped common room. They've just come from Amsterdam, and, like all independent travelers this side of northwestern Europe, they're eager to share the lowdown on substances elsewhere illicit.

In this case, psilocybin, magic mushrooms. The fungal-based hallucinogen is, in addition to cannabis, available at retail outlets in Holland, though only at specific establishments. *Everyone's got a specialty.* Mushrooms have been on my to-do list for a number of years, so this whets my curiosity.

For now, however, I must address my *real* substance abuse problem. I cannot for the life of me understand the dismissal, by certain U.S. officials, of Belgium and France as "chocolate-making countries." Uhm, this is a *bad* thing? Screw the museums and architecture…*this* is why we come to Europe, at least this part of it.

I hold—with what some dismiss as religious fervor, but what do they know?—that chocolate is best served with…more chocolate. None of this jellied fruit crap they keep trying to stick inside otherwise-respectable devil's food cake. Though the odd fresh strawberry makes for a nice accompaniment, and banana even better. But best of all…oh yeah, there it is, sold here on pushcarts on the street: a waffle. Calling it "Belgian" would be redundant.

Since I've never seen it back home, I try the denser, chewier "Liege-style" variety…drizzled with chocolate syrup, of course. Oh sure, it's touristy: I'm guessing not one of this vendor's clientele is local. But really, *so what?*

More awaits in a nearby shop window: all manner of cacaoy bon bons, including a bunch done up as women's breasts—ah, Europe! I resist the pull, however, and offer up a pledge to keep my girlish— uhm, boyish—waistline. Looking up at the church tower looming over Markt, I offer up a mantra to the gods of vanity and good health: *I shall climb every major church steeple or cathedral tower.*

Here in Bruges, that translates into 353 steps. Hardly a challenge for those in decent shape…well, okay, *something* of a challenge: huffing and puffing a bit in the rarified air up top, I take in the sweeping view. Aside from the odd steeple everything's a couple of stories tall, a prairie of humble roofs. All cities looked like this once, before the advent of structural steel and reinforced concrete

To polish off Bruges, I discover—what else?—the town's Chocolate Museum. More than cutesy displays hosted by cartoon elves, this place edifies: Belgium's reputation as a confectionary powerhouse emerged through dominance of cacao-producing regions of Southeast Asia—though the bean itself emerged in Mesoamerica, in the New World.

A surly ticket agent and two more train rides and I'm in Noord-Holland, in Amsterdam. Ditching the hostel scene for a spell, I find a reasonably priced, stylish, newly opened boutique hotel in a flat-façaded four-story townhome on Amsterdam's Rodeo Drive, Pieter Cornelius Hoofstraat. Actually, make that five stories: the little top-floor room they give me feels just like an artist's garret, complete with dormer window. It's close enough to the Rijksmuseum that I hear its carillon chiming on the quarter-hour.

Like every bud-fiend passing through these parts I beeline it to a coffeeshop. John Travolta's character from *Pulp Fiction* had it right: cannabis is legal but it ain't a hundred percent legal. The shops cannot advertise what they're selling, and lighting up on the street is *verboten*. Interestingly, Dutch use of the stuff actually is lower than in many other countries; the coffeeshop contains mostly foreigners, though this is one time I'm happy to have the brand "tourist" stamped on my forehead. On the recommendation of some friends I stop in at Grey Area, a tiny establishment run by some expat Americans—the mellowest ones I've seen. The joint (pun intended) is festooned with colorful signs and bumper stickers; what *is* it with cannabis culture and the overuse of goofy signage?

A friendly trio from Chicago, meanwhile, sits at a tiny round table, perplexed. They turn to me.

"Do you know how to use this thing?"

They're trying to make head-or-tail of the Volcano, a vaporizer parked on the table surface. Its polished conical surface terminates in an inflatable clear-plastic enclosure, a mini hot-air balloon. This is the healthy way to smoke pot—by not smoking it at all. Instead a heating element deep inside this mini eruption coaxes "vapors" out of hashish. We soon figure it out: the balloon inflates with cannabis-infused air, and we take turns emptying it. Soon we're all feeling quite pleasant.

Sightseeing in this state is a new experience—though I doubt I'm the first visitor to do so. I nearly bump into a stern elderly Dutch woman who stares disapprovingly. I check out the Van Gogh Museum and wonder if Vincent also partook—no, he was just crazy. One factoid about the guy coaxes a chill: he painted for only eleven years, dying younger than I am today.

Across the broad grassy park of Museumplein is the Rijksmuseum. Too much to tackle in this addled state...but thankfully most of it's under renovation. Ever since my days as a wannabe filmmaker Rembrandt and Vermeer have captivated: they were really, really into light—or rather, where it comes from. Shafts of sun pour through windowsills while domes of illumination issue weakly from candles.

Nighttime. Amsterdam needs no introduction as a gay mecca, its other lifestyle bona-fide on top of the almost legal weed. I stride down pub-saturated streets, anticipating the grandest gay nightlife scene the world has to offer...

Wait, where is it?

A couple of places in and around the tongue-twistingly named Regulierdrawsstrat look promising: ultramodern furniture, fruity drinks, backlit bars. But they're half-empty, and remain so as the evening gets later and later...even though it should be a busy weekend night in late September.

"Where is everybody?" I ask a classically Dutch fellow from Leiden, tall, long blonde hair, blue eyes.

"This is it."

The subdued bars are no random slow night, he offers. "Better if you're kinky," he adds, wrinkling his nose at one place I'm thinking of visiting. If you're into leather, bondage, big hairy "bears," this is your town. Not so much for those, like me, into pretty boys. The hordes I've been seeing on the streets are (mostly) straight. Leiden boy, meanwhile, has a boyfriend and leaves soon after.

So much for post-gay. I wonder: as Western societies become more open, does the underground allure, the need to push the envelope, commensurately dissipate? Consider the film *Party Monster*, which chronicles the travails of New York City club kids of the 1980s: fleeing repressive small-town America, they congregate in the Big Apple to do drugs, wear outlandish outfits, embark on radical self-expression. But what if they had nothing to flee from? Gazing at the glitzy yet deserted nightspots, I wonder whether Amsterdam can claim to have lost something in its pragmatic policy of acceptance.

Or perhaps my disappointment has an ulterior motive. I'd hoped to make this stop my Rome *à la* Fellini *Satyricon*: willful indulgence as part of my bid to clean the mental slate. Perhaps this is a herald from the travel gods: try as one might, destinations are what they are, anticipation and expectation be damned.

Maybe the city's other reputed vice will do the trick: testing out my Bruges hostel-mates' theory, I happen upon one of those smartshops—oh, who am I kidding, I looked it up online—where magic mushrooms are clinically displayed in small illuminated acrylic cases.

"You probably want to start with something not too strong," says the elderly lady behind the counter. "Like these."

She pulls out a set of little fungal balls. The crisp white label reads "PHILOSOPHERS STONES." I head back to my garret: a safe, comfortable place is a key component of any hallucinogen trip. I'm a bit nervous as I'm without a "trip guide"—a sober friend to ensure nothing untoward happens—and my mental state is still on shaky ground. But I feel the need to have this experience partly for those reasons.

It takes a while, but the Stones do start me up: lying in bed, I stare at my arm and find its fine, dark hairs twirling into spiderlike shapes— and in spite of being a mild arachnophobe, I don't find this disturbing or upsetting. Meanwhile, running my hand along the wall almost feels as if I'm coalescing into the plaster.

But it's the mental trip that does it: I daydream I'm at a big gathering, a barbecue or some such, with anyone who I've ever endured conflict, distancing, falling out. Only here everyone's con-genial. A mantra echoes, again and again: "We can all be friends." The carillon of the Rijksmuseum chimes every so often, clanging accompaniment to the reverie. It's cathartic, an aspirational dream of what could be, somewhere, sometime. I now understand why ancient pagan faiths included hallucinogens in their religious rites, and wonder if this is what's missing from religion nowadays.

Hours pass. As reality begins to reassert itself, I feel the need to wander the city in the lurid night. I stroll through the red-light district—obviously I'm not its target market but the place captivates for another reason: it's the oldest part of town, its streetscapes narrow as any in Bruges, though with a lot more neon and crowds. Crossing over the canals I come upon a building that looks oddly familiar: an incongruously modern-looking edifice trying to fit into the cityscape, brick walls and angular bay windows straddling a many-arched concrete base.

I've been here before.

In my childhood mind's eye, I remember it resembled one of my grandmother's nightstands. On a layover to Canada from the Middle East sometime in the seventies my family stayed here overnight. But in this altered state, that otherwise-banal recollection takes on phantasmagorical significance: a marker stone in my nomadic life. I find myself overcome with gratitude at this welcoming, sheltering city that housed my clan of errant travelers, long, long ago.

So much for willful debauchery. Here in Europe's pleasure capital the fates spur me toward deeper experiences. Even—especially—those chemically enhanced.

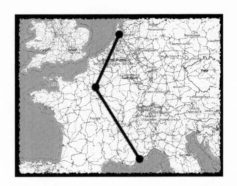

La Belle et le Bad Boy
Paris & Nice

*E*ven with a Eurail Pass, this train commands a burly surcharge. But it's *so* worth it: curtained windows and plush appointments all in burgundy. The whole train is painted burgundy, in fact, livery of the super-express Thalys line that makes the run between Amsterdam and Paris. We rocket into France at 300 kilometers per hour, the wheat fields and trees out the window blurring into impressionistic stop motion. I'm served a lunch of cold fish—doesn't sound so appetizing but surprisingly is. Most scintillating of all: Wi-Fi Internet access on board. Oh, I really don't need to surf the web, and all those travel homilies about unplugging from the grid are not misplaced…but it's just *way too cool* to avoid entirely.

I'm not sure what I will think of Gay Paree. On the one hand, I adore cities, and Paris is perhaps the Platonic ideal of one. On the other, I'm somewhat blasé about the whole French thing after a childhood lived in the world's second-biggest franco-town.

Arrival at Gare du Nord, a couple of metro rides, and I emerge on a street near Place de la Bastille and all misgivings evaporate.

Wow, it's beautiful.

It's just a random long, straight Parisian thoroughfare: five-ish-story apartment blocks of almond and cream, wrought-iron curlicued balconies, black mansard rooflines. Neon-lit green crosses denote local pharmacies offering a bewildering array of beauty products. A gas station blends perfectly into the fabric, a tiny curbside affair with a couple of pumps. Everything's so well-proportioned, so harmonious, so *Paris.* I pull out my iPod and put on the slo-mo thump of MC Solaar's "Le Belle et le Bad Boy" to complete the effect.

Dinnertime. To heck with guidebook recommendations: I speak the language and want to test out the city's foodie rep. I'll pick a place more-or-less at random. I wander, partly aimlessly, westward from the sprawling traffic circle of Place de la Bastille. Its gold-leaf angel monument prances skyward in the dusky light while serpentine Art Nouveau metro signs beckon away from the street. But I stay above-ground, on foot, reaching the Seine and one of its islands, Île St-Louis. Settling in as a *brasserie* (or is it a *bistrot?*), I order a plate of grilled duck and cross my fingers as it arrives.

Magnifique! Succulent and flavorful, arguably one of the best preparations of the dish I've had. I now comprehend Julia Child's religious conversion over *sole meunière.*

Lightning strikes again the next morning: seeking a place to go online (my somewhat fleabaggy hotel is not so endowed), I pop into a neighborhood *brasserie* and order a dish in a hurry. Smoked salmon, poached eggs and cream, all in an ice-cream-sundae-style cup…impossibly delicious.

Focus on the unexpected. That's my mantra in a city of clichés. At the Musée d'Orsay I spy a more obscure bit of pointillism: *Les Îles d'Or,* the golden islands, by Henri-Edmond Cross. Simple, Rothko-like sea-and-sky blues, a dreamlike hazy blur.

Never mind the Eiffel Tower: nearby and uncrowded, the Arc de Triomphe is climbable…though at 200 or so steps, probably a feeble effort to burn off calories earned in this town. Still, a view beguiling in its symmetry in the blue haze: in one direction, the super-broadness of the Champs-Élysées; in the other, the Grande Arche of La Défense—a supersized hollowed-out cube of steel that presides at the center of the city's skyscraper district. A city core as perfectly wrought as this chose a generation or two ago to relegate its modern towers of business to the outskirts. This could be brave urban planning or museumification. I'm not sure which…but then, what part of this place would you tear down to build taller?

Back on the ground and back to matters gastronomic. The waiter spots my English-language guidebook, hears my respectable French and inquires sunnily, *"Canadien?"* So far I've encountered none of the reputed snobbery against *Quebecois* French. And my pizza is as delightful as any local cuisine: I try a four-cheese impregnated with full-on slices of brie and crumbles of blue cheese. *Formidable.* I wonder if the Italians will be able to top it.

"All it is is a bunch of people pushing and shoving and there's *so many better things* to see in that museum."

So offers Ryan during our weekly chat. Paris is the one city in Europe he's visited, and like most everyone else I've spoken to over the years, he echoes the received opinion of the "Mona Lisa": underwhelming. I could be mistaken, but I also sense he's eager to offer up this point: *see, I've traveled too.*

As I enter the Louvre through the iconic glass pyramid, I plan on spending maybe three minutes gazing upon Mona, like that scene in *Fiddler on the Roof* where paterfamilias Tevye, after ranting and raving about the urgent need to see his granddaughter, waltzes into his daughter's home, glances at the newborn, then turns and marches out. Mission accomplished.

I snag a *haute technologie* multimedia guide; the world's biggest art museum has embraced the future, replacing those tinny canned-audio devices with handheld touch screens. Makes Mona that much easier to find. Not that I'd need much help: entering the long gallery, I see them, the ever-present beehive of amateur photographers fawning over the art world's red-carpet celebrity. No velvet ropes, however; instead, a wooden railing extending a dozen feet in a semicircle around the painting. The work itself is covered by glass and flanked by two security guards, just as everyone's said.

And yet…I gaze at the art world's biggest superstar and she coolly gazes back. Even some distance away the effect is hypnotic. *I can't take my eyes off it.* It's inscrutable, confounding, serene. I feel—wait for it—a tremble. Yes, the work is gloomy—due to dirt no one dare remove for fear of disturbing the paint—lending it a foreboding that clashes perfectly with its luminous play of light.

Downstairs, another marquee work fascinates: I never got what was so special about the "Venus de Milo", parodied endlessly on T-shirts and souvenir mugs. *It's the arms, stupid.* Or rather, the absence of them: nobody knows what they looked like. The stumps provide glorious incompleteness, perpetual embrace by invisible limbs.

The museum's too big to see in a day, and probably a week—but the multimedia guide has a solution: compact, self-guided walking tours. Here again, I want to know how this place became what it is. Ah, perfect: an architectural history walk.

The Louvre wasn't always a museum; instead, I discover, it was the original royal palace, the home of French rulership until Louis XIV decamped for Versailles in the 1700s. Consequently, the place is a hodgepodge of periods and styles; the pyramid, alternately reviled and revered—thank you, Dan Brown—is but the latest addition. Building this newest bit unveiled the oldest: the foundations of the original castle were then discovered. The guide's digital screen walks me down to the lowest levels where smooth walls and round medieval turrets of stone are backlit by halogen lights.

I always thought of Paris as a sunny counterpoint to gloomy London, but the two cities actually share similar climates. A raw October wind blows drizzle as I cross the small bridge on the Seine to Île de la Cité. They say it all started here: the Parisii tribe of Celtic Iron Age nomads found this convenient place to ford the river, and from that a settlement sprang up. Of such caprice great cities are made. Nowadays the island is better known for a lumbering Gothic beast, the cathedral to end all cathedrals. Notre Dame de Paris.

It took almost 200 years to complete. It feels to me like every gray stone on Earth went into its construction. With flying buttresses holding up its gargantuan core like spider legs, a central nave stretching on for what feels like forever, and an imposing triple-arched front entrance replete with stone-carved figurines, I'm quickly overwhelmed—probably the intended effect for a religion long on pomp and circumstance. I spend well over an hour wandering and exploring its chapels and nooks and still come away feeling like I've barely scratched the surface.

Religion again. It's ironic that now-secular Europe basks in so rich a religious architectural heritage, while spiritually fervid America must content itself with banalities like the Crystal Cathedral. And yet, for all that this place is a wonder, I remain unmoved by its intended aim.

Why isn't this doing it for me?

Maybe those mantras about traits skipping a generation offer clues: my grandparents rejected religion too. On my father's side, a family scattered all over the world left tradition behind: there's an early photo of my dad sitting under a huge Christmas tree—not out of devotion to Christianity but out of my grandparents' bid to keep up with the Joneses of the time. My mother's side saw a keener pull toward Jewish peoplehood—but in the form of radical secular Zionism. It was my parents who rediscovered religion, sending us all to Hebrew schools to study our heritage. But it never stuck, and I cultivated a pronounced uninterest in piety. Seems I'm not alone: after *la révolution* the cathedral was reconsecrated to "The Cult of Reason."

I'm more captivated by a diorama showing how the place was built; it arguably was one of the engineering and architectural triumphs of the age. As with St. Patrick's in Dublin, faith may have catalyzed but human ingenuity willed this wonder into creation.

The wind and rain give way, gray clouds now punctuated by shafts of sun. A view would be nice. Up the funicular railway at Montmartre to the top of the *butte*, Paris's only real hill. At the top, Sacré-Coeur Cathedral, a faux-Byzantine wedding cake of a place from the late 1800s. *Now who's Disney-fied, bitches?* The French probably fail to appreciate how theme-parky are some constructs in their midst. On the way down, a *boulangerie* beckons with baguettes; I'm nearly as much a bread addict as I am a choco-junkie. The waistline isn't thrilled.

I don't know anyone in Paris—or so I thought until Renaissance Man's roommate tells me to contact her friend Ashley from the States who's studying here for a spell. We meet at the Moulin Rouge windmill—though at €90-plus a pop for its floor show we move on, opting for a neighborhood *bistrot* instead.

"Try the pork loin," she suggests, between talk of Paris student life and travel tales. It's in a honey-curry sauce and is predictably spectacular. Then the grandest news of all: a *gâteau au chocolat fondant*—a molten flourless wonder.

"Oh, yeah!" Ashley exclaims. A fellow choco-addict. As a weak nod to portion control we partition it when it arrives, though it's dense enough that half is plenty. Oh, that waistline.

The RER commuter train to Versailles is surprisingly grungy. Though perhaps I shouldn't be surprised: as we ride out, Paris's picture-perfect *arrondissements* give way to the battleship concrete high-rises of the *banlieues*, the city's suburbs. It's America inside-out: the money's in the inner city. Not that this arrangement is much better: the nation's segregated Muslim minority rioted out here a couple summers back.

The Palace of Versailles itself, meanwhile, is akin to an American suburb: a planned community palace. King Louis had his motives, though, for *haute*-flight to the burbs: easier to manage those drama-queen nobles in a compound out here in the country.

To modern eyes it's blindingly overdone, an orgy of curlicued detailing and chandeliers and canopied beds and gilt-encrusted everything. I'm almost grateful for a temporary Jeff Koons exhibit: cute balloon sculptures—the big silver ball reflecting the Hall of Mirrors in fun-house distortion is especially beguiling—cleverly inserted between the frills and gold leaf.

Like latter-day suburbia this place is all open spaces looked after by a horticultural army. An even line of perfectly trimmed conical bushes in the Orangerie stands at attention against the cream-toned building and the ink-stained gray of a cloudy sky. That's right: this place was a *summer* palace. With fountains switched off the iconic gardens feel as lonely and barren as a wintertime Minnesota parking lot.

Okay, enough museums and treasures. Time to be *un bad boy*.

To start with, a bar in the Marais. I'm heartened that Paris's gay town is also in one of its most distinctive quarters. As I become more familiar with the city I find myself drawn to its unreconstituted medieval parts, such as this neighborhood or the *quartier latin* on the Left Bank. Baron Haussmann's nineteenth-century bout of urban renewal, wide boulevards and endless mansard roofs, has begun to feel monotonous.

Just like riding a bike. Or so I hope: my rusty Montréal French has been useful enough for ordering food in restaurants, so now time for a *real* test—chatting up a gorgeous local. There he is, across the room: tall, long blonde hair, aquiline nose...and aloof in a way that suggests inexperience. I soon find out why from the chattier, not-so-cute friend.

"*Il est un modèle.*" He's a model. And eighteen.

So nothing doing there. They leave and I grow chummy with two other cute guys, this time *en anglais*: a pair of expat Americans, early twentysomethings doing the study-abroad thing. I'm more into Michael, the lean, square jawed Midwesterner, but his friend Erik, a Latino from New York, is more into me. We dance together, though it's decidedly chaste—especially since Erik works to keep his drunken friend apart from a Spanish boy who fancies him. *Le cock bloquage.*

"We always go home together," Erik states. Hooking up is so *gauche*, he implies. Bros before hoes. The *faux*-propriety of youth.

Off to another venue that takes full advantage of the Marais's medieval mojo: CUB is tucked into a brick-arched basement, catacomb-like but for the laser lights and disco beats. We dance till dawn, close the place down—Paris nightlife runs late—and ride the metro home as it reopens in the early morning. Erik and Michael decide they want something out of the vending machine parked on the platform but the contraption has other plans. It eats their Euros and gives back nothing. They start banging and kicking it like rowdy children.

"Come on! *Fucker!*"

Pinched Parisians begin to stare, and I can see it in their eyes: *les americains*. I keep my distance, pretending to gaze at subway maps.

One more roll of the dice the next night, this time at MIX in Montparnasse. Buried under a tall 1960s-era skyscraper, it's another glitzy mega-club like Heaven in London. The glitz is matched by its drink prices—steep—which given the dollar's already weak exchange makes me grateful I'm a modest tippler. Emboldened by a solitary vodka and Red Bull I try chatting up a cute bespectacled boy, another early twentysomething, this one a Parisian native.

"*C'est la plus belle ville au monde*," he asserts. The most beautiful city in the world. A typical boast, though from what I've seen not necessarily misplaced. Still, the brashness grates a bit.

"You were *really* staring at me," he smirks. "Why don't you get us a drink?"

Really? I'm hoping I misunderstood over the din and my grasp of the language. Or maybe not. *Presumptuous too*. I let it slide, forking over €10 each for a couple of so-so fruity concoctions. He downs his quickly and then:

"Buy me another."

Okay, that's enough. Time for the universal "Go fuck yourself" cue. I excuse myself to go to the bathroom. When I return, he's blessedly nowhere in sight.

I guess one stuck-up Parisian over an entire week isn't too bad, but I take it as an omen: time to pack it in.

The seaside café in Monte Carlo affords a splendid view of the yachts, super-yachts, and cruise ships docked in the harbor. Blue skies, balmy temperatures, and little humidity complete the canvas. I see where Charles Trenet got the inspiration for his song "La Mer," covered in English by Bobby Darin as "Beyond the Sea."

It's only 450 or so miles from Paris—about the distance from Boston to Washington, D.C.—but this might as well be another planet. A good thing too: I don't know if it was my fruitless quest at a boymance there and in Amsterdam, or the incipient chill in the north, but I was finding my mood up there starting to flag. Echoes from the past summer stand like troops massed outside the gates of my subconscious.

Nothing like the sun to offer tonic, though to tell the truth the contrast between here and blustery northern France took me by surprise. For one thing, that speedy TGV train evaporates the distance. Nice's narrow streets of Second Empire structures vaguely evoke Paris—by way of Santa Barbara. My wee hotel is a comfy upgrade from my dank Parisian digs—and a good bit cheaper.

I keep coming back to these Mediterranean climates. It's easy to see why, what with their Goldilocks weather and eye-candy geography. All of them—there are only five such regions on Earth—owe their perfect climate to a delicate combination of factors: moderate latitude, well-placed mountains, cool ocean breezes. Well, except for here: the sea is too warm and we're much too far north; Marseilles is at practically the same latitude as Minneapolis or Montréal, a dispiriting fact I learned in French class one frozen February morning. So what makes this place so special?

For one thing, the Alps. Yes, those snowy mountains so associated with Julie Andrews belting it out in *The Sound of Music* in fact terminate right here. I see them, rising up from the coast. *Les alpes-maritimes*, the French call them. They funnel wind down the Rhône Valley, blowing away all that moisture and chill while keeping humidity from the Mediterranean at bay. The wind even has a name that brings to mind a Greek deity: the mistral.

I know just how to explore this place: on two wheels. I rent a motor scooter from a nearby shop—I've got one back home, so it's all pretty familiar—and head along the coastal corniche roads going east.

Rounding the curve of Villefranche harbor, I spot a cruise ship flanked by smaller boats, a mother goose with babies in tow. The water is that distinctive Mediterranean deep blue—caused by its salinity, they say—with coastal peaks a blend of pearl-shaded rock and emerald forest. An occasional centuries-old building looms around a bend. So far the Riviera's living up to its hype, beating out similar such drives in California with richness of flora and history.

I reach Monaco and its best-known district, Monte Carlo. It's been settled since prehistory, more-or-less continuously ruled by one family, the Grimaldi, since the 1200s. Leave it to tinseltown, however, to draw in the crowds: memorials to Princess Grace, Grace Kelly, who married one of the royals and was killed in a car crash in 1982, are everywhere.

City-states are fragile things, and without creative means of keeping themselves afloat they often perish. In Monaco's case, casinos did it—a scheme later adopted by Las Vegas and Macau. It's more of a business center these days than my James Bond-recollected fantasies: industry tends to gravitate toward tax havens like this one, though no doubt the climate doesn't hurt either.

Perhaps for that reason, Monaco is…something of a letdown. The cliff walks and medieval streets near the palace are entrancing, if a bit touristy, but the rest of the town feels bland: a thicket of soulless high-rises climbing the hills above the bay. The casino's still oh-so old-world—jacket and tie required to enter. *Ixne on that*, I consider, gazing at my backpacker duds. Instead I scoot past on my motorbike, 007-style, sending tourists and pigeons scurrying out of the way.

Up on the Moyenne Corniche, the middle road, I stop in Èze, a small hilltop town halfway between Monaco and Nice. The ruins of a fort sit atop a hillside astride an arched viaduct. The blue sea is in the background, perfectly framed by the fecund triangle of the valley. At a small weekend market, people—tourists mostly—buy trinkets, souvenirs, food. Another Disneyland? Maybe: the man himself spent some time here. But Èze doesn't feel forced. My curiosity is whetted: when does a place tip from popular to overrun, from charming *au naturel* to cloying and artificial? So far I haven't crossed the tipping point, and familiarity hasn't spelled the death of wonder or crimped my efforts to find emotional escape.

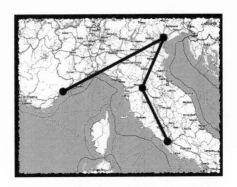

Il Paese Eterno
Venice, Florence & Rome

*I*t's early evening as my Trenitalia "Eurostar City" stops at Verona station. I spy two gentlemen on the platform but doubt they're aware of the Shakespearean significance.

Nice to Venice isn't terribly far, but the journey across the flared top of Italy's boot is an all-day affair: two trains, a missed connection in Milan—trains in this country are as tardy as legend suggests—and a breakneck sprint across the platforms to catch the second leg, which departs minutes after my ticket is re-issued.

Arriving in Venice after dark, I follow a flock of tourists trying to figure out the different *vaporetti*—the water buses that ply the canals of the city. At first I mistake the covered black-and-yellow rectangular floating piers for the ships themselves until one pulls up and it all makes sense. I board and, though weary, am quickly captivated by the Venetian night: arches of buildings are grandly lit, facing the stone balustrade of the Rialto Bridge over the Grand Canal.

My little *residenza*, bed & breakfast Italian-style, is just a few hundred feet from Piazza San Marco—but even my legendary sense of direction is confused by the warren of ever-narrowing alleyways, veins dribbling into capillaries. At last I find it, on a street skinny enough for me to touch buildings on both sides with my arms outstretched. Not something I'm wont to do, however: Venice so far looks to be the dirtiest European city I've visited.

Age is probably a factor: like Bruges, this place hit its peak in the 1200s. Those Oriental building touches—especially the elongated archways—come to us courtesy of eastward trading patterns, as the city once controlled a chain of ports all the way to the Black Sea.

Much as Paris has been endlessly analogized—Chicago as "Paris on the Prairie," Beirut as "Paris of the Middle East"—so too Venice: both Bruges and Amsterdam term themselves the "Venice of the North." Imitations back home range from Venice, California—where a real-estate developer put in actual canals complete with gondola rides—to the Venetian hotel in Las Vegas (gondola rides available there too). Perhaps the city should cash in on its cachet and whimsically brand itself "The Venice of Italy."

The city also birthed something darker, with etymology to match: a small section of town once held a metalworking shop, or foundry— "geto" in old Venetian. Back in the bad old Middle Ages, the district was repurposed into a segregated quarter for Jews: the world's first-ever ghetto.

I almost miss it: basically just a cluster of buildings around a couple of small squares accessible only through a once-gated alleyway. The buildings themselves are unadorned, flat-façaded, numerous stories densely packed. Laws at the time limited the height of the buildings Jews were allowed to live in, but the population kept growing (at its peak it was around 4,000). The solution, the only one the authorities would permit: build ever-tighter floors.

In its day the district had five synagogues, and feeling a bit heritage-minded I book myself on a walking tour of them. An Italian woman with a large key ring locks and unlocks a myriad of doors up walk-up steps: most of these are just a couple of rooms in the cramped edifices. And they're humble—in many, wood is faux-painted to simulate marble. Only one, the synagogue frequented by once-prominent exiles from Spain, boasts richly hued paneling.

I'm traveling solo and on something of a budget, so a ride in one of the city's romantic gondolas isn't in the cards...or so I thought.

There are only three bridges fording the Grand Canal. To aid matters, a number of aging gondolas have been pressed into service as mini water-buses, *traghetti*. I hop on one with two or three other tourists and enjoy the romance for fifty (Euro) cents.

Not that this changes anything in the blueballs department; some romance looks to be happening at my *residenza* but it doesn't involve me. One morning I meet at breakfast a young English couple here for a few days. So, so friendly—Eva, a tallish brunette, and Chris, a lanky, soft-spoken lad with dusky blonde hair. *Boy are you lucky*, I beam in Eva's direction. They're both so jovial, laughing, and sweet that I want to follow them everywhere. I don't, of course—I don't need "stalker" added to my resume. Bollocks to all the plaints I keep hearing from women: why are the best ones straight—and taken?

Water, water everywhere. One afternoon I circumnavigate the city in a *vaporetto*: up the Grand Canal and through the broad San Marco Basin that divides the city's main cluster of islands from the more isolated district of La Giudecca. Crossing under the Ponte della Libertà, the only road link to the city, I see cars for the first time in days: there are no roads in the city to accommodate them; motorists park near the train station and must navigate the city as we tourists do, by boat.

It's really a place that has no business existing: all my life I've read about its battles with the sea, its stinking canals, its sinking buildings. Visitors and writers describe the city as a lost cause, a place fated to be lost to the waves like Atlantis. Now I see why: many places have canals, and other regions wage war on the water—New Orleans (not so successfully), the Netherlands with its dykes and windmills. But Amsterdam lies inland, reclaimed from lakes that were surrounded by more land. Venice, by contrast, sits on a series of marshy clumps half a mile out in the Adriatic. It may have seemed bold in the 1300s for a maritime power to headquarter itself so—but that was before climate change and rising sea levels. Nowadays, with waves lapping at the base of its crumbly buildings and wooden walkways at the ready for the yearly floods (these happened a few weeks after I left), the fate of *la serenissima*, the Most Serene Republic, is uncertain.

Alighting at Piazza San Marco, I take in the marquee attractions: the Basilica de San Marco, all Byzantine domes on the outside and dazzling gold mosaics covering every surface on the inside—the world's biggest and most artful disco ball. The Palazzo Ducale, the

Doge's Palace, plain and unadorned on the outside, a long off-white structure of repetitive pointed arches. But the inside is magic: as the seat of government of the Venetian Republic, its council chambers, anterooms, even staircases are a fantasia of intricate décor and marble-gilded ceilings. The Bridge of Sighs is a letdown: suitably atmospheric looking out its slit windows, all that condemned prisoners would see before meeting their ultimate fate; but the exterior is buried under the blue-and-white of some building-girdling advertising signs. Serene Republic for sale.

And yes, a clock tower to climb, the Campanile. To prep for it, I rediscover my love for gelato—dark chocolate and chocolate with nuts and chocolate mousse. Then I discover from a harried-looking ticket-taker at the entrance: no stairs. Access to the tower is by elevator only. *Great*. Does he want my gelato calories back? The view's remarkable in the orange afternoon, a sea of red tile surrounding the open spread of the piazza. The Campanile, however, could be totemic of the city's fate as a whole. It looks unreasonably newish, and it is: the original fell over in the early twentieth century, and even this reconstruction is in constant need of shoring and repair.

Back on the train. Italy's jumped on the high-speed bandwagon as well, with express lines running down the spine of the country connecting Venice, Milan, Florence, and Rome. Eurostar Italia, they call it. Doesn't help with punctuality, however: over and through the green Tuscan hills we pull into Florence an hour behind schedule.

Then I get lost again. This time it's Florence's unusual address-numbering system, two sets of numbers on the same street, one for businesses, another for residences. To make it more interesting, my *residenza*, on a couple of higher floors of a walk-up apartment building, once was an actual residence.

Florence is also my first stop on the Family Heritage Tour (well, unless you count London, where my parents first met), a city whose place in my lexicon far outweighs its modest size (population under 400,000): my father lived here for two years as a young student in the late 1940s, and tales of the city filled my home. To this day my father is fluent in Italian, and hefty tomes on the art treasures of the Uffizi and Pitti galleries grace my family's bookshelves.

After the unreality of Venice and the seascapery of the Riviera, it's good to be in an honest-to-goodness *town* again: thrift stores, clothing shops, leather markets, places to buy (and sell) used books. Vespas are everywhere, their buzz echoing through the narrow streets where palazzo rooftops seem almost to touch. The city also remains a big college town: on my initial afternoon reconnoiter it seems half the young females are studying for art-school exams.

For good reason: the city could justifiably be called capital of the Renaissance. Botticelli, Machiavelli, Brunelleschi, Michelangelo, Donatello…the list of luminaries who made their home here is staggering. A modest Roman settlement, Florentia, it was catapulted by the then-nouveau-riche Medici family—who patronized all those artistic greats—into World Heritage status before UNESCO termed it such. They were an interesting lot, the Medici, a bit like the Kennedys in America: rising from mercantile means to the pinnacle of political power; just as JFK nabbed the U.S. presidency so too did a Medici become Pope. A stone's throw from my *residenza*, in fact, lies the Cappelle Medicee, where the Michelangelo-crafted tombs are located. It's modest, but only by Florentine standards: a tall vaulted space capped by fresco. The sculptures inside, heftier in the bodice as was the fashion of the time, intricately depict undulating curves of human flesh. And this is *marble*, one of the most temperamental materials to shape.

Something even grander looms nearby: that familiar-looking tent of red tile, ruddy in the afternoon light. Basilica di Santa Maria del Fiore. Brunelleschi's dome.

It's impressive, to be sure, but its clean lines obscure the fact that it was, for the 1400s, the moon shot or Channel Tunnel of the age. The building sat domeless for decades until a builder as clever as Brunelleschi conceived of the engineering to make it happen.

Inside it's a simpler affair than the gothic witchery of cathedrals up north: unadorned white-vaulted ceiling sitting atop square stone columns. The fresco inside the dome is where it goes wild: a dizzying array of vignettes getting ever smaller before capping off in an octagonal window revealing a sliver of cloud and sky.

And not one but two leg-straining options to choose from: the dome itself or the adjacent Campanile, the clock tower, 414 steps. The waistline is grateful.

For caloric replacement, gelato beckons again: I meet two friends, Tim and Emilee, who beeline me to a gelateria. Tim's a colleague from years past, a blue-eyed dark-haired former surfer from Southern California turned software programmer turned student of Tibetan Buddhism at a small institute here in Tuscany. His unlikely blend of life choices partly inspired me to embark upon this journey. Emilee's his new wife, dark-haired, of Filipina descent by way of Cornwall, Ontario, and Yuba City, California. The chattiest of the bunch and a budding chef, she directs me to the glassed-in counter of swirling frozen mounds.

"We've tried a whole bunch of places and we keep coming back here."

Who am I to argue? A dark-chocolate-with-almonds combo is even better than the blend I sampled in Venice. Tim and Emilee indicate the place offers flavors other than chocolate. *So what?*

Back to Michelangelo: the crowds at the Accademia are blessedly light, allowing us to gawk at my namesake sculpture, the "David", for something like half an hour. For once, it's a real-life sculpture bigger than I expect: the hands are especially outsized, intended as it was for a pedestal, out of doors. Another anatomical feature isn't so blessed.

"Don't you think it should be bigger?" I ask, pointing at the lad's not-so-privates. My friends laugh.

"Come on! Can you imagine him with a big-old honking one just hitting you in the face?" Emilee offers.

Uhm, I sure can.

Later I learn that smaller endowment was prized at the time. Still, looking at the sinuous body curves, curly hair, and serenely focused stare, it's hard not to develop a crush on the thing. That's probably in part intentional: only twenty-nine when he completed it, Michelangelo labored for three years on a block of marble other artists said was unusable. If this fetching fellow in marble isn't evidence of the artist's fixation on other guys, I don't know what is.

Tim and Emilee take it easy in the afternoon—they've been here before—but I'm determined to see more. Not too much more, however: this city's giant museums could take a year to explore fully. Instead I head around the back of one of them, the Pitti Palace, and stroll through its luscious gardens terracing their way up a verdant hillside. Diverse sculptures flank the path: here, a pair carrying a vine of grapes suspended by a branch; there, an oversized head. At the top, a cherub in the center of a fountain presiding over a forested valley dotted with red-tiled villas. A friendly young pair from Kansas takes my photo. I'm not sure if they're together, but that fellow's high-pitched sibilants leads me to suspect he may play for my team. *I should have asked.* All this romantic imagery isn't helping the blueballs.

I only visit one exhibit inside the Pitti, but it's richly worthwhile: a display of implements collected by the Medici family centering on the science and engineering of the period. Brass clocks, pendulums and astrolabes sit underneath a richly frescoed ceiling. The Medici invested heavily in the sciences; work done in mathematics in the city led directly to Renaissance-era perspective painting and its feel of three-dimensionality. This, for me, is the truest inspiration: for those who think of science as soulless, offering nothing of beauty or humanity, I offer this up as proof that it's all more connected than we realize.

Nighttime. I rendezvous with Tim and Emilee again in the Oltrarno district, south of the river, at an eatery-cum-food shop to try the local specialty, *bistecca alla fiorentina.* Olive oil infuses steak with uncharacteristic lightness. Talk shifts to the Steve/Bradley debacle, and it leads us back to matters of spirituality and faith.

"It's really hard," Tim says. He's been studying Buddhism for years with rigorous academic focus, and still labors to apply it to everyday life. Bradley wasn't all that religious, but Steve's spiritual quests seemed, paradoxically, to go hand-in-hand with his underlying instability. Tim nods.

"Yeah, I hear ya. I know some addicts too."

He offers that not all spiritual awakenings catalyze conflict the way that mine did, but I'm not so sure: to me it too often feels that religion or spirituality offers recovering addicts a palliative to substance use, one that doesn't always aid in making the best decisions. At least that's how it seemed to me.

But again, enough of that. More distraction awaits.

Wandering about, we come upon clusters of youths sitting on ancient church steps in floodlit piazzas, talking, drinking, and (of course) smoking. I continue the evening with a foray into Florence's gay nightlife: small, just a handful of unprepossessing watering holes. I even try curing blueballs with an unusual remedy: a visit to a bathhouse. I'm not against these places *per se*, though even in my current no-strings-attached state I find myself unmoved by completely anonymous sex; even those one-night-stands I've enjoyed bear some resemblance to romance. I needn't worry, however: the place is deserted, only a handful of chubby older fellows bearing zero resemblance to all those comely sculptures. Blueballs continue.

Next morning I encounter my only other Florentine letdown. The storied River Arno…brackish and muddy.

Okay, Mediterranean Italy isn't exactly river country. Still, I have a reason to stroll the Ponte Vecchio, the famous bridge with all its shops: one of them, specializing in works of coral, once did business with my grandfather. Its proprietor, Ugo Gherardi, greets me warmly and shows me some of his wares. I have early memories of a magnificently carved polished peach rose sitting in my mother's jewelry box that came from this shop.

So much more to see…Donatello's Mary Magdalene in the Museo dell'Opera del Duomo: hands coming together as if in prayer; hair frozen in place like an icy waterfall; hard, angular, weathered face. Michelangelo's Slaves back at the Accademia: unfinished shapes bursting from the marble like emergent life forms in a science-fiction film. The Palazzo Vecchio, the old palace, seat of the Florentine government in the 1500s and like the Louvre a hodgepodge of styles: modest exterior stonework gives way to gilded octagonal flourishes in the ceiling of the assembly halls; a touch of deep-blue compliments the gold leaf. And all of the Uffizi, which I never visit. I leave the Renaissance capital with many of its stones unturned.

Wow, it's a first: the train from Florence to Rome is actually *on time*. Stepping off the platform and onto a crowded subway, it hits me: *back in the big city*. Smaller than Paris or London but more chaotic: graffiti throughout, vehicle horns afire, pedestrianism a euphemism for "game of chicken with speeding vehicles." Intimidating to some, but mother's milk to me.

My little hotel in this city lies on a quiet residential district of rose- and dun-colored three-story apartment buildings. The odd palm tree puffs lazily out front. Stretching for blocks and blocks is a long, many-arched, half-ruined structure of long, slender bricks. *It can't be.* It is: one of the original Nero aqueducts. I've been in Europe more than a month now and have become blasé about layers of history piled together in one place. But not like this, not two-hundred-year-old apartments and two-*thousand*-year-old watercourses.

I hope that surprise isn't the last, because my pop-cultural Rolodex runneth over with references to the Eternal City: *Gladiator*, *Rome: Open City*, *Bicycle Thieves*, *La Dolce Vita*, *Roman Holiday*...too many. Encountering the ruins of the Trajan Forum the next morning, pillars broken and fallen over, all I can think of is Mel Brooks: "Columns! Columns! Get your columns! Doric! Ionic! Corinthian!"

Movies and video games are perhaps a signifier of my generation, because when I think of archeological ruins the first thought that bubbles up is: *boring*. As a boy on family trips to Israel I was dragged from one pile of rubble to another, exasperated relatives wanting and wishing for me to be as excited by it as they were. I haven't laid eyes on wrecked antiquity since. That is, until today, when I stand at the foot of Palatine Hill, the very heart of ancient Rome, beside arguably the most famous ruin of all. The Colosseum.

It may be shoulder season here in Italy, this warm day in the middle of October, but the crowds are thick around the massive edifice. They don't detract—this place was a sports stadium, designed to be bustling. But my architectural reverie is soon quashed as I fire up the audioguide I rent—perfect for dodging long lines, by the way: this was a place of savagery. Mass slayings of wild beasts in celebration of imperial military conquests; the iconic gladiatorial contests—really little more than stylized fights to the death. They say a million animals and half a million humans lost their lives in this place, while the hordes in the stands drank and cheered. Puts those football hooligans into perspective.

The ruins behind cure me of my youthful boredom: at the Forum of Augustus three columns forlornly hold up a single stone where once they supported a building. Palatine Hill itself is sleepy, park-like, its many visitors disappearing into the shady paths. I hear lots of Hebrew spoken, and I soon learn why: it's holiday time in Israel, and Rome is a short flight from the Levant. A bunch of them stare at me photographing myself giving the Arch of Titus the finger.

"For the Temple," I say. They nod appreciatively and walk off, laughing. This monument commemorates the Roman sack of Jerusalem in 70 AD, though I'm not quite sure what possessed secular me to care so much. Perhaps a tribal sense of injustice that transcends religion.

The city may be ancient but the country isn't: on the other side of the Roman relics lies a huge neoclassical wedding cake of a place— much newer, much photographed. Every time I saw it in a movie I wondered what the heck it was: the Victor Emmanuel monument, built to commemorate the nineteenth-century Italian luminary who helped cobble together disparate city states and Papal lands into a single nation. Or so says the museum housed inside. America—nay, Canada!—is older than Italy.

Not far away lies my *real* site of pilgrimage: Gelato di San Crispino, reportedly the best in these parts. At this point I can't even tell them apart: they're all stellar and leave me in a murky chocolate haze. Across the street, meanwhile, sits the most intact of antiquity's structures care of its reconsecration as a church and its inclusion in Dan Brown's *Angels & Demons*: the Pantheon. My time in America, surprisingly, renders it familiar: the Founding Fathers, citizens of the Enlightenment all, were obsessed with classical forms. To wit: Jefferson's Monticello, and Washington D.C.'s Capitol, White House,

Supreme Court, and piles of others. But its mysteries are what truly enchant: modern science still hasn't deduced the exact material used to build the dome. It rises, airy and unsupported, crowned by a hole open to the sky.

I leave Antiquity behind and enter the Middle Ages. Rome's Centro Storico and Tridente bear the telltale signs: the close-in buildings, the narrow streets. So narrow that the hulking Trevi Fountain practically hits me in the face. It looks so Renaissance, all marble sculptures and capacious blue pool in front, but here too, the layers of the city: it once marked the end of a Roman aqueduct supposedly discovered by a virgin. I can only hope she got some after making this discovery.

Tourists must be lazy: the nearby Spanish Steps, the broadest stairway in Europe climbing one of the city's hills, teems with seated squatters. But hardly anyone actually *climbs* the damn thing, or so it seems this late afternoon. I do, and it's worth it: from the small Piazza Trinità die Monti at the top, the view to the west takes in the spires of St. Peter's Basilica fronting a weary orange sun. Then a dusky stroll through the hilltop Pincio Gardens, green and quiet, rock and tree and winding street in perfect harmony. This clinches it: Rome's my favorite Italian city of the three. The hills, the vegetation, the sunlight, the narrow streets, the historic structures, even the graffiti-ed buildings…it's the perfect blend of urban and Mediterranean. Back home these are not to be found together—to wit: the perennial dichotomy of Los Angeles and New York.

I may be unmoved by faith, but the Vatican's still worth a visit. Actually, the tale of how Rome went from the capital of Antiquity's most potent empire to the core of one of the world's biggest faiths is enough to bring me here. It transcends Constantine, the Roman emperor who Christianized himself in 313 AD. Centuries after his conversion, power shifted east—to the Byzantines of what is now Turkey. Unhappy with this state of affairs, scheming Romans found a way to get back in the game: they allied themselves with Germanic tribes to the north to form the Holy Roman Empire.

Walking from the metro station in Trastevere to the Vatican nearby, I spot nuns and priests hurrying about as government officials might around Westminster or Capitol Hill. The apparatus of organized religion. When I arrive at the huge ovoid of St. Peter's Square, I find the place crowded and cordoned off: it's Wednesday, the morning when the Pope does his weekly general audience. It's just ending but I catch a glimpse of the guy parading in his vehicle around the crowds.

The Vatican Museums offer explanation enough for what prompted Martin Luther and his band of ascetic reformers to cry foul: this place has it all, from Egyptian artifacts to ornamented arched ceilings gloriously backlit to hefty stone railings wrapped around broad spiral staircases. Then, at last, after a long spin through numerous hallways, the gilded excesses of Rafael's Rooms and the Sistine Chapel. I prefer the former to the latter, though here it's the crowds that spoil it: unlike the Colosseum this is supposed to be a place of quiet, but the wall-to-wall press of people makes that impossible. Looking up, I'm likewise a bit dispirited.

They don't look right.

Michelangelo's frescoes, that is. I've heard the refrain countless times that this is how they were intended to appear; that it was only generations of soot and candle smoke that gave them that somber shade before restoration a few years ago. And yet…the moody look just *worked* better. They now have the feel of the world's most artfully conceived cartoons.

More gelato burning, this one the biggest so far: 551 steps to the basilica's cupola. From this height the over-the-top nature of the place becomes clear: it was purpose-built to project the importance of the Catholic imperium. The interior—creamy arches, gold-leafed ceiling, wavy wooden pillars supporting the main altar—straddles somewhere between Old Europe and high kitsch.

After dark, an encounter with the Jews of Rome. They've been in this town longer than the Christians, though the crowd I meet is mostly around my age. I rendezvous with a penpal of my dad's, Gloria, and her sister at a tidy little flat in Trastevere. A quick drive across the

Tiber—another middling Mediterranean waterway—to a hilltop flat for a gathering of friends. It's *Sukkoth*, they remind me—I'm almost as oblivious these days to celebrations of my own faith as I am of others—the Feast of Tabernacles, where Jews traditionally erect grassy shelters, the eponymous *sukkahs*, to remember those years wandering the desert. Sometimes it seems every Jewish holiday is designed to commemorate the miseries of our ancestors.

"*Ciao!*" says Gloria's bearded friend as he answers the door to their palatial, high-walled flat on a hillside back near the Colosseum. They use the word for both hello and goodbye. A gang of us sits in the *sukkah* on the capacious terrace, graze on a bit of dinner—the combination of Jew and Italian means I'm practically force-fed by my hosts—and share travel tales.

"You travel by yourself?" I'm asked, not for the first time. They can't conceive of doing so.

"Uh-huh," I answer. "Though it feels kind-of familiar." I bring up my hectic relocation patterns. Gloria shrugs.

"Here, we Romans, we stay. We stay." She points to the earth. Not only have these folks lived in the same city their whole lives...but so have their forebears. Rootedness over uncounted generations. The traditional North American icebreaker question, "Where are you from?" holds no currency in this place.

I'm intrigued: they're the diametric opposite of me and my unceasing restlessness. *Did they have it right all along?* I wonder about the Old World and its rooted folk. At the first sign of trouble I've typically picked up and moved on, but not this crowd. We find lots of common ground—Rome and San Francisco share similar living costs (high), public transit (less than you'd expect), and urban upkeep (middling, with dirty streets and graffiti). But in this fundamental area we're like night and day. Perhaps it's fitting that in this multilayered, seven-hilled city in a storied land—*il paese eterno*, I dub it, the Eternal Country—I would find a populace whose roots run so deep.

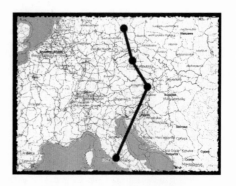

Habsburgs, Ghosts & Cabarets
Vienna, Prague & Berlin

*A*nother former center of empire. Sometimes I think Europe's just one big graveyard of them.

Vienna, however, is on the opposite side of the age spectrum from Rome: the Austro-Hungarians ran the show here until the end of World War I, less than a century ago. This renders the city a paradox: on the one hand, it's modest, no bigger than Portland or San Diego. On the other, it's got grandeur and pomposity to equal the Continent's mega-centers.

The pattern is familiar: an urban palace that's a hodgepodge of styles, and further-flung complexes at the edge of town. I start with the former, the Hofburg, in the city's heart. In use right up to the end by Emperor Franz-Josef, it's predictably a lot less ornate than the insanity of the Vatican or Versailles: the *kaiserappartements*, the former royal residences, are plainly done up in cream-colored walls with thin fragments of gold leaf; some furnishings wouldn't look out of place in a house today. Franz-Josef, the last emperor, reputedly prided himself on living simply and working hard like some latter-day middle-manager.

Still, high drama persisted, as the Sisi Museum next door reveals: the Empress Elisabeth, Franz-Josef's wife of many years—"Sisi" was her nickname. A classic gilded-cage melodrama of a girl of regal breeding married off at fifteen to the emperor…who, creepily enough, was also her cousin. Miserable and reclusive, she traveled around Europe incognito, dressing in black after the death of her son and obsessing about youth and beauty. She was felled by an assassin, an Italian anarchist, in 1898.

And, of course, more churchery nearby: the Stephansdom, bearing stonework more ornate than its Gothic cousins to the West. A carved stairway with near-fully-sculpted busts seems ready to pop out and terrify unsuspecting visitors.

I'm starting to see what's going on here, and it's baser than religion or architecture: human nature being what it is, I can just imagine the towns of old embarking on ever more ambitious cathedrals to see whose is the biggest. *Size queens*. Judging by today's skyscraper Olympics, I'd say little has changed.

Still, 343 steps to the top deserves a reward, and Vienna offers many options: those storied Viennese coffeehouses are everywhere. Plushy furnishings, arched ceilings, racks of newspapers bound on wooden slats. At least that's what the granddaddy of them all looks like, the Café Central. It's crowded around lunchtime so I'm seated at a small circular table across from a primly dressed local, slight and middle-aged, engrossed in the Viennese papers. Scanning the menu, I figure I should try the city's iconic chocolate cake, the *sachertorte*, ostensibly invented at a nearby hotel. It looks heavenly, until I take a bite and make a face.

"Something wrong?" inquires my tablemate.

"What's *in* this thing?" I ask. To my dismay I learn that *sachertorte* features a layer of apricot jam in the middle, which I find repellent.

"But this is *sachertorte*. It is famous!" he exhorts with Germanic militance when I suggest that chocolate go unsullied. No matter. I try eating around it but the stink of fruity goo pervades the concoction.

Time to socialize. In search of a convenient, friendly bar, I find one—right in the lobby of my hostel. I picked Wombats for its congenial reputation, and staying here hammers home that hostelling has come a long way: another solo traveler about my age sits at one of the lobby's two Internet kiosks. A family with small children scurries about, trying to get their laundry done. And in the bar adjacent, lots of cute young guys and gals—*really* young, high-school young. The United

States of Europe has opened up in a big way, and between trains and super-cheap discount airlines it's become commonplace for youngsters to take "flying weekends" around the Continent. A trio from northern England who find my Canadian accent charming say they're planning to visit Schönbrunn the next day and invite me to tag along.

Harry, Emma, Eve, and I board a tram for the ride to the outskirts of town. Harry's been studying in Vienna this semester; a slightly heavyset, bespectacled lad distantly reminiscent of his magician namesake, he begins rattling off info about the place. In a way he reminds me of, well, a younger version of me, too eager to impress. But as with most of the Brits I've encountered to date, he's unfailingly pleasant.

"So are you seeing anyone?" Emma asks. As with most kids of their generation the gay thing scarcely fazes them. *It's complicated*, I muse, considering the Ryan situation and the boy hookups and my efforts to drown out ex-boyfriend angst. I ask if *she's* seeing anyone, which prompts her and Eve to smilingly look at each other.

"I'm not sure," she answers. She's into two different guys, she says, but rumor has it they're really into each other.

So I'm not the only one whose life is complicated.

Schönbrunn, meanwhile, is amazing, straddling an obscene amount of open woodland and manicured gardens. Harry explains it once hosted the likes of Mozart, age seven; Nikita Khrushchev and John F. Kennedy in 1961; and the end of the entire Austro-Hungarian Empire in 1917. The Versailles analogy is apt: Empress Maria Theresa, the 1700s-era monarch, probably borrowed a gold leaf or two from the French as Marie Antoinette was her daughter.

Sympathetic to my choco-plight, the Brits haul me to another place to try *truffeltorte*, a concoction laced with chocolate cream and unsullied by fruity nastiness. Then a bit of shopping: Vienna's got both an open-air market, the Naschmarkt, and a pedestrianized upscale-ified downtown center that, if you squint, could be Grafton Street in Dublin or Dam Square in Amsterdam…right down to the Zaras and H&Ms and Gaps. The relentless march of globalization.

Wombats is booked for the last two nights of my stay, so I decamp for a place with a slightly different party vibe: instead of a bar on the ground floor, this gay-oriented bed & breakfast features a bathhouse on *its* ground floor.

It sounds promising, but in fact it isn't: it's a pleasant enough spot, with the fluffiest, cushiest pillows I've ever had the pleasure to rest my head. But at breakfast it's a motley crew of forlorn-looking, leathery-faced gay men gazing dispiritedly at their eggs and toast like figures in an Edward Hopper painting. No one speaks or socializes.

What's up with that? I'd heard once upon a time that gay men are intrepid and adventurous, willing to go anywhere and try anything. Compare with the cliché of the straight guy hanging out with his friends at the same sports bar week after week or married with kids. My experience so far is the opposite: I'm meeting a vibrant mix of younger straight vacationers wherever I go, but see none of my homo cohorts out in the world—and when I do, it's cliquey small packs or middle-aged couples doing everything five-star. On the one hand, this is great: my forays to nightspots have enabled me to meet locals. On the other, well…I consider my blend of backpacking and B & Bs, of youth hostels and gay guesthouses, and can't conceive of any of my peers doing it this way.

Then again, maybe it has more to do with national tradition: Americans—and Canadians too—are granted very little time off compared to Europeans. Those who want to take big trips to faraway locales must do it when they're young and pre-employed; once they get in the workforce opportunities are limited. I wonder if this, more than isolationism or scale of the United States, is what keeps Americans from leaving home in greater numbers.

Meanwhile, on the subject of the home front, a political first: I drag myself to an Internet café and send off by fax a dozen or so pages of my first-ever vote in a U.S. election. It's historic in many other ways, of course, most especially in that it's the first time a black man has been in the running.

Meanwhile, I see why all those Florida seniors were so confused back in 2000: a typical U.S. ballot sports a dizzying array of national, state, and local figures coupled with bizarre means of marking one's choices; the San Francisco variant is a form of connect-the-dots. It takes me twenty minutes just to figure out the damn thing.

It's dusk. The most romantic time of day deserves a spin on this city's famed Prater Ferris wheel, where hopefully some comely guy will follow me up one of the burgundy wooden cabins for an afternoon reverie…or maybe not: as it gets dark the place is overrun by hordes of families and seniors. Still, the view is beguiling, all those lights popping on in the city beyond the fairground.

Then it's back to Wombats, where my teenage British pals are in the midst of some melodrama: too much alcohol, a successful hookup for one, and a failed romance for another. *Sigh*. A reminder that my magnetic attraction to youth may be part-and-parcel of my social grief back home: Bradley and his friends used to have such episodes. Of course, it doesn't take much to distract me: a charming, adorable Finnish boy—eighteen—comes sauntering into the bar dressed as a girl; one of his hostel-mates loaned him the duds for an impromptu Halloween costume. A bit tipsy and a lot friendly, I'm within inches of making a pass at him…but figure this might be time to play the better part of valor; I don't think Euro boys are *that* open, and this one claims a girlfriend back in Helsinki.

I wrap things up with a stroll along the Ringstrasse, Vienna's former city fortifications that were transformed in the 1800s into grand boulevards. The marquee edifices—the Parliament, the City Hall, some elegant hotels—are magnificently floodlit; one building is gilded with tiny blue icicle-style lights the entire breadth and height of its seven or so stories. The city feels as if forlornly waiting, waiting, waiting for a return to relevance. One day it was the capital of an empire of sixty million souls and the next day…it wasn't. I doubt that mighty America awaits such an abrupt turnabout, but it makes me wonder.

The second-class compartment is packed to the gills. Still, it's a marvel what a non-event this trip has become: a quick change in locomotives and a terse "Welcome to Czech Railways" announcement over the intercom. Hard to believe that a couple of decades ago this was a stop replete with border guards, gun-toting troops, forensic document checks. The East Bloc has vanished from Europe like a ghost.

The pastoral landscape evokes similar hauntings: autumnal hillsides, trees all manner of oranges and reds. It evokes for me the landscape of countless war films as we enter the Second World War's heartland and arrive soon after in Prague.

Past notwithstanding, Prague is a city of the future: when the Cold War ended and lots were being cast on which spots would adapt best, many guessed this city, with its rich heritage and history of democratic rule, would surge to the front of the queue. Stepping off the metro immediately vindicates this: two large steel-and-glass malls flank the Anděl station, complexes that wouldn't look out of place in Chicago or Minneapolis or Los Angeles. McDonald's, Starbucks, and KFC are everywhere. I'd been warned by the Brits that the town is overbuilt, hyper-touristed, another flying weekend destination. I hope they're wrong: this is still *Prague*, after all. Home to Keplar, Kafka, Tycho, to say nothing of innumerable films bewitched by its ghoulish cityscape.

Under the capitalist sheen I quickly find the ghosts of the city's past: the clean and smartly run metro—built originally by the Communists—retains Soviet-era artwork. The city's old town is spotlessly preserved—though after the tight squeezes of Bruges, Amsterdam, and Venice it feels rather roomy. So too the capacious town square, where I wait with the crowd for the polychromatic, dials-within-dials astronomical clock to chime the hours.

The clock betrays a darker side: one of the cuckoo-clock figurines marching past during the hourly chime is a bearded hook-nosed caricature now dubbed "Greed"; once he carried moneybags and was called "The Jew."

Nearby lies more of this history in the old Jewish quarter of Josefov. Most of it is no longer squalid and crowded like the one in Venice: it was cleared in a nineteenth-century bout of urban renewal and now sports broad streets and elegant art-nouveau boulevards that could have been lifted wholesale—high-tone stores and all—from an *arrondissement* in Paris. Yet commingled with the grand newer edifices are significant pieces of the old: six synagogues, a town hall, a graveyard. The Jewish buildings are striking in their modesty: in contrast to the metallic wonder of the astronomical clock in the main town square, the Jewish counterpart features two simple wooden timepieces—one bears Hebrew letters and spins counterclockwise. The synagogues are similarly austere, almost out of place in the district that once centered on them. Still, the buildings inspire in their own way, if only as emblems of a community's will to go on in spite of all those hardships.

And go on they did, making the most of their cramped surroundings. The best example is the old Jewish cemetery: thousands of headstones tumbling over each other at all angles bearing weathered inscriptions in Hebrew from centuries past. The cemetery sits on higher ground, but for reasons unnatural: earth was brought in to raise it once it filled up, and bodies were stacked one on top of the other—rumor has it up to twelve deep. There was simply no more room to expand.

I come across the place's most famous monument, that of Rabbi Lowe, star of one of Judaism's few ghost stories: legend has it he created a sort of Frankenstein monster, the Golem, to protect the Jews of Prague from their tormentors. The Golem's clay body—brought to life, the story tells, with a tiny scroll of hallowed Jewish scripture inserted in its body—supposedly rests in one of the synagogues in the heart of the quarter. It's still around (the synagogue, not the Golem): the Old New Synagogue remains a place of worship, one of the oldest Gothic buildings in the city. Though it feels strange to call it that: its simple flourishes pale in comparison to the hulking churches and cathedrals of the ruling faith.

The Vtlava River meanders nearby. It's a sunny afternoon and the Charles Bridge's Gothic towers, blackened by soot, loom menacingly over the water. One of the towers can be climbed, and from the top a sea of red-tiled roofs cap frothy white and mustard-yellow facades. The bridge itself is lined with numerous stone statues that glower enigmatically: figures of angels, saints, and kings.

Across the river the city celebrates its favorite son. But instead of chapter-and-verse recitations of his life, the Kafka Museum echoes the man's work with experiential spaces: one room is filled with mirrors, a fun-house sort of place of anonymity and ambiguity. Another offers an endless array of filing cabinets stretching floor to ceiling. A third offers a stairway leading down to nowhere, flanked by walls made entirely of wooden slats like Hannibal Lechter's lair of serial killing. It sounds like cloying trickery, but I leave the place suitably creeped out.

Something similar lurks down the road: Prague's long-anticipated but only recently unveiled memorial to the victims of Communism. The Czechs hated the regime, and the monument—a series of sorrowful bronze figurines on a park-like hillside, each figure missing an ever-increasing array of body parts—is a mite earnest but gets the point across. So does the city's hard-to-find Museum of Communism. Underscoring Czech sentiment, it's housed in a building containing a casino and a McDonald's. It's also empty as twilight falls on the otherwise-bustling shopping street in the city's New Town.

All those over-the-top propaganda posters, hammer-and-sickle flags, and statues of Lenin. Ironic that a system devoted to abolishing inequality probably created more of it than it swept away: shops were often empty, their keepers holding back their best for those who could slip them something extra; Communist Party members with access to hard currency were favored. Not to mention, for a system intended to guarantee happiness and harmony, a police-state atmosphere of betrayal and mistrust.

And yet…looking at these fixtures of the vanquished regime, I'm struck by the historical points we overlook. Communist Party paranoia and intrigue was absurd: they were fixated on the notion that, at any moment, the West was going to invade and enslave them all. Except when one considers the ferocity with which Western nations reacted against the Russian Revolution: the powers of the time fomented a bloody civil war, seemingly willing to stop at nothing to destroy the "Red Menace." Or the level of paranoia America itself endured under McCarthy in the 1950s. That said, if any of us had to choose an America in the thrall of McCarthy or a Czechoslovakia under the Communists, with the jackboots of Stalin never far away…

Prague's ghostly aura prompts delving into darker shadows just outside town. Early the next morning, I pile into a comfy SUV together with a middle-aged couple from Philadelphia. Our driver-cum-guide is taking us to Terezín, a town an hour's drive away. As urban Prague gives way to suburbs and then to countryside, he recounts the backdrop of what we're about to see.

"Czechoslovakia was divided by the allies in 1938." We history buffs nod: he's referring to the fruitless appeasement bid dreamed up by Neville Chamberlain to ensure "Peace in our time."

"What no one realizes is why the Germans really wanted the Sudetenland."

"Wasn't it because it was an ethnic German enclave?" I offer.

"That's what they said. But the Sudetenland runs like a belt around the rest of the country. And it's the high ground."

He continues. "All of Czechoslovakia marched to stop them. But the rest of the world told the Czechs they would be responsible if they started a war. They forced them to retreat."

With conquest of the country sewn up by 1939 the Nazis set upon retrofitting Terezín, a garrison town with an adjoining fort, into one of the lynchpins of the Holocaust.

"The Czechs cooperated with the Nazis," our guide explains. "They weren't just anti-Semitic. The Nazis bribed them with Jewish homes, Jewish treasure."

We pull up to the small fort just outside the town, walking from the gravel parking lot into my first-ever concentration camp. Its mustard-yellow entry arch is emblazoned with a painted *Arbeit Macht Frei*—"WORK MAKES FREE"—in imitation of the bigger death camps out east. It's foggy and freezing—although we're barely forty miles from Prague it feels many degrees colder. We tour the squalid facility—barbed-wire atop high stone walls, barracks with wooden-slat bunks, an assembly yard where prisoners were made to stand in the Czech winter for hours on end. Meanwhile, beyond a stand of trees are officers' quarters and soldiers' barracks, looking for all the world like elegant country homes. There's even a swimming pool the Jews were forced to build with their bare hands.

At the edge of the prison, a sign reads, "KREMATORIUM." Although I've seen any number of documentaries about this grim period, my hands shake as I snap a photo of it and the facility that it marks. Although the world has seen other genocides come and go— some even more brutal and savage—I think none have yet matched the single-mindedness by which a major industrialized world power devoted itself so completely to mass murder.

And yet, amid all the darkness, some hope: since 1989 the post-Communist Czech Republic has devoted significant resources toward research and upkeep of this facility. Much of the Communist-era slant—which glorified the role of the liberating Soviets while downplaying the facts of the genocide—has been replaced by more balanced history-telling. As we tour other museums in the town, we learn about the treatment of other minority groups interned here: gays (yes, the Nazis would hate me on two counts), Jehovah's Witnesses, political prisoners. Also heartening is the presence of numerous high-school tour groups, many from neighboring Germany; the German educational system has made it a priority for its young to see this for themselves.

Another striking detail: since Jews of all stripes from throughout Europe were pouring into this place, it saw a sizeable share of writers, musicians, artists, and other luminaries. Some of this work is on display; in addition to the much-popularized children's drawings are adult works of striking proficiency.

We return to the city and I wander the streets for more than an hour, trying to shake the haunting sights out of my head. I rest up, then rise very late that evening for what I anticipate will be a happier occasion back home.

It's the first Tuesday in November, Election Day in America. The *Prague Post*, the local English-language daily, hosts an overnight party at a sports bar in New Town. I walk in to a place crowded with big-screen TVs showing not soccer but CNN; I realize it's been over two months since I've laid eyes on Wolf Blitzer's beard.

Ironically, for such a coming-together type of gathering, the crowd is initially aloof: I try sitting at one table and a couple of middle-aged men shoo me away with a gruff "these seats are taken." Everyone's in tight groups of friends or colleagues. It's another of those *remind me why I'm traveling alone again?* moments.

Fortunately, some space opens up next to some friendly youths; they're Czech economics students and they impress me with their grasp of the American political system. I've come to take for granted how much Canadians know about our neighbor to the south, but I'm struck by how the same is true the world over.

As the tide of the election moves in Obama's favor, the crowd livens up; even here in the heart of newly capitalist Europe there's no love lost on Dubya's Republican successors. Finally, at five in the morning, the results are announced. History is made, and even from 4,000 miles away the Obama echo resonates.

For me it spawns a different resonance: in giving up on places, leaving them, I've dismissed the possibility that they or their denizens can evolve. But they can and they do. Perhaps this is my homeland reminding me, broadcasting a subtle signal that things may be different next time…should I choose for there to be a next time.

A train ride the next afternoon brings me north, to Berlin. Close to two months in Europe means I've seen train stations aplenty, but Berlin's Hauptbahnhof feels like a different sort of creature: gargantuan and new, with more retail than some shopping malls. A ride on the city's elevated S-Bahn and subterranean U-Bahn whisks me to Friedrichshain, a district in the former East Berlin that's now something of an arty student district. As I step out onto the impossibly wide Frankfurter Allee, it's clear this is a European city like no other: broad, straight streets lined with trees, their leaves almost gone in the November chill. Brawny brick-and-stone apartment houses. No medieval alleyways, no Tinkertoy churches. This city looks like it belongs in the New World.

For the first time since London, I replace hostel and guesthouse living with a real-life apartment as Renaissance Man hooks me up with a couple of friends: Jen and Jesse are two twentysomethings sharing a two-bedroom flat, a nicely done-up place with pale hardwood floors, expansive living room, and cozy wooden kitchen. I nearly faint when I learn what they're paying—even in über-strong Euros, it's still less than half what a comparable place would cost in London or San Francisco.

Jen's headed out of town to visit a boyfriend in Stuttgart; she's about as weary and worn-out as I am as she too was up late at an election-night party. Jesse, the other flatmate, is out most of the weekend at his own girlfriend's place. They give me the run of the place—Renaissance Man's hospitality is matched by his pals'. Jen even points me to a good hair salon; I'm starting to get a bit shaggy after all these weeks on the road, and need to look my best if I'm to tackle this city's nightlife.

It's coming not a moment too soon. City after city of museums, churches...and sexual frustration. The only chapel I see—and in passing at that—is the partly ruined shell of the Kaiser-Wilhelm-Gedächtniskirche, a memorial of sorts to wartime bombing. Otherwise, it's time to take Liza Minnelli at her word, and see if life in this town really is a cabaret.

I develop a near-instant crush on Dmitry, a hunky blonde Ukrainian I meet at glossy lounge bar Heile Welt. He's friendly enough, but only enough. His friend Paolo, meanwhile, a Filipino who grew up in Sydney, Australia, is chattier.

"You went to the wrong part of town," he says. We're in Nollendorfer Platz in Schöneberg, Berlin's storied (read: less hip) gay district. "All the cute guys stay in the east, in Kreuzeberg and Prenzlauer Berg."

But we're here now, might as well make the most of it. We pop over to Goya, a glitzy mega-club a few doors down in a capacious domed space. Surprisingly, the place is half-empty throughout the night. Maybe Paolo's right.

"It's the cover. Most Berliners can't afford the €10."

There's a reason for that cheap rent: Berlin still is struggling to recover from all those decades of turmoil, a world war and decades of East-West divide.

But I'm not quite ready to go home yet. I take the train back east—it runs 24 hours on weekends—and pay a visit to a bathhouse in Prenzlauer Berg just north of my temporary home at Jen and Jesse's. As expected, this place is a lot livelier than similar such places in other cities. But again, I'm not too into encounters that random. After a bit of play I sit at the bar and engage in a chat with the barkeep, a fellow named Jens with the same black-dyed hair as my ex, Bradley. We even exchange numbers and pledge to meet up again. Now *that's* a first, at least for me: an oh-so-conventional—and chaste!—pickup at a sex club.

Okay, the town deserves a *little* sightseeing: I roam around Mitte, the central core of the city containing the Brandenburg Gate, the Reichstag, and other monumental, if sterile, official buildings. As with much of Berlin, many of these are newly built as the reunified Germany completes its move of the capital from Bonn. It's an odd vibe: a storied world center utterly bereft of the expected pomp and solemnity. Nearby is the city's Holocaust memorial, though it's hard to tell what it is even up close: essentially a sprawling grid of large blocks of different heights, divided by passageways of varying depths. No plaques, no maudlin explanations or pithy Santayana quotes. The conclusions one draws are solely one's own.

The resurrected Reichstag, the German parliament, bears its own subtle bit of memorializing: the new Norman Foster-designed dome, a pageant of steel and glass, distantly echoes the burning of the building in 1933 that provided the pretext for Nazi dictatorship. The dome can be climbed—if one can bear the two-hour wait in line. I'm too hungover to try.

The Reichstag and Brandenburg Gate sit astride what was once the no-mans-land of the Berlin Wall; the same is true of Potsdamer Platz, once a lonely open plaza now filled in with a glitzy retail mall—what else?—care of Sony. The divide has been utterly erased, yet riding the tidy, efficient U-Bahn and S-Bahn I start to wonder: *how did they divvy up the trains?* With typical German efficiency, of course: a once-tangled array of blocked-off trackage and "ghost stations" where trains ran but did not stop. The whole system was only stitched back together a few years ago.

Nevertheless, relics of the divide persist: East Berlin's jolly street-crossing indicator, the Ampelmännchen, remains prominent and beloved throughout the eastern sector. I can see why: he's a cartoonishly hatted green man in a hurry, looking like he's about to stride off the signal post.

Ironically, with the city whole again, East Berlin has had the last laugh: much of Mitte lay within the eastern sector and this district is once again "downtown." West Berlin's city center around Charlottenburg has resumed its role as an upscale shopping and residential district, another Back Bay in Boston or Upper East Side in Manhattan.

All those images of people stealing souvenirs of the Berlin Wall led me to think it's all gone. But no, a part of it remains as an open-air museum to what was: the East Side Gallery, a mile-plus of the Wall running along the River Spree. Once graffitied, it's now festooned with true street art. One highlight: 1970s-era Russian and German leaders Leonid Brezhnev and Erich Honecker locked in a kiss while sitting in a Trabant.

Further along, the old Checkpoint Charlie remains, though it's now reduced to a tourist trap replete with ersatz guard for the posing. Even though it's in the middle of a humdrum shopping street, the starkly officious "YOU ARE LEAVING THE AMERICAN SECTOR" signage retains a certain aura. Maybe it's those Bond films or that goofy 1980s teen flick *Gotcha*, where a young Anthony Edwards—full head of hair pre-*E.R.*—is berated by a joyless East German border guard rattling on about "ze dee-dee-ahr."

As darkness falls I ride a couple of trains to Pankow, a quiet streetcar suburb in the east beyond upscale Prenzlauer Berg. Here lives Jens, the bartender from the bathhouse. He and his black Labrador meet me at the train station and we head for a nice dinner in an Italian joint that lets us sit outside with doggie. Well, sort of: it's a heated, enclosed patio that keeps out the chill.

"I grew up on the eastern side," he tells when I ask about life post-reunification. "They acted like they knew everything," he says about the *wessies*, the former West Germans. Nowadays, though, he complains about different problems for a gay man in the city—homophobia from ultra-nationalists and immigrant Muslims alike.

"It's why I have the big dog."

It's not the only thing that's big. Back at his tidy one-bedroom in a newish apartment block, I unzip his trousers and find something impressive underneath; let's just say the antithesis of the sculpture of David. Soon I'm enveloping his stiff manhood with a condom in preparation for a righteous rogering, as the Brits call it.

Cabaret indeed. *Auf wiedersehen*, blueballs.

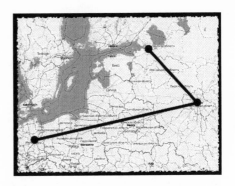

Legacy of the Kievan Rus
Moscow & Saint Petersburg

*I*t's all so overwhelming.

It had to happen eventually: I've been wading slowly from the proverbial shallow end of the familiar—Denver, London, Montréal—into the murkier depths of foreign tongues and, now, foreign alphabets. Still, it surprises, given the ease of navigating Europe so far. If I came to the Continent in search of mental distraction, here that takes the form of struggling to swim with the stream.

It starts on the train: the AeroExpress from Domodedovo Airport is noisy and run-down. Seats recline awkwardly; cracks in the bunched material between cars let in gusts of chill air. But the real fun begins at Paveletskaya station—one of Moscow's nine rail hubs: a huge neon sign reading "MOCKBA" is not the only thing in Russian-only. I spend several minutes figuring out how to exit the airport train arrival area: my ticket was already scanned once, upon departure, and checked again by an actual person en route…but I learn it must be slid through *again* in the exit turnstiles or they won't let you out. A kindly old man helps me out in broken English.

The Moscow Metro is the busiest in the world—more passengers than London and New York combined. But ticket-buying remains decidedly old school: lines form—who said *those* went out with Communism—in front of beat-up wooden kiosks in the grimy marble-white metro entry hall. I repeat, like a mantra, *"deh-syit"* again and again; when I reach the *babushka* behind the counter, I say it again and receive ten tickets in exchange. So far so good.

Inside the ludicrously busy tunnels the signage is hopeless: subway lines are supposed to be color-coded but the wording and symbols have all faded to a dull purplish-gray. Fumbling with my guidebook's inadequate maps—English only—against metro signage—Russian only—I arouse the attention of a sympathetic-looking young blonde lady.

"Where in Canada are you from?" she asks in perfect English, motioning at the flag on my backpack. Suddenly this oh-so-predictable Canuck traveler practice pays off. She's from Vancouver.

"Here," she points on the map in my guide. "This is where you want to go."

A couple of trains and I'm at my destination, a hostel near Tsvetnoy Bulvar not far from the Garden Ring Road. It's a first for me: a shared bathroom. Thus far I've been scouring online listings and hostel review sites and obtaining (relatively) inexpensive ensuite rooms…but not here. Moscow accommodation prices are the highest in the world. It works out okay, though: the place is clean and cheerful, and my room's just across the hall from the commode on the second floor of a brick apartment house in a respectable residential area.

Still, I need a break: I take the next day off, hanging out, doing laundry, catching up on my blog. This becomes a pattern repeated every half-dozen or so destinations: every so often even the most intrepid of explorers needs a recharge.

Red Square blows me away.

You'd think—for a traveler who's already seen Big Ben, the Eiffel Tower, the "Mona Lisa", the Colosseum, and the Reichstag—that a large rectangular plaza on a November Moscow morning wouldn't be that big of a deal. But it is for those of us who came of age in the final spasms of the Cold War. Standing at the site of all those parades of missiles and marches in lockstep, with aging Soviet premiers stiffly looking on…it feels weightier to me than all the cathedrals in Christendom (most of which I feel as if I've seen as well).

Oh yeah, there's a family connection too: none of my forebears actually hail from here, but I think for anyone of Eastern European stock, Moscow has the feel of mothership. The Kievan Rus, the ninth-century tribe for whom the country is named, are long gone, but their Slavic influence extends deep and wide. This was their heartland, Moscow the pinnacle of their legacy. My paternal grandmother prided herself on her Moscow-accented Russian, a Tsarist equivalent of the Queen's English. On my mother's side, meanwhile, one great-grandmother attended dentistry school here, a feat far from mundane for a Jewess from the provinces of the pre-Revolutionary Russian Empire.

The city's big and newish like Berlin, though unlike Germany's capital, still recalibrating from past depredations, Moscow's packed to the gills. It's not just the subway that's mobbed. The inaptly named Garden Ring—one of several girdling the city in concentric circles—is fourteen solid lanes of bumper-to-bumper traffic running in a six-mile oval around the city center.

Contrasts between old and new Russia are so blatant as to seem staged: walking the footpath between my hostel's street and the metro station, I spy a grimy Lada parked next to a shiny black Mercedes; when's the TV-commercial crew turning up? Though the old Russia—ahem, Soviet Union—had its bits of elegance: the city's monumental old skyscrapers, hulking Gothic and Art Deco-inspired affairs reminiscent of the Chrysler Building or Chicago's Wrigley Building. That's not an accident: the Seven Sisters, as they were called, were ordered at the behest of Stalin to show that Soviet-kind, too, can build skyward. The pomp, however, conceals a darker truth: most of the magisterial edifices were built with slave labor.

So back to Red Square. After drinking in the Kremlin's rust-red walls on one side, the G.U.M. department store's Edwardian spires on the other, and the polychromatic onion domes of St. Basil's at the far end, I make for midway down the plaza to meet the most famous mummy of all: Vladimir Ilyich Lenin himself.

Entry is free, but the gauntlet of guards—whose sole purpose seems to be ensuring you have no cameras on your person—is daunting. I check my photographic gizmos at a nearby cloakroom, then descend a dimly lit ramp into the mausoleum. I enter the chamber where the body lies, stuffed and preserved, the skin a dull grayish hue, the fingernails an unnatural purple. He seems so slight for an architect of a mighty revolution. Now that the Soviet Union is no more, secrets of the body's preservation are out: it's cleaned regularly to keep it looking fresh. Oh, here another family connection: my late grandfather actually shook those hands. Around the time of the Revolution he was a student active in the Communist Party.

The moody mausoleum is matched by nearby St. Basil's, a cathedral like none I've seen before: instead of the capacious naves of the Gothics or the sunny domes of Italy, this Russian Orthodox varietal is a beehive of small chambers that rise up, rocketlike. The interiors of those slender onion domes are hollow. The rooms are covered wall to wall with icons—compact squares bearing gilded depictions of religious figures that presaged the use of the term in computer operating systems. Click here to worship the Virgin.

The G.U.M. store across the way is probably the most transformed of the Red Square landmarks. As a boy I remember hearing from travelers how it symbolized Soviet austerity, its large shop windows barren. Nowadays it's resumed its role as a luxury mall, a Harrod's or Saks of the East. Here the backpacker budget kicks in, as everything but a cappuccino—which I do enjoy—is out of my price range. *Oh, Bradley, you woulda loved this:* like many gays, that boy could shop me under the table. I content myself with a gaze at the architecture, which provides uplift enough: modeled after the great railway stations of the Victorian age, the arched steel-and-glass roofline and white marble-and-limestone gallery windows have been immaculately restored—the cleanest place in the city so far. Among the upscale shops is one called "Pinko"—I'm not sure if they get the joke.

Renaissance Man's friend network reaches all the way to this end of Europe: another chum of his from London, Geraldine, is here in Moscow for the season. She's a budding art-world prospector and I meet her after dark at an artist's studio on an island in the Mosvka River just south of the Kremlin.

"It's a symbol of this place. The shopping. The commodities," the artist explains to Geraldine and me—I've been deputized as assistant prospector—clicking through photos of his installation art on a laptop computer. In the works he's wrapped himself in giant wads of cellophane and styrofoam, a man-sized slab of meat in a display case.

Geraldine's father lives here and arranged for a car and driver—a much easier state of affairs than my tortuous metro navigation. We cross the river past a Kremlin gloriously floodlit, then dine at a Central Asian eatery—in addition to sushi having taken the Russian capital by storm, this kebab-and-flatbread cuisine is also popular.

A sharply attired art-prospector brunette and a gay male backpacker are hardly the likeliest pair to hit a Moscow adult nightspot. Most probably wouldn't let us in. But Club Bordo's run by Geraldine's father, and can be counted on to exclude us from the Studio 54-style "face control" that has become *de rigueur* among trendy Moscow nightspots—even the racier ones.

"It's the Moscow club everyone fantasizes about but never finds," she says, as dance beats thump and provocatively clad ladies swirl. One of them makes for me and leans into my lap.

"You are having good evening?" she asks in that warbly accent.

"Uh, sure!" I reply, smiling guiltily. She picks up on my vibe right away.

"You are gay?" she asks sweetly. *Yup.* We all have a good laugh and move on to discuss stiletto heels.

Behind the scenes, the club sounds like a better arrangement than most: Geraldine says the girls are free agents, paying only a nominal fee to work the place for whatever its patrons desire that they're inclined to give them.

Like Stephen Colbert I must miss the Cold War: the next day I make for the Contemporary History Museum, as this former paean to the Revolution has been renamed. Housed in an elegant mansion that was once the Moscow English Club, it's a surprisingly effective display of the last century-plus of Russian history. This is a land that has suffered mightily, something we often forget in the West. Twenty-seven million died in the Second World War alone. Millions more in Stalin's purges. Considering all that, it's remarkable they've achieved even moderate proximity to First World living.

After last night's pricey dinner and twenty-dollar-plus meals at even the modest spots near my hostel, I break down and visit—yes—a McDonald's. The menus are in Cyrillic only, but though I no longer patronize fast food eateries back home I'm American enough to know the items by heart. I also have a suspicion that American fast food is actually of better quality in some international locales. My lunch seems to support this: the McChicken sandwich here is not half bad. As a plus, this McDonald's offers free Wi-Fi Internet access; I get to chatting with some cute blonde lad on GayRomeo, a European dating site. He's free this afternoon so we decide to meet up.

Anton isn't quite as cute in person, but he's fetching enough. He's not much of a conversationalist either but is into other activities: after a spot of afternoon tea we head back to the hostel for a bit of afternoon fun. Our postcoital chat sees us compare relationship information; he's recently broken up with a boyfriend of two years—impressive given he's only nineteen.

"I love him," he says with some intensity. It's a sweet moment, though I can't help but muse, *I guess that makes me the rebound.* That's okay: for me this entire *trip* is something of a rebound.

Lenin and sex clubs and gay boys, and I still haven't seen the inside of the Kremlin. All those movies led me to believe it's a monolithic structure, like the Capitol or Buckingham Palace—in fact, it's a whole campus of buildings cluttered with military troops and gold onion-domed cathedrals. The word "Kremlin" is in fact a generic term for "fortification." I almost take a wrong turn into the presidential offices before being curtly ushered by a guard toward the section for tourists. No meetup with Medvedev in the cards for me.

The sites fascinate but the overall effect of the place, with its omnipresent guards and beefy walls, is about what I expected: this country's rulership takes itself very, very seriously—always has. Interestingly, relics of the *ancien régime* persist: the towers along the walls are still capped with Communist-age ruby-red stars.

Unlikely though it sounds, my dating life here remains pretty lively: I hear from another GayRomeo boy and arrange to meet up at a bar near Kitay Gorod. It's Moscow's oldest part of town, probably the only district with winding medieval streets. I almost lose myself in them but a few phone calls and I'm at Propaganda, a sometimes-gay bar-and-grill joint. Vlad is there waiting; this one *really* doesn't look like his photo: a heavyset blonde with a bitchy demeanor. He hails from South Africa and has come to Moscow for the opportunities—he's in business too, though I don't quite catch what exactly.

With the evening a dud, I decide to head back early—and make the mistake of accepting a ride in Vlad's Audi. Nothing unseemly, he just doesn't get the hint. After dropping me off he starts texting me and doesn't stop, professing his love and promising to wait outside the hostel, Romeo-like, for me to emerge. I hole up inside. Hours later I peek out my window that overlooks the street: he's gone. My Moscow stalker.

After two brawny urban behemoths, Saint Petersburg feels light as a feather: canals and columns again dominate. Even better, for little more than my hostel in Moscow I score a spot in a mini-four-star hotel just off Nevsky Prospekt and a stone's throw from the Hermitage. The proximity works out well: Moscow's autumnal cool has been replaced by early tendrils of the harsh Russian winter. Blasts of wind and gloom come rumbling off the Neva River as I huddle with my backpack onto a quiet side street.

Saint Petersburg has to be the only city built on malaise: in this case, Peter the Great's weariness of the suffocating intrigues of imperial Moscow. He dreamed of a gossamer capital modeled on the European metropolises he'd visited, the first Russian Tsar to do so. *You and me both, Peter.* Even in my far simpler life I've done no shortage of fleeing, when the going got tough, to more welcoming locales.

The Hermitage and Winter Palace are a wonder, the façade of robin's-egg-blue, white and gold a perfect complement to the perennially weak sunshine: we're so far north here that midday feels like late afternoon, though the flip side of this is the White Nights of eternal summer daylight. But I won't be here for that.

Instead, it's a day at the world's second-biggest art museum (the Louvre is number one). Astoundingly comprehensive, spanning prehistory to the postmodern. And yet, as with the Vatican or Versailles, the place overwhelms. Not because of the art, but because the building itself is just *so damn breathtaking*. It's almost impossible to focus on the art. Arched gilded ceilings, gilded columns, gilded wooden doorways, gilded red-velvet thrones…it feels like a deliberate, near-obsessive attempt to outdo Versailles or Schönbrunn, akin to those single-minded Soviet Olympic training programs of years past. They don't do things halfway here.

Geraldine's in town as well, taking meetings with artists in this city. We meet up at a cozy bistro with wood-burning fireplace. Apparently this town's arts scene is pretty lively as well: she's had a hectic, full day sandwiched between overnight train rides. After our meal we stroll through Isaakievskaya, one of the city's grand squares, snapping photos of buildings dazzlingly floodlit.

"We're like a traveler's fraternity!" she says of Renaissance Man and his crew as she plies me with more travel tips. I give her a warm embrace farewell: this crowd of Euro-explorers has done so much to buoy my spirits just as I'd lost faith in my nearest and dearest back home.

Crossing the Neva the next day, I reach the Peter & Paul Fortress. No relation to the folk-singing trio, but rather the original islet where the city was founded. Never used as an actual fort—Peter's victory over the Swedes in the early 1700s was decisive—the place is home to a hodgepodge of structures, including the cathedral where Tsar Pete himself is buried.

One museum here especially captivates: a history of Soviet and Russian rocket development and space exploration. The biggest surprise? It's located on the site where much of this actual development took place in the 1930s. One of the founders of modern rocketry, Konstantin Tsiolkovskii, hailed from Russia.

Inside the uncharacteristically plain-looking building is a long hall filled with rocket engines, their tangle of tubes and piping evoking organic circulatory systems. At one end, a replica of Sputnik, the world's first human-built satellite; it's small, basically a three-foot sphere with antennae protruding from its orb. Hard to imagine the stir it created back in 1957, beep-beeping through the October sky.

Back to the mainland. I pass the Bronze Horseman, the statue of Peter the Great erected by Catherine the Great. This one had more than mere ceremony as its motivation: Catherine married one of Peter's grandsons, then proceeded to boot him out of power. Her obsession with matters European—echoing her grandfather-in-law—explains why I can sort-of read the inscriptions: they're in Latin.

Speaking of obsession, it seems I'll do almost anything to see a big dick. I head halfway across town to a most unusual little museum housed in, of all things, a working STD clinic: Saint Petersburg's Museum of Erotica. The exhibits are nothing special—a variety of figurines in various coital positions, among other things—but the real draw is a pickled phallus, said to be that of Rasputin, the "Mad Monk" who bewitched the last Romanov Tsarina. Further weirding-up the story, he was said to be something of a womanizer and was hugely endowed. Yeah, pretty impressive, though the thing's a funny shape.

To beg forgiveness of the gastronomy gods for my Moscow McDonald's transgression, I sample a bit of local quick-serve; as with many nations, Russia now has its own fast-food joints. At Teremok I try blinys—basically a Russian variant of a crêpe, with similar sweet or savory fillings—as well as some borscht. They're both pretty good: too many stale memories of being forced to choke down such stuff at my grandmother's are safely put to rest. Best of all: a chocolate-banana bliny, consisting of an entire banana enrobed in rich sauce.

I vote this the greatest legacy of the Kievan Rus.

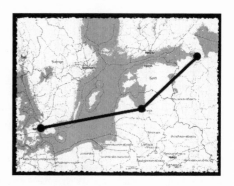

Forefathers & Friends
Riga & Copenhagen

A buzzing green-and-white airBaltic prop plane lifts off from St. Petersburg's Pulkovo Airport and heads southwest. A final stop behind the former Iron Curtain to complete the European portion of my Family Heritage Tour: my father's entire extended family—his dad was one of ten kids—hails from Riga and its surrounds.

Latvia's past as a Soviet Republic feels almost as erased as Prague's: an airport spotless and new, signage in Roman letters—I can *read* again!—and English widely spoken. In addition to the generally relaxed feel of a smaller center—Riga's metro area is under a million—there's also that intangible feeling of being back in honest-to-goodness *Europe* again. No surprise, that: Latvia has joined the EU and touts its capital as more of a Scandinavian city than a former East Bloc burg.

More low-season bargain hunting scores me yet another find, an elegant, three-star boutique hotel smack in Riga's medieval Old Town. Its ornate neoclassical façade belies an ultramodern interior. My en-suite bathroom sports designer fixtures; all-glass shower doors; and patterned one-inch black, gray, and white tiling that could have been lifted from an interior design brochure.

I *love* a nice bathroom. Too bad I'm only here a couple of nights.

The city, meanwhile, seems unusually lively. Crowds gather by the promenade fronting the Daugava River. Soon a parade starts up, complete with marching soldiers, flags, emissaries from other countries, and a fly-past of Latvian military jets and helicopters.

What *is* this? And who knew Latvia had a *military*? I ask a youngish Australian couple standing next to me.

"It's Latvian Independence Day. We didn't know about it either," one of them says.

It's the country's ninetieth, to be exact, commemorating its post-World War I separation from the Russian Empire. Though a better term for it might be "re-Independence Day," since for over four of those decades the country was absorbed into the Soviet Union. Only in the last ten years has the country again emerged as a distinct entity on the world stage.

After dark the festivities heat up in the wintry chill: the bridges spanning the Daugava are brilliantly lit; the crowd cheers as a massive fireworks display springs up. Afterward, meandering back from a late dinner, I encounter a familiar swirl of white: the first snow of the season and my first on this trip. Circling the medieval churches and narrow streets, it transforms the place into a giant snow globe.

I rise early the next morning determined to learn more about my ancestors. The city is quiet after its Independence Day binge as I walk out of Old Town to the "new" part of the city—still more than a century old—to a stately brick structure that contains Riga's Jewish Museum. Before World War II this building was a Yiddish-language theatre, evidence that my forebears were not alone in making this a sizeable Jewish center.

The two old ladies running the place tell me it doesn't open for another hour: I had already looked online but found precious little on this spot aside from its address. No trouble: I now have an excuse to explore Riga's turn-of-the-century central core (and drop off a bit of laundry).

The city was once known as "little Paris," and it's a moniker that's not undeserved: the town is positively crawling with Art Nouveau buildings, much like Josefov in Prague. I wander Elisabetes iela and Alberta iela, two of the more prominent Art Nouveau streets, and imagine my forebears—some of whom struck it rich early in the twentieth century—residing in one of the elegant structures.

Back at the museum, I learn about the Jews of Latvia: it's not as old a community as those in Poland or Lithuania, which lay within the Russian Empire's "Pale of Settlement" where Jews were permitted to reside in Tsarist times. But starting in the 1600s, a vibrant culture flourished in spite of ever-present prejudice and repression.

I don't expect to find anything specific about my family and instead wander the galleries with a visiting British fellow; upon learning my surname, however, he points me to a display case: in it lie a number of 1940s-era Soviet documents, including a death warrant for one "Jacova Judeikina"—one of my grandfather's brothers.

Ohmigosh. I've heard stories of my great-uncle's fate—a prominent businessman, he was among those targeted by the Soviets—but have never seen my surname in a museum. Especially not for something like this. On my way out, I chat with one of the old ladies and she nods; in broken English she tells me some of my kin residing in Israel have paid this place a visit before.

I want to take a trip to the outskirts of town, to Rumbula Forest, where in the winter of 1941 Nazi *Einsatzgruppen* carried out mass executions of Riga's Jews—including my great-aunt Rosa and her family. I'd heard stories about this at Holocaust commemorations and such; it may have seemed irrelevant and boring to me back then, but coming here ignites it with new purpose.

To my surprise, neither the museum staff nor anyone else has any idea how to get there; finally I decide on a taxi. It's only a few kilometers out of the city center, past battleship-gray Soviet-era apartment blocks and the odd industrial park.

The entrance to the memorial, at the edge of a pine forest, is a simple demi-arch latticework of iron with stones trapped inside, something of an impressionistic take on barbed wire. It's a cold day and snow from the previous night thinly coats the ground. The place is deserted.

We pull into the muddy parking area. I hop out and walk a little way up the snowy path to the memorial itself. It's made up of rough-hewn stones suggesting a graveyard, laid out in a pattern that from overhead forms a six-pointed star, the Hebrew Star of David. In the middle is a twelve-foot-high metal menorah, the seven-tipped Jewish candelabra, made out of iron tendrils resembling branches or roots penetrating the earth.

Every stone is marked with a name: families who were killed here. Since they're partly wet from the melting snow, it's hard to make out the inscriptions, and I search in vain for anyone familiar. Then, as I am about to leave, I spot them: my great-aunt and her family, their surnames carved into the rock.

I stand for many minutes, paralyzed by emotion. My family's airbrush scatter of adopted homelands—not to mention my own cycle of wandering—have trained me to expect no trace of my lineal past to linger. But here it is. This is my Ground Zero. The presence of these names cements my connection to this place across the decades and centuries.

As dusk falls I return to town and take a final spin around the cobbly streets, now tranquil after the previous evening's reverie. Although the curves and proportions of the buildings betray a faintly eastern sensibility, the place distantly reminds me of my hometown, Montréal: the gray of the stone, the trees, the river, the frigid climate. I can see why my grandparents, having left this land behind, chose to settle where they did. Coming here feels like I've completed a circle somehow left unfulfilled by their passing. I've now experienced it for myself, if only briefly, the land where my forefathers lived, worked, loved, and died.

I have yet more friends to visit before taking my leave of the Continent: an old college chum working for a Danish clothing firm relocated to their head office in Copenhagen a few years ago. After a speedy plane ride and an equally speedy train into the city, I head to Cindy and her husband Jonathan's place in Islands Brygge. Once industrial docklands, it's now a tranquil but hip residential district just across the water from the central city; the cylindrical concrete structure in which my friends live was once a grain silo.

"Let's take a look at that," says Jonathan, a warmhearted stocky English fellow with a penchant for gadgetry that exceeds even my own. I'd misplaced my camera's battery charger somewhere in Russia and he, of course, just so happens to have a spare on hand.

It's been almost a decade since Cindy and I last saw each other, yet our catch-up makes the years evaporate. Well, some things have changed: she presents me Thomas, their shy, adorable two-year-old son wearing a Mr. Bump T-shirt. His fair features and towhead makes him a dead-ringer for my nephew Jacob. To prove the point, I show them a picture.

"Thomas!" he exclaims, pointing at the kid in the photo.

They're hundreds of miles apart, but in my mind's eye I almost confuse Copenhagen and Amsterdam: both smallish, orderly, well-run Northern European capital cities straddling Germany. They bear similarities, to be sure, but Copenhagen sets itself apart in one area: it's overflowing with smart-looking ultramodern structures and, within them, implements of efficient design—all those gorgeous can openers and ergonomic chairs we snap up for a premium back home. Sweden, just across the Øresund Strait, gets the acclaim for name brands like IKEA, Volvo, Saab (and, of course, ABBA); but the Danes are unsung masters of simple stuff that works. They even have a museum for it, the Danish Design Centre, a prim modern space of black steel and reflective glass windows. I delight in the displays of sleek teapots, high-efficiency reflective lamps, and minimalist yet comfy chairs. My fondness for this stuff becomes ever more obvious as I browse their gift shop replete with compact travel devices…and discover I already own several of them: backpacking demands space-saving goodies.

The Danes are just as fastidious about the past: the nearby *Nationalmuseet*, the National History Museum, recently remodeled and free of charge, impresses me with its dynamic, effective exhibits with nary a trace of stuffiness. Its section on Danish prehistory—complete with ambient mood music and lighting—schools me that that horned Viking helmets greatly predate the Vikings; they actually stem from the Bronze Age. Hägar the Horrible would be crushed.

The next day, the weather having cleared—though temperatures remain low and I'm still freezing—I walk over to Nyhavn, the picture-postcard old harbor district of colorfully painted many-windowed buildings overlooking a canal. Figuring it would be empty with the onset of winter, I embark on a boat ride around the harbor. Instead, the boat's packed to the tits: locals as well as tourists shopping in nearby Strøget apparently make this their pre-Christmas excursion. Venturing out onto the windy stern to escape the crowded glass-enclosed interior, I see more elements of Danish Modern: the Opera House, not as famous as its Sydney counterpart, its bubble-shaped glass front capped by a jutting flat roof like the prow of an aircraft carrier; the "black diamond" of the Royal Danish Library, something of a cross between the Jawa Sandcrawler in *Star Wars* and the monolith from *2001: A Space Odyssey*; and—on the traditional side—the copper dome of Amalienborg Palace, winter home of the otherwise-modest Danish monarchy.

The boat also churns through the canals surrounding Christiania, Copenhagen's hippie haven, which events conspire me to miss on this outing; too bad, as I'm told it's a ramshackle but lively quarter of artists, squatters, and (somewhat) freely available weed.

Our last stop: Denmark's Mona Lisa. They call it the little disappointment as it's, well, a lot smaller than everyone expects for a mythology so grand. Still, I find the Little Mermaid statue haunting and sad. Fairy-teller Hans Christian Andersen is Copenhagen's favorite son: there's a street named after him and a statue in the center of the city where one expects monuments to warriors or politicians. The darker side to his fairy tales—all those themes of alienation and ostracism—are no accident: Andersen was bisexual and had little luck with either gender. Maybe that explains the resonance for me and many gays: in my more closeted days even the happy-ending-ified Disney version of this fairy tale held strong resonance.

Hopefully I'll do better than Hans. I'm staying at a gay-owned guesthouse on the top floor of a massive five-story brick building fronting on the water. It's Saturday night, and as I'm making ready to go out I hear a bunch of guys out my door gabbing away in Danish.

"We're going to a party," they tell me. "You should come."

Sounds tempting, but first I have dinner plans: yup, it's another of Renaissance Man's friends; the guy seems to know half the damn Continent. Anna's an auburn-headed twenty-six-year-old student with a background similar to her London chum: her family too was part of the hippie-missionary circuit. We dine at an intimate Indian place, where I discover why Danes tend to eat at home: our meal comes to around US$40 per person.

Anna heads home early but I stay out. I can't find the guesthouse guys and their party so instead I head to Foxy, another in my series of two-story nightlife affairs, this one in the heart of Copenhagen's low-key downtown. Walking to the place, I notice something I haven't seen since my days in the alcohol-soaked American Midwest: lots and lots of tipsy folk stumbling about. Maybe that bodes well: Amsterdam may have the party rep, but these folks look hotter to trot.

Foxy is positively hopping, and the crowd is cute, drunk, and very friendly. As I'm completing my initial circuit of the place and am about to head down the stairs, a *very* good-looking guy, ice-blue eyes and gray wool cap, eyes me, stopping in his tracks. Clearly inebriated but still lucid enough, Christian offers me a drink then leads me onto the dance floor. It starts innocently, then moves in the direction of bumping and grinding. He's into it: I can feel his hardening, substantial member under those designer jeans.

We head back to the guesthouse and spend the night, going at it twice before passing out, and once again the next morning. He's one of the best-looking guys I've been with, body lithe and toned, face like a movie star. Too often looks like these come paired with arrogance, conceit, power plays. But Christian is none of those things: twenty-two, a business school student, son of a well-to-do diplomat, he delivers a night of good conversation and even better sex.

We emerge the next day for a late-late brunch. On the way back he leans against a building, tilts his head into the sun, and closes his eyes.

"You okay?" I ask.

"Oh yes," he replies. "We don't see the sun enough here."

Indeed, it's brighter, warmer, and sunnier than I've seen in some time. A kiss farewell, then he heads home and I meet up with Jonathan, Cindy, and Thomas one last time. Tivoli Gardens, Copenhagen's iconic nineteenth-century fairground, has just opened for the Christmas season and is a pageant of decorations amid the tall trees and even taller thrill rides. Thomas looks a bit overwhelmed.

"Give him a year or two," I tell Cindy. I saw this pattern with my nephews. "Soon you'll have to drag him out of here."

Darkness falls. The lights come on, a million of them twinkling on fences and trees. It's fitting that I end my European ramblings here, in an amusement park that once inspired Walt Disney.

"Would you ever move back?" I ask Cindy. She's let on about the high taxes and the near-impossibility of amassing a savings here.

"No way. It got so stressful for me back home." She looks off at the fairyland décor. "I think this is where we're going to stay."

Her point resonates as we say goodbye among the dazzle of lights. I begin to wonder how my life would have gone had I taken Cindy's path, chosen Europe instead of America as an adopted home. They seem to be onto something, the Europeans, with their clean cities and efficient trains and social safety net and five weeks of vacation. Maybe those higher taxes are worth it. The Continent has felt great, served as worthy tonic for a frazzled mind. It even leads me to speculate: would I have fared better with friends and lovers had I settled here instead of in helter-skelter America? Maybe not: people of all stripes inhabit every place. And yet, I come away from these lands, a civilization at once older and more recently transformed than our own (to wit: the ending of the Cold War, the EU) wondering if they have life's fundamentals a bit more figured out.

Fittingly for the last of my travels in Europe, I've got a rail journey ahead—my longest, an overnighter into Germany to make a couple of flight connections. I cross the street from Tivoli to the train station, where a waiting Deutsche Bahn CityNight sleeper train hums softly on the platform.

It's deserted; November isn't exactly high season for this sort of thing. Consequently, I have a two-person cabin all to myself. I fold down the lower bunk, revealing a twin-sized bed that amply fits my six-foot frame. Given the carousing of the night before, I'm pretty wiped out and manage a full eight hours following a quiet meal in the train's dining car.

A quick knock rouses me the next morning.

"We're an hour late," the steward advises. *What?* This is *Germany*, for heaven's sake. Actually, there's a bigger worry: I'll have just enough time now to catch my flight out of Frankfurt, but no more.

I burn up more of that time trying to buy a ticket for the airport train: the Euros I withdraw from the ATM are too large a denom- ination for the ticket machine. Finally, gum purchased from a convenience store to get change and ticket in hand, I charge onto the platform just as the airport train is about to leave. I spy a half-empty compartment and make it inside just as the doors swoosh shut. I fail to notice that the seats are a slightly different tone than the rest of the train, and diminutive "1" signs festoon this portion of the carriage.

As we exit the warren of tunnels and leave the city behind, two uniformed train inspectors enter the car and begin checking tickets. They seem a tad curt, admonishing the other passengers in German about…well, I don't know what. I have my ticket, and show it to them when asked; they look at it and shake their heads, clucking in disapproval.

"You are in the wrong compartment," one of them says. "This is First Class." He points to the signs. The fine for this transgression: forty Euros.

Fuck. I don't have that much European cash on me, and don't have much time—but with a "don't worry" hand gesture the older guard dismisses the younger, and I think it's all good.

We arrive at the airport and I rush out; glancing at the monitors I see it's barely forty-five minutes to my flight. Behind me I hear "stop" in an assertive growl. I turn and see the younger inspector motioning me to wait while his senior cohort metes out fines to other passengers.

Chat, chat, chat. The clock is ticking. I know one of my flights is chock-full. I'm starting to envision hours rebooking flights and all manner of penalties.

Guard Number Two finally comes over.

"No fine for you. But in Germany, you know, you do *not* board First Class with a Second Class ticket!"

"Even on a train to the airport?" I ask. The ride is maybe twelve minutes.

"Yes!" he says, eyes widening for emphasis. At last he lets me go. I sprint to the check-in counter, making it with nary a minute to spare.

The connection is no less interesting, as I hear the words dreaded by every traveler:

"You can't check in."

This is one of my award tickets, and to prevent people from cheating and skipping flights—though I fail to see how that's cheating, but never mind—you must fly all segments on your itinerary. One of mine was not yet logged as "flown" by British Airways. To rectify the matter, they send me to the award-issuing carrier, American Airlines.

"You need to go back to British Airways and fix it with them."

"I already tried that—they said it's been updated in their system," I reply.

No one can help. Finally I make a call on my mobile to the American Airlines elite traveler desk—a perk from my consulting days. I'll say one thing about back home: they know customer service. It's a good half-hour on and off hold—even with a global SIM card that's not cheap—but the friendly lady with a Texan accent on the other end calls both airlines, reissues the ticket, makes all it okay.

Maybe the Continent didn't want me to leave.

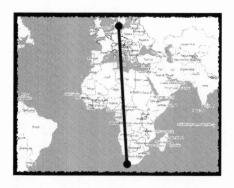

The Far Side of the World
Cape Town

A landscape could arouse the sublime only when it
suggested power, power greater than that of humans...this
is the lesson written into the stones of the desert and the
ice fields of the poles. So grandly is it written there that we
may come away from such places, not crushed, but inspired
by what lies beyond...
- Alain de Botton, *The Art of Travel*

R enaissance Man gifted me this book on my way out from
London, and its words ring true, here at the bottom end of
Africa over 800 foot cliffs, cobalt waters swirling into foam
below.

It's out of my way but has been on my radar for years: a shot clear
across the southern flank of Europe, the Mediterranean, the Sahara,
and the Serengeti to Cape Town, South Africa. Three of my grandfather's siblings settled here in the 1920s. I have more relatives down
on the Western Cape than I do in my Canadian hometown—and I'm
curious to see what they've wrought.

Heathrow's cavernous new Terminal Five presents row upon row
of parked 747s in various stages of preparation: service vehicles tend
to the lumbering beasts like make-up artists doting on a starlet. Dusk
falls as my flight is called. Two middle-aged ladies sit next to me,
chattering quietly in Afrikaans. Like many white South Africans their

near-stereotyped Nordic features, ruddy complexions, and fair hair echo their Dutch ancestry.

I sleep poorly, as I usually do on planes, and awake at daybreak. Wisps of cloud hug the still-dark ground below. We're over Namibia, only the second time in my life south of the Equator.

It's a brilliant cloudless morning as we turn on final approach: the sea is a rich blue and the brownish splotch of Robben Island lies offshore; it bears the prison where Nelson Mandela was held for more than two decades under the apartheid regime. Admittedly, part of my motivation for coming to this land is curiosity: how has it moved on from its Cold-War-era pariah status and racial divide?

I'm picked up at the airport by a driver sent by my bed & breakfast; this is all very unfamiliar after two months of self-service train travel. Having heard of the country's growing crime problem, I do a quick double-check with the fellow to ensure he is in fact sent by the guesthouse. He is, and acts as a pretty friendly welcome wagon.

"Look at Table Mountain," he gestures at the iconic flat-topped peak overlooking the city. "From here it looks like a man lying down."

As we pull onto the main highway, I see crowds and clusters of buildings, horribly built out of scrap timber and metal. It's the shantytowns of the Cape Flats, the open plain halfway between the airport and the city center. Nearby sits a huge billboard, proclaiming with WPA-era optimism "SLUMS WILL BE CLEARED" amid drawings of people frolicking among idyllic suburban tracts.

My guesthouse, the appropriately named David's, occupies a compound of two turn-of-the-twentieth-century townhomes in Green Point. The district is a gentrified seaside neighborhood just beyond Cape Town's smallish city core. The whitewashed buildings with double-decker balconies have the feel of another oceanic once-British enclave, Sydney, Australia. David's is run by a gay couple but they're away the morning I arrive; instead an elderly friend is in charge.

"When you open the lock you need to turn it this way," he explains. He continues explicating minutiae, from the buttons on the alarm clock to directions to the main street a scant hundred yards away.

I think I got it covered. Still, I indulge him his grandfatherly assistance. The staff, meanwhile, busily tidies the place; all have pitch-black skin and lilting, accented English that reveals it's not their first language. This country has eleven—eleven!—official tongues.

I take a stroll down Main Road, Green Point's shopping drag. Across a grassy park by the water looms the towering skeleton of the World Cup football stadium, set to be completed for the 2010 games. The area could easily be mistaken for a similarly upscale-ified part of Los Angeles or Miami, with one exception: gangs of young people milling about—not homeless but decidedly impoverished, very probably unemployed, occasionally too eager to make your acquaintance in search of coin. All have dark skin.

I continue to the Victoria & Alfred Waterfront, another bit of postindustrial urban renewal like Darling Harbour in Sydney or Pier 39 in San Francisco. This variant has the same candy-colored buildings and touristy, overpriced shops, though it's nestled amid a still-working port: dazzling white yachts and oil-stained cargo vessels compete for space among the moorings. It's brilliant, warm, and sunny, the sky a cobalt blue and in the background, the rugged flat-topped crag of Table Mountain.

I missed Copenhagen's hippie colony, Christiania, but have an opportunity to see something similar here, 5,000 miles away: Oude Molen Village. A tangle of white former barracks once used as a mental institution, the expansive compound now houses environmental groups, NGOs, craftspeople, and filmmakers. No weed for sale, alas. An old college friend of mine who used to work for Lucasfilm has friends out here, a pair of special-effects animators who've turned some of the spaces into studios and apartments. I meet Ree and Nina for brunch and spend half the time gawking at the digs: an entire floor, some 7,000 square feet, artfully festooned with pottery, white-upholstered modern lounge sofas, and old-style wooden chests. It's a space I'd kill for—and in any major American city would cost a fortune.

Then it's family time: after brunch I'm picked up by Leon Jedeikin—my father's namesake—and his son Darron, a fellow about my age. Leon is almost the cliché of the kindly middle-aged pediatrician, with tanned skin and melodic South Africanisms such as "I was in my rooms" in describing his office; "is this where you stay?" when asking about housing; and my favorite, one they all use: "the robots"— a traffic light. It's off with them on a sweeping afternoon drive down the Cape Peninsula south of the city. As in California's urban centers, the clot of urbanity quickly gives way to natural splendor: the peaks of the Twelve Apostles tumble into the blue Atlantic; inland, green wineries nestle against emerald woodlands while low clouds hang over nearby mountains. I see my first examples of Cape Dutch architecture: the curlicued gabled roofs of Holland adorning whitewashed buildings, Amsterdam mixed with Monte Carlo.

And more instances of the ever-ominous crime problem: back in town, we stop at a liquor store; as we do, a fellow wearing an orange reflector guides us into a parking spot. Darron hands him a banknote.

"Is he the parking attendant?" I ask.

"Not officially," Darron replies. "But if you don't give them something, you may find your car vandalized."

Leon and his wife Maureen's house in suburban Milnerton is a sprawling, one-floor ranch-style affair. Here I meet my doppelgänger family of Jedeikins—this Leon also has four kids. The youngest of them, Jonty, is a software geek like me, and it's the usual struggle to avoid lapsing into shop talk and boring the rest of the clan hopelessly. His older brother, Harry, a husky, jovial fellow with an Israeli wife and two young children, offers a way out—or at least the kids do. Once they find out I live in California, they ask the all-important question.

"Have you met the Jonas brothers?"

I need a way to get around. No convenient subways here: in addition to climate and mountainscapes, Cape Town shares with Los Angeles a pronounced lack of good public transit. The shared-ride taxis that impoverished locals rely upon might be an adventure for some, but I seek a safer experience than those rattletraps choking their way down

Main Road. Two wheels to the rescue once more: I rent a scooter from a shop downtown—a 125cc number that creaks a bit but proves a trustworthy steed for a couple of days.

Cape Town's central city and inner-ring suburbs cluster around a semicircular valley known as the City Bowl. On the motorbike I ride up Long Street, the city's funky shopping avenue filled with pubs, used clothing stores, the odd backpacker hostel. As it ascends the hill, Long Street turns into Kloof Nek—totemic in its blend of English and Afrikaans names. To the right looms Signal Hill, the peak overlooking Green Point. It's chilly at the top—Cape Town's "southeaster" is much like San Francisco's westerly blasts off the Pacific—and some odd-looking chicken-like birds roam about.

"What are those?" I ask an elderly couple.

"Guinea fowl. They're indigenous," the lady replies. The birds cluck around frenetically, black feathers speckled with white, blue heads and ruddy beaks.

On my way down I tool around Bo-Kaap, a hillside district of small bungalows painted in flaming pastels: purple, green, red…I lose count. It's an old Malay district, and in spite of the cheeriness of the buildings, the vibe's a bit menacing: locals eye me suspiciously. I avoid stopping or pulling out my camera and instead ride home.

Cape Town, South Africa's Mother City, is reputed to be the gayest place on the continent. To test that theory I head out to some clubs in De Waterkant, the neighborhood adjacent to mine. It's maybe a fifteen-minute walk, but my guesthouse people warn: "Take a taxi."

I hop out in an urbanish area, dodging the ever-present "Can I help you?" gangs on the street. I pop into The Bronx, yet another in a series of gay bar/club hybrids the world over. This one's done up in dark wood paneling and emerald green. The crowd is cute and seems awfully friendly: lots of stares, smiles, and glances.

"I'm Pierre," says a handsome late-twentysomething I've been eyeing: deep tan, darkish hair, bloodshot blue eyes. In spite of his French name he's Afrikaner, from a farm up north near the Namibian border; now he lives in a Cape Town suburb. I may be thousands of miles from home but my gift for picking up suburban farm boys remains intact.

A bit of dancing, then he drags me into a restroom stall. I learn the reason for the bloodshot eyes: he's been snorting "ket," known as Ketamine in my part of the world. A dissociative anesthetic, it's not really my thing; besides, I detest snorting, but I'm a good sport and have a little with him. I'm more interested in what comes next: Pierre and I start making out and he even delivers a bit of oral below-the-pants action. We don't linger too long, though: it is a restroom and he's in the throes of drug-fueled attention deficit. But we dance and talk the rest of the night.

"You'll have to excuse my English," he says. "I only learned it three years ago."

He comes home with me and in spite of our slightly (well, in his case, not-so-slightly) drug-addled state, we have a good go of things in the bedroom. He leaves early the next morning; Graham, the stand-in innkeeper, bids us a good morning and me a knowing wink. Gotta love those gay B & Bs.

The city proper isn't much of a sightseeing mecca. Besides, I've seen enough cathedrals and museums over the past couple of months to last a few lifetimes…nevertheless, the spirit moves me, and I soon find myself downtown outside the Castle of Good Hope, the oldest standing European structure in the country. More a walled fort than an actual castle, its low-slung stone walls and mustard-colored barracks offer a history lesson: South Africa's European colonization dates back to the 1650s, almost as old as North America's. And as with New York, Cape Town began life as a Dutch colony before being seized by the British. There's a fair bit about early wars against the indigenous Khoi-San, as well as on the Boer War between the Brits and the Afrikaners. The divide between these two white colonials distantly echoes America's struggles between North and South; as with back home, I get the sense the scars are far from healed. Refreshingly, this museum reveals the cruelty of all sides; no sanitizing the past here as far as I can tell.

One tourist turn deserves another, so after the stint at the Castle I hop on one of those open-topped double-decker buses that have become a fixture in so many major tourist cities. If there's ever a place where independent-minded travelers should relent and bother with one of these, it's got to be here: we roll through the city's modest center, head up to the base of Table Mountain, then cross Kloof Nek over to the Atlantic side to the upscale beach town of Camps Bay. I jump off here and have a spot of lunch—given the exchange rate, it comes out to maybe eight dollars for a top-shelf beachfront eatery overlooking two chunky palm trees that frame the pale blue sea.

I go to bed a little under the weather and hope this isn't my first bout of traveler's sickness. Maybe not: the soreness is in my throat, not my belly, and South Africa isn't on my list of "don't drink the water" countries. When I rise the next morning, my throat feels as if a tiny gremlin has been at it with some sandpaper; a glance in the mirror reveals small white growths around my tonsils. I break out my mini-medical kit—now I'm happy I packed one—and take my temperature; it's at 101.

If I could have picked *anywhere* to come down with strep throat, an English-speaking country where a nearby relative is also a doctor would probably top the list. A quick consultation with cousin Leon and he sends me on my way with an antibiotics prescription. After a day and many hours of sleep I'm in much better shape.

Ree and Nina have some time the next afternoon and take me on a leisurely car ride out to the Cecil Rhodes Memorial. It's a pretty setting on a verdant hillside, complete with teahouse and, on the slopes below, wildebeests and zebras as part of a game enclosure. The Greek-styled monument, a cavalcade of steps and columns topped by a bronze horseman and lions, obviously evokes the heroic. Nina and Ree have a different take.

"He's partly to blame for it all." They fill me in on past colonial depredations, then start inspecting the monument. "People sometimes deface it," they explain.

Yeah, colonialism: glory-grubbing explorers carving up whole swaths of globe, unforeseen consequences be damned. Rhodes is the fellow for whom Rhodesia—now Zimbabwe—is named, a country whose present-day troubles give Cecil's ghost a lot to answer for. On a brighter note, he also established the eponymous scholarship, willed into existence by his estate.

In spite of what their actions wrought, there's a shard of these vainglorious men's spirit I respect: the will to seek places anew, to undertake what must have been real-life risks for them out here in the unknown. They could have been ruthless and ambitious back home to probably equal or greater success. Instead they chose to strike out for the far corners of the Earth.

Hopefully our voyages are better for the world than theirs, and we travelers in our own small way leave places better than we found them.

Afterward more family beckons: cousin Lionel hails from another branch of my sequoia-sized family tree; he and his wife Jeni pick me up in their Range Rover for another hop to Camps Bay. His family is younger than Leon's. To wit: I've been Facebook buddies with his two teenage kids for the past year or so before ever meeting the grownups. Jessica's a quiet, dark-haired, fair skinned girl whose good looks belie the fact that she's the brains of the operation.

"I told him how to invest his barmy money," she says of her brother David's Bar Mitzvah haul. David, meanwhile, is a buff, athletic fourteen-year-old with the distinction of being, far as we know, the only other David Jedeikin in existence. This is a lot more scintillating than it sounds: my unusual and unspellable surname was the butt of much teasing in school days; I wear it as something of an outlaw badge of honor. I gladly pronounce my namesake worthy of the moniker: he's a down-to-earth, outgoing, easygoing fellow—not something that can be said for most adolescent boys.

Fuck, this thing scares me.

It's just a pint-sized Opel Corsa for which I've traded in the scooter to see farther-flung destinations. But it's wrong-hand-drive for a cars-on-the-left country, and manual transmission to boot. Surprisingly, the combination works well: one needs to pay attention in either case. After tootling around Green Point and neighboring Sea Point for a spell, I feel ready to take on a more demanding excursion.

High winds have closed the winding road on the Atlantic side, so I take the False Bay route all the way down the eastern side of the Cape Peninsula. Here tidy hillside towns climb peaks rocky yet green; since it's an inlet, the water is much calmer, bereft of the crashing south-easter-driven waves of the open sea. More Cape Dutch buildings front main streets in a number of towns I pass.

The rocky, verdant hillsides at the bottom of the peninsula are bereft of human settlement: the Cape of Good Hope is part of a nature preserve. I pull up to the parking area and pose for the requisite photo in front of the sign: "THE MOST SOUTH-WESTERN POINT OF THE AFRICAN CONTINENT." The knifelike winds explain why mariners called it the Cape of Storms. They rage all around as a scattering of us tackle the otherwise-easy hike up the cliffs to the crest of the Cape. It's a fetching view, craggy off-white-colored rocks coated with greenery zigzagging down several dozen feet to foamy surf.

The Cape Peninsula isn't the true southern tip of the continent—that distinction goes to another spot ninety miles away, Cape Agulhas. I think, though, that the human penchant for spectacle made this place the more well-known. But pretty as the Cape of Good Hope is, something even grander awaits.

A rumbling green funicular crowded with chattering Brazilians climbs to the top of a hill. More fine views, but nothing too different than what I'd seen so far. Then I get off the funicular, walk a little ways—and discover what sublime really means.

It's all those uplifting musical scores of a nature documentary or IMAX movie rolled into one. Without moving, it feels like I'm a movie camera flying over coastline as I behold the phenomenon that is Cape Point: a monstrous, heaving slice of mountain and rock tumbling 800 feet before slicing into blue ocean waters wracked with foam. Greenery flourishes wherever the incline permits. Birds soar and pinwheel about on updrafts. The end of dry land for thousands of miles, past the storm-swept latitudes of the Roaring Forties and Furious Fifties of the Southern Ocean, all the way to the ice floes and emperor penguins of Antarctica. This is the far side of the world and doesn't let you forget it. All the shards of my existence at this moment—the humdrum logistics of travel, the sour memories of the recent past, the

fact that I'm freezing in the roaring gusts—all crinkle into insignificance against the cliffs, the rock, the roiling sea.

I wander around rocky manmade trails, the remnants of World
War II-era fortifications, and pass the lighthouse erected high atop the
Point. Too high, in fact: it was frequently obscured by fog and another
had to be built closer to the sea. The best-laid plans.

The Rand is still cheap and the exchange rate favorable, so I
splurge a bit and dine at the elegant restaurant at the base of the funicular. Done up in modern glass and dark-stained wood, the establishment perches atop a pavilion with expansive views of cliff and sea.
Outside, in the parking lot, some primate friends pay a visit: baboons
frolic and play, some brazenly sitting on the tops of cars. Later I see a
bunch galloping on the road before dashing into the brush. Shyer are
the Rock Hyrax, or "dassies," cute brown bunny rabbit-like creatures.
These have a peculiarity all their own: they're a genetic close-cousin, of
all things, of the elephant. A weirdish, wild place this is, in Dr. Seuss
parlance.

It's the weekend and Pierre offers to take me on some adventures.
I drive out to his part of the world, the suburb of Bellville some
twelve miles down the N1. Most of Cape Town's Afrikaner population
lives in the burbs; at Bellville's Tyger Valley mall, where we lunch at a
local burger chain, Pierre orders in Afrikaans rather than English.
Aside from that, however, suburbia here feels pretty much the same as
back home: the shopping center's sprawl is matched by tract homes
and broad, trafficky main streets. Some new development shows signs
of change: Pierre lives in a complex of smart midrise apartments with
retail stores within walking distance. We visit one of these where he
works. I now see where he obtains what seems like an endless array of
tight-fitted collared shirts. Then we stop in at his apartment to swap
cars and have a quickie—can't forget that—before setting out on our
way.

"You want to try biltong?" he asks. No, it's not another party drug;
instead, it's a sort of gourmet beef jerky eaten by the early Dutch
voortrekkers as they crossed the African bush north from the Cape. We

stop in at a local deli-style market offering a wide range of these. Perfect snack food for the journey ahead.

"My dad used to make it," he says. "I was overweight for years from eating it."

I can see why: more tender and flavorful than jerky, it's curiously addictive.

He then takes me to Paarl, to a hilltop where a modernist series of curvy concrete obelisks rise above a grassy park: the Afrikaans Language Monument. Notwithstanding the language's controversy in South African history, the monument to it is in a splendid spot overlooking the green valleys of the Cape Winelands and the mountains beyond.

The Winelands are our real destination for the day. We stop in at one of the wineries around a town called Franschhoek. Comparisons with Napa and Sonoma are inevitable; but this area's topography is even more interesting: craggy green peaks present an ever-interesting Rorschach of shapes over the rows of vines. The wines are pretty good too: South Africa seems to have reached the point where its varietals compare favorably with the rest of the world.

"So does your dad know you're gay?" I ask Pierre as we sample a medley of reds and whites.

"No. He wouldn't understand."

His folks still live on the farm, apparently in more ways than one. Though Pierre hasn't left all of his background behind, as I find out as we pass a slow-moving, overcrowded shared taxi filled with dark-skinned folk.

"*Fokin' kefirs!*" he cries out. Now I'm no expert, but I'd heard that word was actually banned in these parts nowadays. He motions to some nearby shantytowns, enraged.

"They take our electricity. We pay for it. Everything they use." He proceeds to give me a harangue on the parasitism of the blacks. I nod and keep the conversation light. I'm not from here and don't know all the details, but I'm pretty sure I've just encountered real-life, untrammeled racism.

"It's nothing like that!" my relative Jeni exclaims when I repeat Pierre's harangue. "I can't believe someone that age who would say that." Apparently such retrograde notions typically are confined to Afrikaners of another generation. *Sure, trust me to find one.*

"If one of my kids was there," she adds, shaking her head, "they'd have said something." She agrees that it was wise for me to steer clear. My own country's ideological issues are enough for me, thanks.

The grown-ups have a function to attend that evening and I'm too tuckered out to hit the bars, so instead I order take-out with my young cousins and stay in. It's weird after all this time away: being a home-body. David and I trade songs on our iPods—I garner an appreciation for the South African indie scene while bequeathing him a few oldies. Jessica's boyfriend Shai-Am is over, a handsome young Israeli fellow whose South African twang is tempered by a bit of British. They're all so *nice* to each other it's sometimes hard to remember they're still teens.

I've been here more than a week and have yet to go up Table Mountain. There it sits, beckoning out the kitchen window on a calm, sunny morning. I'm determined to see it today, but fate has other plans: now that the winds have died down, the lines for the aerial tram—the "cableway" they call it—are long.

"No worries," Lionel says, with far more enthusiasm than I can muster this early. "We're taking you on a hike up Devil's Peak."

We drive a little ways past the cableway station to the trailhead—Devil's Peak is one mountain over from Table. It's one of those picture-perfect Mediterranean-style mornings I used to dream about while digging cars out of snowbanks...I'm actually able to pull a "when I was your age" quip in context. The hike is spectacular: views of Table Mountain, the City Bowl, the harbor, even Green Point all the way on the other side of town where I stayed earlier in the week.

"Look at these." Jeni holds up some brightly colored pinkish wildflowers. "All this is the Cape Floral Kingdom." The area around Cape Town is one of the most diverse in the world.

The hike's not too taxing, so Lionel and Shai decide to make it so. A hearty, daredevil type, plastic surgeon by trade with a graying ponytail, Lionel starts running down the hill—down a path that looks too steep for running—with his daughter's boyfriend right behind. Jeni shakes her head in wifely fashion.

"I hope he doesn't kill himself."

Saying my goodbyes to this side of the family, I head back over to the Milnerton relatives for an evening of "potje." Yet another tongue-twisting Afrikaans word (pronounced "*poy*-kee") from days in the bush, it's a rich stew of meats and cooked over flame for oodles of hours in a cast-iron pot; apparently my cousin Harry's been working on this one since ten-thirty in the morning.

He's jovial, but Harry's hiding a recent trauma. I'd heard it referenced, so I turn to Tsilla and ask what happened.

"He was driving home from work when he was carjacked. It was a gang of kids on some kind of drugs. They tried to put him in the trunk, but look at him." They motion to his portly frame as he laughs with friends over the potje pot.

"There was no way he was going to fit inside, thank God. He knew if they put him in there, it would be the end. Instead, they just ran off as quickly as they came."

His mother, Maureen, a retired speech therapist with a voice like Queen Elizabeth and a demeanor as gentle as her husband's, chimes in.

"There's not a family in this country that hasn't been touched. More than economics or politics or anything else, the crime is what's making people pack up and leave."

Not that it seems to have dissuaded my cousin. They ask him if he wants to move away.

"Can't," he says, cracking open a beer. "We're having the house remodeled."

I feel I need to better understand this country's underside. I'd heard there are actual tours of the shantytowns and that they're locally run and pretty good, but my cousin Teri, another of Leon and Maureen's kids, offers to go one better.

"I work with crafters in the townships," she says. "I think I could get one of them to take you."

Teri works for a nonprofit cooperative that sells the works of shantytown artists. At their shop downtown I meet Jim, my guide for the day. Wearing a "One World/One Love" T-shirt, shiny gray pants, and a colorful cap, he could be mistaken for one of those hipster types back home with a tech job and a live/work loft.

"I come from Zimbabwe," he says on the drive over, one of many fleeing his home country's descent into chaos in recent years. "Not like many people here," he adds as we drive into the township. "At least I have an education and a trade."

Through The Wire, the company he runs with a couple of friends (a play on words since they're all from across the border), transforms bead-and-wire and scrap metal into intricate artforms and statuary. In their shack of a studio they show me one piece in progress, a giraffe over seven feet tall.

The township is as dispiriting up close as it was from a distance. Homes are built out of whatever spare materials can be foraged: cinder block, odd-sized bits of wood, corrugated metal. Mangy dogs wander about while nearby, heavyset women hang laundry. Jim shows me his home, a space crowded with clothes, a cot, a hotplate. Toilets are outside. But for all its squalor, the place functions: there's Internet access and electricity; a convenience store next door sports a Coca-Cola sign—chalk one up for the new colonials. Nearby is a shop where broken-down vehicles are made roadworthy. Mechanics in these harsh places need greater ingenuity than their rich-country counterparts to coax life out of machines long past their prime.

It's not all silver lining, however: as we walk down one path, four tough-looking youths pass us with menacing stares.

"If you were alone, there probably would have been trouble," Jim says once they're out of earshot. For his part, he avoids going out after dark, and has his own struggles as a foreigner in this place. Poverty can make strange bedfellows but is no guarantee of solidarity.

I give Jim a respectable donation and an earnest—hopefully not too earnest—thanks. He hands me a bandana in the colors of Rastafari—red, green, and gold with a cannabis plant in the center. Clearly he knows his audience. Oh, of course he does; we shared a joint earlier in the day. For the future, Jim hopes to parlay his skills and his refugee status into legal residency in South Africa, and in so doing leave the townships behind. I drive off hoping I return to this land to see him so situated. I often fancy myself an immigrant, with my myriad of cities and rootless family past. But my experience pales in comparison to what I've just seen.

I'm late and flustered—a no-no on South Africa's mean streets, even here on trendy Long Street. I'm meeting Ree for a drink and seem to have miscounted the blocks. A scruffy teen notices and starts following me.

"What you looking for?"

I wave, "I'm okay."

I hurriedly turn into a shop—only to find it's closed. When I turn around, the kid's right in front of me, his arms spread to prevent me from leaving.

"Don't fuck with me, man."

More on adrenaline than anything else, I brush away one of his arms and blurt out, "I'm *late!*" He doesn't follow, and moments later I meet Ree on a sun-dappled café patio.

"Are you alright?"

Yup, I'm fine, if a bit shaken. We chat a bit about the incident but soon segue into lighter conversation, discussing matters of romance and less-than-romance: Ree's been on the friend-with-benefits treadmill too. I observe how the locals—Ree, my cheery cousin Lionel, my recently traumatized other cousin Harry—seem to hold the ability, Zen-like, to take all this turmoil in stride. Maybe you need that to soldier on here without losing it entirely.

I say my final goodbyes to Ree, to the Western Cape, to Africa. The traffic is heavy heading out of the city toward the airport, and for once I'm grateful: it's turned cooler again; a blanket of fog—locals call it the "tablecloth"—hangs over the flat roof of Table Mountain. I feel a twinge, and not simply for the beauty or the sublime. Here in this faraway place, where great beauty collides with such heartbreak, I wonder if my mental holiday is up: sooner or later I'll have to address the demons that have been fermenting in my subconscious for so long.

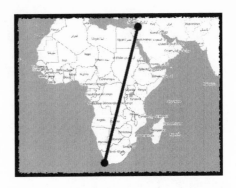

Nabatean Kingdom
Jordan

T
he contrast couldn't be greater: from a midday visit in a South African township to sunset in a British Airways Club World lounge. The flight back to the Northern Hemisphere is the first of several on which my award ticket grants me Business Class.

"Something to feel guilty about," my relative Maureen said to me earlier. Actually, I've never seen it that way: economists speak of "positional goods," products aimed at high-end consumers as a means of differentiating them from the great unwashed. But I hold out hope for more equalizing change, where luxuries of today become commonplace for the everyman and everywoman of tomorrow, just as the toilet and dishwasher did for much of the world in our time.

Call me an idealist with a champagne flute.

Those fabulous airplane seats I've always had to walk past are now mine: this one's a wide ergonomic recliner with a footrest several feet in front; the whole thing folds down to become a flat bed. After a terrific dinner and some sleepytime-inducing wine, I pass out for a full eight hours—a feat I've never managed before on an aircraft. Better yet: the following morning, a hot shower in the arrival lounge before setting off for the next leg.

Signs of what's to come greet me at my connecting gate: it's the period of the Hajj, the pilgrimage to Mecca, and in gates adjacent to my flight to Amman are a number of others going to Saudi Arabia. The departure lounge is filled with Semitic men wearing the *keffiyeh*, the Muslim head covering; quite a few others are garbed in the full-bodied flowing white *thawb*. I'm leaving that nebulous construct known as "The West" for the first time in my life.

Jordan's a good place to start: it's a land known for its hospitality. My overnight stay at a midrange hotel in Amman sees me greeted with a chilled glass of mango juice on arrival; they also provide me with helpful information on how to get to Wadi Musa, my destination for the next day. No trains here, and the comfy, tourist-oriented JETT bus leaves at the crack of dawn—not going to happen knowing my sleep patterns. The alternate is to take local transport: a minibus leaving from one of the open-air bus terminals not far from the hotel.

The next morning a taxi takes me to the bus station. It's an honest country too, with official fares posted to destinations all over the country: for 117 Jordanian Dinars—about US$150—they'll take you all the way to the "IRAQI BOARDER," as the sticker posted inside the cab window effusively states.

The minibus is a tidy blue-and-white twenty-seater, with uni-formed officer literally riding shotgun. The crowd is a blend of young and old, religiously attired and not. These buses leave when full; fortunately that isn't too long after I arrive. They aren't air conditioned, but that's not a problem here in late fall, when the temperature is just right.

After an hour or so we stop at a dusty roadside shop; next door is a rundown mosque where some of the more religious-minded folk head in for prayers—probably the real reason for our break, as Muslims must do this deed five times a day. The food at the store—some mangy grilled meats—doesn't look so appetizing, so I settle for something packaged, a bag of cashews.

"Where you from?" amiably asks one of the younger guys on the bus. I'm the only foreigner on board and their curiosity is disarmingly pleasant. These guys live in Wadi Musa but work in Amman, making this three-hour commute twice a week. We actually have something to share here, as I was once an itinerant multi-city contract worker myself.

It's not much of a town—really just a dusty entrance to Jordan's biggest archeological treasure. But I figure it merits at least a stroll as the sun goes down. Stone and cinderblock structures are the norm here, along with traffic circles no doubt borrowed from British Mandate days. On the front of one building, in Arabic and English, a sign reads, "NO GOD BUT ALLAH, AND MOHAMMED IS HIS MESSENGER." In the sandy yard of one home, children stop when they see me and yell out, "Hi hi hi hi hi hi hi!" as I pass.

My little inn near the center of Wadi Musa is likewise just-right hospitable: it's run by a young, good-looking fellow, Ibrahim, and his mother, who cooks us a hearty meal of kebabs, humus, and other Middle Eastern dishes.

"Here, have a look." Ibrahim's playing around on his laptop, and shares with me and a couple of Belgian guys what he's looking at. It's his Facebook page, crowded with fetching females.

"She was here last month," he says, pointing to one from Germany. "She says she's coming back next summer." *Shit, Ibrahim's a player.* He's also into Hollywood comedies, judging by his DVD collection.

"This one's my favorite," he tells us, pulling out *Eurotrip* from the pile. "You want to watch?" *Sure, why not.* it makes for a perfect, if unlikely, end to a day of travel and settling in.

Next morning begins early. I'm a bit trepidatious, having dragged myself halfway down this country to see more ruins. Happily, I'm captivated up front: the Siq is a marvel, an entry canyon barely twenty feet wide walled by jagged, curving rock soaring straight up a hundred feet or more. Slivers of sky form knifelike cutouts between the peach-hued stone; overall, the effect is the natural world's answer to a medieval town street. *These guys sure knew how to make an entrance.* Along both edges run grooved channels, mini-aqueducts where water flowed into cisterns after the flash floods endemic to the region.

I round the final curve in the Siq and there it lies: *al khazneh*, the Treasury, a monumental Greek-styled façade carved into the auburn rock. It's the grand first edifice of Petra, the "rose-red city," principal outpost of the Nabatean Kingdom. They ruled these lands for more than a thousand years, establishing a far-flung network of caravanserai, rest stops for the trading caravans of ancient days. It's a sight of cinematic proportions…which is partly what's drawn me (and, I'm guessing, the sizeable horde of other Western tourists) to this spot:

they used this place for the climactic final scene of the third *Indiana Jones* film. Inside, however, no warren of caverns, no knights from the Crusades, no home to the Holy Grail: the Treasury's interior is small and nondescript. All the money's in the façade, like a storefront on the set of an old Western. Maybe the Nabateans were better showmen than we give them credit, the Spielbergs of antiquity.

Petra was more than just a warren of caves, though little remains of the freestanding structures; a colonnaded street and a crumbling amphitheatre suggest the grandeur of what was. The valley floor bustles with tourists, vendors of trinkets, donkey and camel rides. I decide to break from the crowds and hike the path to the pagan ritual ground, a semi-ruined set of stone-block structures that make up the High Place of Sacrifice.

Passing a scattering of vendors and a few watchful cats, I reach the summit, a couple hundred feet up where a vista of the valley awaits, along with a quartet of young female travelers. American English speakers all, they too hail from San Francisco. Something tells me if I were straight this might have been a bit of a pick-up; instead we snap photos and they head back down the mountain, leaving me alone with the reddish-brown rock formations and killer views.

I sit for a long time. Something about this place—its seclusion, its long-ago role as a pagan ceremonial alter, perhaps even the fact that I am for the first time away from the distraction of gay-friendly lands— brings to the fore the emotional turmoil I've been pushing away all these weeks. *How did everything go so wrong?*

If there's one thing I've learned in all my years of moving around, it's that the folks you leave behind often view your departure as something of a betrayal. You are, in a sense, rejecting them in favor of someplace else.

It all began over a decade ago: I was a struggling wannabe screenwriter—before the tech bug bit me—when I met Steve, a Liberal Arts major at USC. A reserved intellectual with a biting wit, our friendship back then weaved from intense dependency to old-married-couple bickering. Yet in spite of waxes and wanes our bond strengthened through the years. That is, until 2001, when I became another tech-crash layoff statistic and had to relocate just as Steve began a descent into drug addiction. While under the influence he wrote me nasty, hateful e-mails as a goodbye. More than a year later, clean and sober, he expressed contrition and slowly we rebuilt the trust that had been broken.

Flash forward a few years to about six months after the surgery: Bradley and I headed to San Francisco on our scouting foray, dividing our time between Steve's place in the East Bay and a hotel in the city. Platitudes about "visitors and fish stink" fail to capture how badly it went. Steve's acerbic humor clashed with Bradley's propriety—though I saw deeper forces at play: some was the not-uncommon antagonism between a spouse and a close friend. More came from their respective histories of substance use, with Steve a recovering addict and Bradley something of an unacknowledged problem drinker. Maybe heading for happy hour to get better acquainted while I caught an early-evening snooze was a bad idea. The two of them ended the night with a nasty squabble in a hotel parking lot—and I spent the remainder of the trip hearing rejoinders of "I never want to see him again" from both parties. *Terrific.* Just what I needed on an assessment tour of a prospective hometown.

Back home in Boston the mood now changed: Bradley's parents, quietly acquiescent about our California adventure at first, began to agitate for their son to stay put. After one further hospitalization incident—Bradley endured a couple of these after the transplant, not uncommon in these cases—his mother admonished that he'd probably always be indigent, might never be well enough for the big bad world outside their care. My independent lifestyle and inability to offer him health insurance worried them too—though I still held out hope for a solution that would make everyone happy.

Bradley, meanwhile, revealed his intentions another way: on a Sunday evening before one of my work-related flights he headed out on the town without me. Halfway through the night I awoke to the sound of the bathroom shower running; emerging from bed I noticed the door to the second bedroom was shut. As I was about to open it Bradley emerged from within with most of his clothes off. In the bathroom the shower continued to gurgle.

"Did you bring somebody home?" I asked.

"Just to jerk off!" he replied defensively. I noticed his glassy eyes and slurred speech: *he's shitfaced.*

Disclaimer: we did have something of an open relationship. But not *that* open. Not bring-a-guy-home-and-do-him-in-the-other-bedroom open. Something bigger was afoot. No time to deal with it now, though: my crack-of-dawn flight was waiting. I kept my feelings in check but they lingered like rainclouds over the week. Finally, the following Friday night, Bradley met me outside my doorstep for a stroll around the neighborhood.

"My parents asked what I wanted to do, if I really wanted to go with you. They're planning to get a place in the city, you know." They'd been talking for years about selling their suburban home.

"I guess you know what my answer is."

Even now he can't come out and say it. But the message was clear.

It's over.

Things moved quickly after that and I had little time to think. My condo sold swiftly; the promised work opportunities out west materialized almost as fast. Before I knew it I was living in San Francisco and Bradley was in another relationship. *Classic rebound,* I thought. He talked up the new guy's virtues—a fellow with Hollywood connections—loudly and often. Finally I told him to stop. I couldn't take it anymore.

It pains me to say it, but the feeling that welled up most during those weeks wasn't anger or pain—it was disappointment. *I risked my life for this guy.* I'd always treated the surgery as a rational, carefully considered act, but the truth is, when you donate a piece of yourself—in this case the Jew ironically granting the gentile a pound of flesh—you also impart some of your aspirations to the recipient. And this was not the direction I'd hoped for or considered even in my wildest imaginings. Seeking a sanity check, I decided to make Steve my confidant; given his bias we'd skirted discussion of this so far…which might have been where I should have left it: upon hearing my musings, Steve did a complete about-face and hurried to Bradley's defense.

"Well, you know, you're the one who abandoned *him.*"

Huh? Steve had often prided himself on his penchant for devil's-advocacy…but if ever there wasn't a time. I'd come seeking camaraderie, solace, the sort of bonding soldiers expect in a foxhole. I hadn't expected blandishments about his guilt for prior squabbles with the guy—or for what I suspected this was really about: the fact that I'd abandoned him to addiction all those years ago.

"I can't help the way I feel," Steve added. The conversation segued, as conversations often do, to other matters. His newfound spirituality in particular and how it informed his outlook...over my protestations that this *really wasn't the time*. On we blathered, for hours, and although it was probably the most strained conversation we'd had in years, it felt, by the end, that we reached something of a resolution.

Or maybe not: Steve didn't answer my calls on subsequent days and retreated to his preferred mode of communication during a conflict—instant messaging chat. I find this medium to be precisely the worst for working through things, and sadly I was right on the money: Steve adamantly insisted that I accept his right to an opposing outlook. "You can't tell me how to feel," he wrote. "Deal with it." He went on about his spiritual quests, explaining how he'd labored to conceal them from me, his secular friend. *Who is this guy?* In one breath obstreperous and indignant, in another channeling the Dalai Lama. It felt like I'd re-befriended an entirely different person than I'd imagined, one just as unhelpful in a crisis as he was all those years ago. In an angry e-mail the following day Steve set forth an ultimatum: apologize unequivocally for my hurtful and narcissistic behavior—or never contact him again.

And so, in the span of a few weeks, two of my closest relationships vanished into the ether.

Efforts were made in fits and starts to patch things up, but it all came to naught: Bradley grew ever angrier at my disapproval of his life, which at this point seemed centered more around the new fellow and further drunken bouts instead of a return to school. *I sound like his parents*, I mused, while his real parents continued their role as tireless nursemaids. Steve, meanwhile, informed me of his plans to set up a discussion website, "Where friends can disagree." The cherry on the sundae, the afterburner on the angst turbojet, was the final hostile missive Steve sent right before I flew off to London. *Fuck you and have a nice trip.*

It all reads like the plot of a daytime soap...especially recollecting it here atop a Jordanian clifftop. Though maybe coming at it now holds deeper significance: just as I've shifted continents, headed further into the world, away from the comfortable and familiar, so too now comes an inner shift. *I need to face this stuff.* Understand what it all means, what it spells for the future. This dizzying, kaleidoscopic world journey offers more than mere distraction. I believe each of us, in a sense, is a world in microcosm, a brew of different forces pulling and tugging every which way. And yet, without the fertility of new experience we remain a psychic monoculture, unable to see past ourselves.

No more. This trip is my chance to draw deep, to look further within, to garner the understanding that's eluded me for so long.

I trundle down from the High Place of Sacrifice and find a bunch of camels lounging at the base. I walk up to one of their owners and negotiate a decent price for a ride across the valley, to the steps of Petra's other big-ticket building, the Monastery. It's my first time riding one of these beasts, and in spite of touristic hokiness—some middle-aged ladies looking on let out a chuckle as I mount the thing—it's something I just have to try.

It's an easy, languid ride—particularly since there's a saddle with grips on both sides. The gentle swaying motion isn't for the seasick-prone, but for me it's oddly hypnotic. The driver of the camel leading mine sits with one leg folded over the other, but I don't dare try that—it's a long way down. On the sand the beast's hooves pad rhythmically; they're as soft as the ground itself—unlike the keratinous crunch of horses—and perfect for the desert floor.

"Difficult climb! One hour!" call out the donkey-jockeys, but I ignore them and with my long legs make it to the top in barely twenty-five minutes. There I'm greeted by a broad, expansive plaza that's shadowed by the columned Monastery. Like the Treasury, it's carved into the mountainside as if about to burst forth like those unfinished Michelangelo sculptures back in Florence.

That's a wrap for Petra. Now I need to get back to Amman. Ibrahim has an answer cheaper and friendlier than the JETT bus.

"Go with my friend Ismail," he says, motioning to a middle-aged businessman with a Camry. He's heading up there and offers to take me for a nominal sum. On the road, Ismail offers me some *lafah*, thick chewy pita bread that's a specialty of some Amman bakery. If any food has the potential to replace chocolate as my new carborific treat, it's this.

My evening's free and Amman's a big city, but that doesn't translate into much: the Middle East is one big no-fly zone for me where gayness is concerned. All the gay guides mention death penalties and underground communities and I don't dare try; I prefer to leave the region with all my extremities intact, thank you very much. Besides, I'm not sure how a gay bar would fare in a region where the dominant religion outlaws not just sodomy but alcohol as well.

"Oh no, many places to drink," Ismail offers when I tell him I'm not much of a drinker (I say nothing about my sexual orientation). That Jordanian hospitality again, along with an eagerness to show that *we're not like them*, those other unabashedly conservative Muslim countries. It's heartening; perhaps someday Jordan will break with its more religious neighbors and become a Mideast haven for the homos. Someday. Just not now.

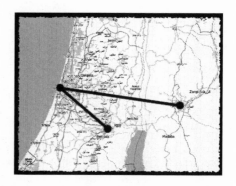

Return to Zion
Israel

*A*mman to Tel Aviv is less than a hundred miles. Back in Europe, or even South Africa, a train or rental car would have sufficed. And yet here I am, sitting at Amman's Queen Alia Airport waiting for a half-hour flight to the Israeli coast.

I'm doing this for a couple of reasons: the road from Amman across the Allenby Bridge slices through the strife-torn West Bank; I'm not too keen on having my trip spiced up by a firefight. Apparently others have the same idea: for a flight that back home might call for a dozen-seat prop plane, here we're on a full-blown Airbus A320, one of four a day that fly this route.

Geopolitics aside, Israel's become something of a Levantine Ireland: from a quasi-socialist Middle Eastern nation it's transformed itself into a high-tech hub. I see the signs right away: a spanking-new airport of steel, glass, and locally hewn Jerusalem stone; multilane freeways; sleek skyscrapers dotting the urban core. Coming here from dusty Amman feels like crossing from East Berlin to West all those decades ago.

Accommodation in Israel is pricey, but I still score a flashpacker-friendly rate at a funky boutique hotel located in a Tel Aviv "White City" Bauhaus-era building from the 1930s. Call it the unintentional benefit of the Nazi rise to power: they kicked out Jewish modernist architects, who came here and continued their craft in whitewashed Mediterranean concrete. Like Miami's South Beach, this place is on the map, having made it onto the UNESCO World Heritage list in 2003.

My lodgings formerly housed a cinema, and vintage projection equipment and posters adorn the undulating curves of the lobby.

It's only a short walk to the seashore, so that's where I head first. It's a near-perfect sunny morning, ample repayment for Copenhagen, Riga, and Saint Petersburg. Tel Aviv's oceanfront boardwalk, meanwhile, has changed beyond recognition in the twenty-plus years since I was here last as a boy: the Bauhaus structures and other less-than-charming concrete apartments on stilts have been joined by a pageant of new high-rises, postmodern luxury towers that could have been lifted wholesale from Santa Monica or Miami Beach. Weekend crowds fly kites along the beach while a herd of cats watch from a rocky mound.

Nothing out of the ordinary for a beach-hound like me, but the sense of déjà-vu here is different: *I remember this place*. Distant childhood imagery comes popping forth. When kids order popsicles from nearby sidewalk vendors, I recognize the brands and flavors—and can even make out the Hebrew lettering. The "clack-clack" of beach racquetball—*matkot*—resonates in my mind. It dawns on me that much of my attraction to beach towns in my adult life—part of why I've been so drawn to California—stemmed from a forgotten childhood in this Mediterranean town. I wonder how many of us possess unexplainable attractions to places, smells, or ideas, all based on half-forgotten influences from when we were small.

I'm almost all the way to Jaffa when my uncle calls me up. He and four of his five kids have just driven in from Jerusalem, and they scoop me up in their minivan minutes later. I've always had a close rapport with Sammy, my mother's youngest brother, only a scant twelve years older than I—yes, I really do have an Uncle Sam. Of my rather large Israeli clan he's one of the few who's been able to make it out to Canada on visits over the years, but this is the first time since adolescence that I've met him in his home country. We get to talking about that long-ago visit as if it was just yesterday.

"I never understood," Sammy says in his languid Israeli accent, "why he was so angry at you guys." He's talking about my late grandfather, who chaperoned me and two of my young sisters to his home in a Tel Aviv suburb. My grandfather was anything but grandfatherly: he was petulant and sullen, so much so that Sammy remembers squabbling with him about it.

"He was annoyed because it meant he was going to be apart from his new girlfriend for a couple of months," I answer. Sammy nods in comprehension: a puzzle piece just fell into place.

My grandmother died of cancer at age fifty-three. A dutiful and devoted husband, my grandfather cared for her to the end while remaining, in my foggy early-childhood memories, a devoted grandpa. All that changed upon her passing; he was never cruel but became detached, uninterested, a non-entity in our lives. Meanwhile, he pursued an ever-deteriorating spiral of shrewlike, abusive women, culminating with one who he dated for twenty years. At the end, as he turned frail and sickly, she stuffed him in an old-age home where he perished soon after.

"Once he was different," Sammy says. He used to be a gregarious, outgoing intellectual until he fell victim to a bureaucratic mix-up in 1950s-era Israel that saw him imprisoned and court-martialed. He was discharged—not honorably—from the Air Force where he worked as an engineer, and apparently was never the same again.

Not on my watch is what floats into my mind. It's the bugaboo that threatens every would-be nomad: leaving your peeps behind. While fights and fallouts are one thing, it should not obscure the importance of keeping one's global spiderweb of good relations in a healthy state. This is what keeps me close to my nieces and nephews, growing up on the opposite corner of the North American landmass.

As Jerusalemites, Sammy and his clan don't get to the seashore often, so we drive up the coast to the Port of Tel Aviv, on the city's northern edge. Yup, it's yet another once-derelict harbor district transformed into a panoply of shops enveloped by a wooden boardwalk. The kids take in the sea breeze, loving it. Who wouldn't?

"All this is new," Sammy points as we drive north of the city, past oases of luxury high-rises. We arrive at a glassy office park in Ramat

Hehayyal, one of Israel's tech hotspots. We're not here to work, however; we grab a bite of dinner then head to Max Brenner, a New York confectionary whose specialty is—wait for it—all manner of chocolatey wonders. This is family and can be counted on to share my tastes. They gawk at my choice of flourless cake, which I graciously let them try.

"I think of all of them, this one's the best," Sammy pronounces. *Hey, who do you think you're dealing with?*

The chocolate haze limits my motivation for later-night carousing, which is too bad since Tel Aviv is something of a nightlife hub—and practically the only gay center in the region. Alas, my timing's off as well: given the country's Muslim/Jewish mix the weekend happens a day early. Friday and Saturday are days off. Sunday is a workday like any other. Although Tel Aviv is the country's most secular, urbane city, I still find things pretty sleepy on the Jewish Sabbath. Ditto for the Saturday night when I venture out: there's just a smattering of places, all of which close relatively early. I visit Blackbook, a small alternative joint with appropriately midnight-toned interior and edgy drum and bass thumping over a diminutive dance floor. I chat with one fellow, a long-haired, dark-skinned fellow whose English is near-impeccable; Israel isn't quite Holland or Denmark, but high-tech has made English a far stronger second tongue than it was in my distant memories. But the boy has to go home—work tomorrow—so I too call it an early night.

The Yarkon River that marks Tel Aviv's northern boundary sits in a pleasant green space lined by brick bicycle paths. The pedestrian bridge that spans it is walled in concrete that's punctuated by Star-of-David-shaped openings, Zionist paper-doll cutouts. Like America, this land wears nationalism on its sleeve. To wit: my destination on the other side of the river, the *eretz yisrael*—Land of Israel—Museum.

Rather than a paean to jingoism, however, it's more a micro-Smithsonian of arts, culture and history, all of which this place possesses in abundance. If you think about it, the term "ancient land" is something of a misnomer: the whole planet is the same age, and the scale of individual geologic epochs defies conception. It is we who imbue the term with meaning. The Levant is the land bridge connecting Africa with Asia; evidence of human activity in the region goes back a million years. In addition to archeologists, fiction writers have taken note: before leaving I borrowed the James Michener epic *The Source* from its perch on my parents' bookshelf. It recounts 10,000 years of history centering on the remains of a Levantine village. The region is riddled with such spots—tells, they're called, earthen mounds formed not by natural happenstance but rather by the weight of one civilization sacking then rebuilding a place, millennium upon millennium. Archeologists digging at these sights find fragments of history going back in time as they dig deeper, concentric tree rings of human activity. This museum is sited on one of these.

The exhibits alone are entrancing: both pottery and glassmaking—particularly blown glass—were in large measure invented in these parts. Some ancient samples of glassware are surprisingly intricate...I'm not one for going gaga over glass containers, but here I am awed: *these people were barely out of the Stone Age.* The tell itself is equally haunting, particularly on this midweek afternoon when the place is empty. City skyscrapers shimmer in the distance, held at bay by a stand of palm trees. The stones glow orange in the fading light, underscoring their great age. I'm not the first to be struck by such spots: the most famous tell of all, *har megiddo*, was the site of so many struggles for its domination that, legend states, the last battle on Earth would one day be fought there.

It's better known by its non-Hebrew name: Armageddon.

The highway to Jerusalem curves and winds 2,500 feet from the coastal plain up into the Judean hills. It's after nightfall when my uncle, his wife Yudit, and their two older children drive me up from Tel Aviv. Eden, my twenty-year-old cousin, does this forty-mile commute every day to her office job in the Israeli military; although military service is still a requirement in this country for youth in the eighteen-to-twenty-one age bracket, for the vast majority of them this translates into a desk job. This is not dissimilar to the situation in America and in most modern militaries.

My time in Jerusalem is more concentrated than in Tel Aviv, partly by design: it's the cultural and spiritual capital of the country and the world's three major monotheistic faiths…which is partly what puts me off. Nevertheless, faith-based-centers, if they can be called that, fascinate in their history and evolution. Jerusalem's got that in spades, and my family eagerly points me in the right direction to find it.

"This was the dividing line," Sammy points as we walk toward Jerusalem's Old City the next morning. This town's been stitched together for a lot longer than Berlin, but there remains a palpable tension as black-frocked Jewish religious types scurry about amid crowds of secular Israelis and—once I enter the walls of the Old City—shopkeepers in traditional Arab garb. No hostilities during my visit, but the place feels as if on break from a giant boxing match; sure enough, the country explodes into conflict a few weeks later, though mostly further south around Gaza.

I'm headed to the other side of the Old City to tour some ruins— Sammy remembers my childhood boredom and promises this'll be different. I hurry through the narrow laneways—no wider than Venice's—before emerging on the other side of the Old City at a spanking-new archeological park erected by a private foundation: the City of David. Like so many developments in this land, this exhibit was controversial: its excavation of Judaic legacy rests at the heart of an Arab neighborhood.

Our young tour guide, bearded and bespectacled and straight out of Brooklyn, starts on the story of this place.

"You probably think the Old City is the Jerusalem of the Bible," he says. *Well…yeah.*

"Jerusalem was destroyed and rebuilt many times," the guide adds. *Hmm.* I figured a center as major as this stuck it out, Rome-like, through thick and thin. Guide: "When somebody came to conquer, they usually burned the city to the ground."

The "old" part of Jerusalem therefore isn't really that old: it dates back to the Ottoman-era 1500s—newer than most European centers, and only a century or two older than the cities of the American East Coast.

"Here is where the *real* City of David once stood, where he established his capital after conquering it from the Jebusites." The guide points to a pile of rubble—what else?—all that remains of the First Temple, sacked by the Babylonians in 586 BC. Another pile denotes city walls dating back to the twelfth century BC. We spin down wooden stairways, lower and lower, past walled outlines of former homes and other structures.

"That's the Valley of Kidron," our guide points at a shallow gulley. "It used to be much deeper." It's been filled in by millennia of human activity. Antiquity's trash heap.

The highlight of the tour comes at the end. As with Petra, every ancient city possessed a delicate jugular: a reliable source of water. That's why Michener named his book *The Source*. In one chapter he details the travails of an engineer, circa 2000 BC, dealing with this problem: the natural spring, the water source, lay just outside the town walls—fine for prehistoric hunter-gatherers who first settled there but a critical weakness for towns threatened by siege. Engineers of old, using stones on hilltops as markers, ingeniously deduced how to dig tunnels shooting diagonally downward under the earth.

Here there's a real-life version of this yarn: our tour ends at the fabled Hezekiah's Tunnel, an aqueduct built to divert water from the naturally occurring Gihon Spring directly into the former city.

"Does anyone want to go in?" our guide asks. Most of the group is older and none are interested. I might be, but first, one question:

"How clean is the water?" I ask over the rushing din.

"Pure underground spring water," the guide replies. *Works for me.* I strap on my miniature miner-style headlamp—once again, I come prepared—and navigate the 600-yard tunnel in my hiking sandals. The water rushes at my feet, strong enough to fell me if I'm not careful. The tunnel curves and contracts in spots, barely wide enough to walk, sometimes low enough that I need to stoop. The pale limestone rock, smoothed some by the centuries, remains uneven: this was dug long before machines and without the precise engineering of imperial civilizations. Nevertheless, the dank burrow enchants, and for me the marvel of this place grants more uplift than anything traditional faith can muster: this literally was a life-giving achievement, enabling townsfolk of old to survive in a hostile and savage world.

I emerge out of the tunnel on a street in the Arab town of Silwan; the tour group is nowhere to be seen. Some kids play in a nearby yard while a woman sweeps a front porch. In spite of this being "Arab East Jerusalem" I don't feel unsafe. I hike back up the hill, check in with the tour center, then head back through the Old City for some lunch. I find a falafel stand—however popular this dish is in the region, Israel seems to have especially cottoned on to it—and order from a character straight out of the soup Nazi from *Seinfeld;* this country's rep for surliness hasn't been entirely vanquished under the aegis of globalization.

My aunt has worked at the Israel Museum for over twenty years. Although much of the museum is in the midst of a multi-year renovation she grants us access to one part of it still open: an expansive model of the city as it looked during the Second Temple era. My uncle is fascinated with ancient civilizations—which I suppose makes Jerusalem an ideal place for him to call home.

"The Romans and the Jews, they were—how would you say today?—not a good cultural fit for one another."

Judaic intransigence flummoxed the Romans: for all its cruelty, the real secret of Rome's success was its willingness to integrate different cultures and faiths. Although desirous of territory and tribute, the empire left local practices alone. But that wasn't good enough for the Hebrews, who wanted no foreign intercession of any kind. Consequently, the collision between antiquity's greatest superpower and its most obstinate adversary ended in tragedy. Well, not for the Romans, which is why they threw up that Arch of Titus that I flipped the bird at back in the Italian capital.

I've always been something of a fan of science fiction, a fanciful trait that stood out growing up in my nose-to-the-grindstone eastern-Canadian enclave. Well, here's where I got it from: Sammy turned me on to Isaac Asimov when I was a teen and retains a fascination for matters speculative.

"How did they do it?" he asks. "These civilizations—they moved rocks, they made measurements precise by millimeters!" Extraterrestrial intervention sounds absurd...until you see these ancient ruins up-close and the imagination is awakened.

It's a country where everything is very old or very raw and new. We segue from the former to the latter as we stroll inside, where there's a temporary exhibit devoted to State of Israel iconography. Some of it could be described as catnip for ultra-nationalists—original copies of the Israeli Declaration of Independence and early designs for the flag—until we come upon one display case: it bears a prayer for peace carried in Yitzhak Rabin's breast pocket the day he was assassinated in 1995; on one corner there's a dried bloodstain.

They say there are only seven storylines, and sometimes I wonder if there are only a commensurate number of personality types. I don't find this reductionist hypothesis upsetting; on the contrary, it reminds us we have more in common than we realize. I consider that when I meet Daniella, Sammy's five-year-old daughter who could be twins with my niece Lola, 5,000 miles and several cultures apart, whom she's never met.

"This is a giraffe. This is a butterfly," she points out in Hebrew, matter-of-factly in her picture book. My rusty command of the language is stimulated. She's just as curious to learn the English names for these, so it's a lesson for both of us.

Her oldest sister, Adar, tears me away for a bit of dinner at a bohemian eatery near my little hotel off Jaffa Road; although Jerusalem lacks Tel Aviv's glitz and operates in the shadow of religious persuasion, the city's still got a lively coffeehouse scene: stone-paved pedestrian thoroughfares are abuzz with young and old sipping drinks and partaking of serious conversations. Over some salad and hearty soup Adar and I add to the mix: a more earthy, intellectual type than her younger sister, Adar's gift for languages is evident as she slips from flawless Hebrew to soft-spoken English.

"I never met you. You were like some faraway story," she laments.

Actually, that's not *strictly* true; I met her when she was fifteen months old and still in a baby stroller.

"I know," I reply. "That's partly why I came." Israel may have posed logistical complexity as I tried to fit it in with the rest of my Middle East itinerary, but so what? There was no way I would neglect this kin any longer. That global spiderweb needed maintaining. Meanwhile, wanderlust has also seized Adar: she's adding Italian to her repertoire, and hopes to attend school there next fall.

"I'll make you a promise," I say. "Go to Italy and I'll pay you a visit when you're there."

It's a deal...not that I need much inducement to return to the land of gelato.

Jerusalem has yet more secrets to disgorge. Back to the Old City the next morning, this time for a tour of passageways under the Western Wall. These hold special significance as they were the flashpoint of the Al-Aqsa Intifada back in 2000 that unraveled the peace process.

The passages front a wall of massive stone blocks floodlit from below. Our guide, an earnest young woman in black slacks and beige sweater, explains that the Western Wall is but a fragment of the massive walled complex that was Temple Mount. Built in its final form, ironically, by the Romans under Herod, the passageways underground confirm the engineering prowess of this ancient empire: row upon row of hefty stone blocks, some a dozen feet long, perfectly rectangular and perfectly fitted. By contrast, various modifications made later in history are jagged and imprecise.

"Why is the Western Wall so sacred?" the guide asks. "There are many other parts of the Temple that are also excavated." She then answers her own question as we pass ultra-religious-garbed men in long black coats bowing and praying in the artificial light.

"Temple Mount is Mount Moriah, where God stopped Abraham from sacrificing his only son, where the Ark of the Covenant was said to rest, and from where the world was created from a single rock—the Foundation Stone. It's closest to here," she points into the wall, "inside the Dome of the Rock."

I may be a skeptic but I can see the appeal.

We emerge in the Arab quarter of the Old City—though really, it looks just like other parts of this walled enclave. I notice that in addition to our guide we're escorted back to the Western Wall by a couple of armed security guards. But otherwise it has the feel of a morning like any other in the centuries of this place's existence: locals sit on stoops, roam about, shop; without knowing the context, one would be hard-pressed to distinguish olive-skinned Arab denizens from Jewish Israelis.

The Wall itself is a broad, open courtyard. After its capture by Israel in 1967, the houses that had been built beside it were torn down and the resulting open space was consecrated as a Jewish place of worship in the Orthodox tradition: signs indicate where men and women are to be separated; they also admonish respect, indicating this is "WHERE THE DIVINE PRESENCE ALWAYS RESTS." Up by the wall itself, bearded Orthodox Jews sway and bob, reciting ancient incantations. Peppered among them are yarmulke-wearing soldiers in military fatigues, most quite young, automatic rifles at their side, just as enraptured as their black-frocked cohorts.

Okay, enough of that. Luckily there's more archeology to keep me occupied—yes, it's official: *archeology is interesting*. The nearby Jerusalem Archeological Park in particular. A pavilion underground does it up the way members of my generation expect: with a CGI-animated re-enactment. The short movie chronicles the journey of a long-ago pilgrim from some small Galilean town arriving in Jerusalem for the thrice-yearly pilgrimage: buying animals for sacrifice; purifying oneself in ritual baths; proceeding with sacrificial rites under the aegis of the priesthood…it's all so mystical, so elaborate, so—dare I say it—*pagan-*seeming compared with what Jews do today.

I leave the holy city to visit more relatives in further-flung corners of the land. This car-rental experience, however, is nothing like service-with-a-smile Cape Town.

"No stamp in your passport? Then we charge you tax," says the surly young lady at the counter.

"How about insurance?" I ask.

"Collision damage is extra." She shows me the price—and it's a lot more.

"I take it there's no deductible?" That's the norm back home for insurance this pricey, and this is one of the big U.S. agencies.

"Of course there's a deductible!" she snaps. You'd think I just asked to race the vehicle in NASCAR.

"Do you have GPS?" The website said they did.

"Go across the street. We don't do it. Maybe at the hotel they'll rent you one but you have to bring it back here."

Well fuck that. I'm supposed to give the car back at the airport so that's not going to work. I take the collision damage but something tells me I'm getting dinged in the rear in another sort of way.

With that out of the way, the car—another pint-sized affair, a fire truck-red Hyundai Getz—is actually pretty fun: I buzz down curves of the hilly Jerusalem-Tel Aviv highway, then turn off and head south, to a kibbutz near the coastal town of Ashdod where my great-aunt Rachel has lived for over sixty years.

Well, at least I *thought* that's where I was going: for the first time in forever my legendary sense of direction fails me. I miss the turnoff to the not-so-well-marked Kibbutz Hatzor, and spend the next hour frustratingly weaving around residential subdivisions. This is also the time my local SIM card chooses to run out of minutes. My poor great-aunt is getting flustered—not something you want to have happen to a ninetysomething. Finally I make it to the quiet agricultural village of rambling shade trees and small bungalows. This is one of Israel's original collective settlements, a once-barren outpost of concrete cabins settled by left-leaning pioneers. It's now only a couple of miles from rows of coastal apartment blocks and close enough to metropolitan Tel Aviv to have become a bucolic bedroom community. Nevertheless, old-timers like my great-aunt persist.

"I was worried about you," she says, her diminutive frame embracing me as she walks out of her golf cart. She rode her bike well into her eighties until she finally was ordered to slow things down.

"Wow, you look great!" I haven't seen her in over a decade and am hard-pressed to see a difference. I hope I end up with *those* genes.

"Yeah, people keep telling me that," she says with a weak smile. I suspect the spry elderly are about as weary of hearing that as children are of "Look how big you got!"

Still, she's not without her opinions: we sit in her tiny bungalow and she fills me in on the family schism.

"You know, your grandfather and I would read the bible, and as children he'd say to me 'I can't believe grown-ups actually believe what's in here.'" Rachel stems from a long line of secular Zionists, folks for whom ambitions of nationhood were shorn of religious connotation. Now members of our own family have found religion—and secularists like her are at a loss.

"I suppose it's kind of like born-again Christians back home," I offer.

"No. It's much worse!" she exclaims, and I see what she's getting at: aside from church attendance and the occasional political leaning, little separates the lifestyles of hard-core American Christians from their secular cohorts. Not so with Judaism: a web of rites and rituals surround observant existence, right down to the most fundamental of human social rituals, that of breaking bread together. Dietary laws make eating a logistical ordeal, driving a wedge between people even if none other exists.

As dusk falls I arrive at my next destination, a place where I witness Rachel's depictions for myself. About an hour further south and only a couple of miles from the Gaza Strip lies the settlement of Tlamim, where my aunt Ella, her husband, Zvi, and a couple of her now-grown kids live. This wing of the family, reared by atheists, turned and ran toward faith in a big way. The first apparent difference comes as I'm greeted by my warm, charming aunt—a tall, thin, olive-skinned woman with long, straight nose and distinctively angled jaw line.

"No hugging, no kissing, but it's great to see you!" she says. Under religious tract, no physical contact between women and non-immediate family. Aside from that, however, it's just like old times: Ella's an accomplished artist and offers rich insights into many of the places I've visited. Their new home, a modern take on the sprawling ranch-style affair, is impeccably decorated. Together with her husband Zvi, an entrepreneurial family farmer, she helps run a faith-based foundation centered on a charismatic—some say psychic—religious leader. Hey, Judaism's got its gurus as well.

Zvi is even more transformed than his wife: his once-Paul Newman-esque blonde hair and tanned skin have been replaced by a pate of thinning gray merging into dense, flowing beard. As we snack on cakes and appetizers, he mumbles blessings before anything passes his lips. Once he was a classic tough guy, a former paratrooper who helped capture Jerusalem's Old City during the Six Day War. Their path in life baffles me, though I notice that faith seems to have softened them. Better yet, they're accepting of me and my gayness, something that can't be said of most born-agains.

One thing hasn't changed: my go-getter uncle spends half the time on two different mobile phones—one a Blackberry, natch—sometimes on both at the same time.

My cousins, Maya and Ruth, also join as the evening progresses: Maya's had a trying few years, raising three small children on her own after her husband was killed in a raid in Lebanon; it's the only time such a tragedy has befallen my Israeli clan. Ruth, also a mother of three, is working on a fourth—the last time I saw her she was about the same age as her little ones.

"I remember you," she says in broken English. "*Ha-cochavim.*" The stars. I was a space-crazed kid when I was last here, beguiled by the brilliant night sky out here in the sticks. It's probably one of her earliest memories, this gawky cousin from Canada always looking to the heavens.

In the months to come things will turn sour for the religious ones: Ella and Zvi's guru comes out of self-imposed seclusion and accuses them of all manner of crimes, from embezzling funds from his foundation to holding him under house arrest. It explodes into a scandal that divides the family and sees them investigated for alleged wrongdoing. It looks like they've gotten themselves on the wrong side of a religious power struggle, something we've seen many times in evangelical America. Although unsurprising to secular cynics, I still find myself greatly saddened: it's one thing to have ideals shattered and drift away from that which you once held dear; it's quite another when the catalyst for that disillusionment is a legal and financial shitstorm. But on this balmy Thursday evening in early December, all of it is still beyond the horizon.

It's getting late as I arrive at my last stop for the evening, the farming community of Ein HaBesor. Ella and Zvi once lived here, and their remaining secular children still do. I'm staying with my cousin Dan—less than a year younger than I but with a life about as different as can be imagined: having inherited and expanded his father's farming business, he and his wife, Ayelet, live in a roomy, pastel-colored home with five (!) kids. A soft-spoken, mellow guy with a shaved head, he and Ayelet share a quiet late dinner with me.

"You loved the tractor," he says. I was always wanting to ride in it whenever we came to visit. "And remember when you forgot your shoes and couldn't walk on the road." *Yeah, I remember that:* it was a hundred fucking degrees and the pavement was egg-frying hot. Oh, childhood. We used to play hide-and-seek in mysterious concrete-covered stairways leading underground. Only in later years did I learn what they were for: air-raid shelters in the event of rocket attacks.

The road not taken. As I nod off in Dan and Ayelet's robins-egg-blue spare bedroom I consider it once more. My parents nearly ended up settling here when I was a boy. They were drawn to this place out of cultural zeal—though they're nowhere near the level of my uncle and aunt on the observance scale, so I hesitate to call their fixation religious. Then they left, disgruntled, after three years. *Sounds familiar.* I wonder if that was the lesson imparted to me as a lad: *if you don't like it, leave.* I've always prized that notion, though the sheer number of times I've acted on it—to say nothing of the aftermath of the last uprooting—makes me wonder.

Agriculture comprises only a sliver of Israel's economy but retains a lock on the nation's psyche. Dan drives me around their operation—in contrast to agribusiness back home, Israeli farming remains largely in the hands of families and local cooperatives. It's also decidedly high-tech: water-efficient drip irrigation was developed here.

"We don't grow oranges anymore," he says. "Not good in the climate. An orange is mostly water." *I never thought of that.* Nowadays they grow lettuce heads and other greens. A die-hard city boy, I always find it surreal to see tidily arranged rows of plants bearing the produce I'm used to finding on supermarket shelves. But it's an assembly-line operation like any other: we check out a packinghouse where pale-blue-attired ladies sort potatoes as they tumble into brightly painted boxes. Interestingly, most of the farmhands hail from other countries, Thailand and the Philippines in particular.

"It's not safe to hire Arabs anymore," Dan explains.

Back at the house, Dan's younger brother, Binyamin, is done for the day, lying in the sun with his MP3 player.

"Top of the morning," he says with a smile. Like lots of Israelis, he's traveled widely. He feeds me some good tips on where to party in Thailand.

From the country back to the city, to yet more relatives. My dad's cousin Robert, a South African who's a dead-ringer for my father—with his ruddy complexion and round head—more than his brother in Cape Town. The vagaries of genetics.

"He's the good-looking one," he quips.

Their kids are grown with the exception of their youngest Yonatan, a slim twenty-year-old who's more aloof at first than his chill-beyond-description Cape Town counterparts. Still, he warms up some when we try to get their Internet connection working—I'm considering starting to lie about my occupation since this is usually what ensues once I tell people what I do for a living.

"I'm also at a desk job," Yonatan tells me when I ask about his military service. "I'm lucky. Lots of the ones who are in combat, they're the ones you'll meet in Goa or in Thailand going crazy on drugs to forget what they've seen."

Israel's hair-trigger existence literally is right before your eyes—at least it is in Kfar Saba, barely two miles from the Green Line.

"That's Kalkiliya," Robert points to the Palestinian town in the middle distance as we walk their dog the next morning. Then he motions further up the hill. "That's an Israeli settlement." Just down the road, meanwhile, lies Ra-anana, another of Israel's glassy skyscraper-soaked technology hotspots.

"They probably won't ever shell here," Robert says. "They don't dare hit one of those buildings."

Seems that even in places riven by strife, business is still business.

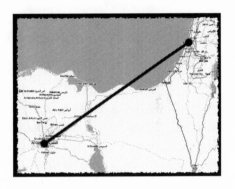

Riddle of the Sphinx
Cairo

O ur flight is delayed. This comes as a surprise as every flight so far has been punctual as a Swiss watch.

This time, it's a plus: my energetic, offbeat seatmate engages me in a chat; Sarah's a project manager who does aid work for the University of New South Wales; she's just completed a stint of economic-aid consulting in the Palestinian Territories, and this delay is the least of her day's ordeal.

"They kept me at the airport for two hours," she says. "They asked me the same questions, over and over. And kept checking my bag."

Apparently, this is typical of what Palestinians endure daily when crossing into Israel under the rubric of security. *Law & Order* has nothing on these guys.

"Are you on some watch list?" I say. Joke: she's an arty-looking Aussie brunette from Sydney with name and demeanor about as menacing as Julia Roberts'. The whole story surprises me—I've long labored under the belief that Israeli security is smart and subtle, cool eyes assessing passengers efficiently with nary a misstep. I suspect it's incidents like this that hurt the country's image in the eyes of the world.

Still, Sarah remains cheery—I'm not sure I would be in this instance—and gives me voluminous advice about spots to visit in Australia. We trade business cards; perhaps our paths will cross again.

And so on to Cairo. *This is it, the big time, baby*: at nearly eighteen million people, my first ever bona-fide developing world megacity. I'm a bit anxious, feeling as if all travel up to this point has been a dress rehearsal for spots like this. As most such metropolises, accommodations come in two flavors: ultra-deluxe and super-cheap (read: shithole). With the former out of my range I bite the bullet and rough it just a bit, booking myself into a widely recommended hostel near Midan Tahrir, right in the heart of town. Better yet, the place provides free airport pickup.

We drive into the city, massive rows of dirty apartment blocks lining the broad expanse of highway. And yet, it's all relatively quiet, the traffic sedate. I soon learn why: I've come during the feast of *Eid al-Adha*, marking the end of the *Hajj* and commemorating Abraham sacrificing a sheep—instead of his son, Isaac—at Mount Moriah where I've just been. This could go either way, visiting a foreign culture during their equivalent of Christmas or Thanksgiving.

The Nubian Hostel is on the second floor of a grimy walk-up on the edge of a pedestrian street. A pair of tiny cats darts into a crawlspace behind the stairway as I hoof it with my backpack. The blue walls, glossy paint on rough stucco, are festooned with colorful yet dusty decorations. My room is private and expansive, but with a tiny window and walls a sickly shade of pink made even less comely by office-style overhead fluorescents. The bathroom—private, at least—is in a metal booth built into the room. The toilet leaks a bit.

After dark the city spectacularly comes to life: the warren of pedestrian streets near my hostel is chock-ablock with *sheesha* cafés and quick-serve eateries. It's dinnertime, but I'm squeamish about street food even though it looks edible enough; I'm determined to dodge the dreaded "Nile Pile," so I make my way to the cluster of high-rise international hotels around the enormous traffic circle of Midan Tahrir. It's abuzz with holidaymaking Egyptians and speeding cars while neon-lit advertising signs watch serenely from the tops of nearby buildings. Negotiating traffic in this city is an adventure that makes Rome seem tame: no traffic lights, vehicles speeding in every direction, a giant game of dodgeball. Coming from jaywalker-friendly Montréal, I love it. The World Series of urban warfare.

The 1960s-era Nile Hilton feels like those once-chic overseas hotels from some old adventure film: a gaudy gold-and-colored-sphere chandelier hangs in the lobby; a mélange of guests, Western tourists and traditionally garbed Middle Easterners. I enjoy a bite of fairly unadventurous dinner in an outdoor eatery overlooking a lush courtyard: decent, safe, and moderately priced, which suits me fine for now. Maybe later in the trip I'll muster up more courage and chow down on street grub.

The Corniche road fronting the Nile is party central; families and gangs of youths mill about or ride music-blaring party boats along the river. The waterway is broad and expansive, its blackness reflecting the crazy quilt of pulsating boat lights. I see quite a number of slender young men walking arm-in-arm: this is by no means a gay gesture in these parts, just the way locals express camaraderie. Though looking at a few of them, I begin to wonder…especially the more gregarious packs who wag their heads at me and exclaim "Welcome! Welcome!" Still, I don't try anything: I'm back in the no-fuck zone. Later I hear from other gay travelers how they were repeatedly propositioned by secretive gay locals across the Middle East; no such action for me.

I've got to get rid of this thing, I muse, fingering my Israeli passport. It's *verboten* at some future stops. Researching online, I find a number of DHL offices nearby…but thanks to the holiday, they're shuttered up tight and will stay that way throughout my visit.

On to Plan B: one of the big downtown hotels. I walk back to the Nile to the Semiramis Intercontinental. I approach from the rear, behind service driveways leading to the main road.

"You walk like an Egyptian," a thinly bearded fellow says. I don't think he's making a Bangles reference.

"Where you going?" *Uh-oh.* I've read about this line: it usually means, "I'll show you the way for a not-inconsiderable sum." But I keep it friendly.

"Just the hotel."

"Go that way," he points. "I'll show you." He invites me down a dark driveway. No thanks.

"Nah, I'm just going to go this way," I motion, pointing at the driveway. At this he gets incensed.

"I'm just trying to help you!" *Right.* I smile and wave him away, but the encounter leaves me a little shaken.

Inside the Semiramis it's a different story: a newer place than the Nile Hilton, their business center on the second floor is polite, solicitous, and charges about the same to mail a UPS package that I'd pay elsewhere—if anyplace else actually was open.

This museum looks like it belongs in a museum: dusty, richly patinaed display cases are stuffed with carvings, statues, mummies…anything the British, French and other occupiers hadn't managed to steal. It's the Egyptian Museum, a low-slung neoclassical beast reclining lazily across Midan Tahrir. Billy Crystal's right: hieroglyphics really do look like a comic strip about a character named Sphinxy.

Old Kingdom, Middle Kingdom, New Kingdom…what's astounding about this civilization was its longevity. If Rome was a sprint, an incandescent flash engulfing the Mediterranean—including Egypt itself—for a smattering of centuries, then this country was a marathon, its Pharaonic dominion spanning millennia. The hieroglyphs, the lavish tombs, the inscrutable pyramids—all this flourished when Rome or Athens were mud huts or less, when Jerusalem was a paltry Canaanite settlement, when the Americas and Europe held thin clusters of hunters, gatherers, and cave dwellers.

The Nile's the reason, but it's more than just the river *per se:* rains from central Africa would roar down to the sea, causing the waterway to flood. Flooding cycles gifted the lowlands with fertile soil—the only region so blessed amid thousands of miles of arid desert. It was the perfect place for agrarian civilization to take hold, and with civilization came writers, artists, engineers—and pharaohs. The word itself is derived from *per-aa,* "great house."

The museum isn't the only bit of faded urbanity: Cairo's city center is a pageant of Mediterraneanized nineteenth-century Paris. With the Nile eventually dammed and contained over a century ago, Egypt's rulers went ahead and ordered up a city core in accordance with the latest European fashion. Meanwhile, on the fringes of this "new" city core sprouted upscale residential districts: Zamalek, on one of the river's islands, a blend of more dirty high-rises—some vintage, others not-so-vintage—and shops on its main drag, Sharia 26th of July. It's something of an expat hangout so more establishments are open here than in the city center; for lunch I find a French-themed place that serves a pretty mean Italian-style pizza—call it "European fusion." After a wander of quiet side streets—more crumbling apartment blocks—I hop a cab back to town. I'm probably being overcharged, but refuse to haggle over what I calculate is probably four dollars.

After fighting Corniche traffic I disembark at Garden City, a quiet knot of old mansions canopied by shady trees. Late-model Mercedeses float serenely down winding streets. I snap a photo of one wedding-cake-white home, beautifully restored, only to learn it's an embassy. The guard outside is firm but surprisingly kind.

"Canada?" he says, learning where I'm from. "*Parlez-vous francais?*"

He hails from one of the franco-African nations; sadly, linguistic kinship doesn't grant me consideration: he makes me delete the photo of one of the few edifices in this city not coated in grime.

En route to the pyramids. Like the guidebooks say, the Giza complex really does lie right at the edge of the city. But this banal factoid does little to prepare one for the sight of these great structures looming behind a sea of grimy high-rises. They're just *there*, imposing and monstrous, perfectly wrought triangles that just so happen to be four-and-a-half thousand years old. Their geometric perfection is equaled by their tonnage: they're pretty much solid stone inside.

My hostel offers a reasonable car-and-driver option to get to the pyramids; typically it's *caveat emptor* for hotel-based excursions in scam-prevalent Egypt, but this one looks more on the level. My driver, Jamil, a heavyset middle-aged fellow, brings along his quiet, sweet seven-year-old son, Mustafa, who's off school for the holiday week.

"You should go to the Papyrus Museum before we go to the pyramids," Jamil says. *Okay, sounds good…*though I'm still unaware of the ulterior motive.

Drivers in poorer countries derive commissions from dragging foreign tourists to shops thinly disguised as "museums." This one specializes in papyrus art—the demo of how this ancient proto-paper is made, from crosshatches of wet leaves, is quite interesting, but it's immediately followed by a nonstop sales pitch. *Sorry fellas.* That poster-sized $500 piece isn't going to fit in my backpack; still, I do find something compelling and small, a painting of the jackal-headed god Anubis holding some Pharaonic dude's hand. Homoerotic subtext? I miss it at first—though I suspect its sellers do as well.

This episode is just the opening salvo in what I term the Great Tout War that must be waged to reach my objective, the pyramids themselves. I make the mistake of offhandedly mentioning to my driver that I might be interested in a camel ride.

"You know," he says, "the pyramids are too crowded. You see nothing. Maybe just a camel ride?"

I'm not quite clear what he's driving at—I want to do both—but I'm still an amateur at this game. He drives me over to camel stables some distance from the Giza complex.

"Three hours, around the complex, full panorama," the fellow running the place says, drawing lines in the sand by the outdoor table where we sit. "625 pounds"—around US$100. I'm no expert, but this sounds like a lot. I say "no thanks" and get a harangue about how awful the pyramids really are up-close, how they're not worth the admission, and so forth. Finally my driver rescues me and we're off.

"Very bad price! You almost could buy the camel!" Jamil exclaims, though a part of me wonders if he'd be singing the same tune if I went for it. I'd planned for this to be a low-key day like my visit to Petra, but obviously that's not how it works around here.

"Just drop me off at the entrance," I say.

"One more place," he offers. "Right next to the entrance."

Okay, fine. At this place a fellow in a *thawb* insists the camels are top-notch: "This is a *government* stable," he asserts…whatever that means. This one's not inside the Giza complex either, which means the view will be akin to watching a ballgame from nosebleed seats. No thanks. I tell Jamil and Mustafa I'll be back in a couple of hours. Dodging a bunch more vendors selling tickets that aren't tickets, I buy the real thing from a not-terribly-well-marked booth. Like something out of Willy Wonka the actual ticket is gold-fringed; with it I pass through a security check and enter the pyramid complex on the Giza plateau.

They say most of the vendors and touts have been kicked off the complex proper but there are still loads of them, mostly selling postcards and knickknacks on dusty rugs beside the footpaths. Yet another camel jockey is not so demure: I'm starting to learn that "no thanks" here is just an invitation for more haggling. This fellow chases me for a spell quoting ever-better prices—some of which are actually compelling—but at this point I'm too annoyed to go for it. *What part of fuck off don't you understand?*

Trying to shake these aggravations out of my head, I come upon the Sphinx. Cutesy platitudes about "smaller in real" life fail to capture it fully: this thing is *small*. Since part of it is below ground level, it rises barely a couple of dozen feet. All those pictures of it, shoulder-to-shoulder with a pyramid in the background (including mine—I can't resist perpetuating the illusion) are tricks of perspective as the huge monoliths are some distance away.

It gets quieter heading up the path to the granddaddy of them all, the Great Pyramid of Khufu. Up close these structures have jagged, craggy surfaces, but that's merely the product of age and vandalism: once upon a time the pyramids were encased in polished limestone; what we see today merely is the inner layer. The scale is spellbinding: each block is several feet square, almost as large as one of the camels waiting at the base. The scene is captivating enough for a photo, and this triggers the next round of the Tout War.

A boy of maybe thirteen, curly hair and a white hoodie, hurries up. I indicate I'm not interested in a ride, but he insists on posing for my pictures with *keffiyeh* and whip in hand.

"You have to take picture! Free! Free!" he keeps shouting. He tries to fit me with the *keffiyeh* and the whip.

"No thanks," I say again, though it's almost futile. I wave him away—but not so fast. He stops me, rubbing his fingers together.

"*Baksheesh.*" A tip. I tell him I have no small change so he offers to change a bill of mine. I hand it to him…and he smiles, spirits it away, and dashes off.

Doing the math, I realize I've been swindled out of maybe two dollars, and yet somehow this breaks my mental camel's back. The voraciousness at which I've been pursued and accosted, again and again…it's almost an insult to the great monuments. *Does it really have to be this way?* I try the whole "put yourself in their shoes" exercise and come up blank: the circumstances that spawn such behavior lie beyond my grasp. Egypt is the poorest country I've visited, and these folks seem almost *angry* about it—vengeful, I'd say—when confronting tourists who to them must seem impossibly wealthy. It's sobering: however dysfunctional our society—or my modest life—may seem, it doesn't amount to a hill of beans, in Bogart parlance, when measured against this place.

Visitors are allowed inside the pyramids, a privilege that may not last much longer. It's a tricky climb up a narrow, steep stairway-cum-ladder to the tomb at the top. An echo of what I saw in Jerusalem: the great stone blocks rise at an angle for hundreds of feet, perfectly shaped and fitted and, as my uncle said, accurate by millimeters. Those extraterrestrials again.

The king's chamber at the top is little more than an empty room; the treasures within have long since been looted or placed in museums. Light filters in through shafts leading diagonally upward to the outside. Apparently the pharaoh at first wanted to be buried underground, but then later chose this room with a view to spend eternity.

Circling the pyramid on the outside, I pass the two other monuments in the place, the Pyramids of Khafre and Menkaure. The latter structure, smallest of the three, bears a gouge in its side from an attempted dismantling in the twelfth century; hard though it may seem to believe, for many generations the Muslim rulers of Egypt frowned upon these structures and anything related to ancient Egypt: too pagan. Though coming here back then must have been easier; probably no scrum of touts.

I find a way to leave them and most everyone behind by climbing the sandy heights of the plateau behind the pyramids. At the top of the ridge, in the distance, lies a cluster of tourists, camels, vendors, and the rest. But between them and the pyramids…nothing. This stretch of the plateau is as forlorn and empty as it has been for millennia; I get sand in my hiking sandals as I plod upward. In the shimmering calm of the desert, the press of civilization recedes into insignificance.

I meet Jamil and Mustapha back at the entrance and we drive south, to Memphis, toward the step pyramid of Saqqara. The two-lane road parallels a water channel running from the Nile that renders the place an oasis. But while the parkland outside the Saqqara complex is a paradise of fluffy palms, the village en route is the real Egypt: squalor, dirt, almost more dispiriting than the townships of the Cape Flats on the other end of the continent. The muddy brown channel is polluted with trash; unfinished, rundown structures lie alongside. Still, people make do: women carry buckets of water on their heads; kids and old men ride donkeys along the side of the road.

A lunch of kebabs and freshly baked pita at a shady outdoor eatery is followed by one last bit of salesmanship: this time it's a "rug museum." The fellow here shows me one carpet after another in spite of my protestations that none of these will fit in my pack.

"If you have a magic carpet, I'll buy it," I tell him. *Maybe now he'll shut up*. He laughs and keeps right on selling.

The Saqqara complex, home of the step pyramids, is much quieter. It has the feel of a dress rehearsal for Giza: these pyramids are stair-stepped, as engineers were still learning how to build in true pyramidal form, limestone blocks bearing weight at an angle. Mustapha asks if he can tag along and I'm happy to indulge: we evade one elderly tout, cane in hand, who insists on showing us around the intricately hieroglyphed tombs. Instead we sneak photographs—they aren't allowed, but my camera snaps them without flash—and pose like characters in the paintings. Walk like an Egyptian indeed.

I'm still squeamish about street food. On advice of guides both printed and online, I'm not even drinking local tap water, at least not without purification. Luckily I packed in my James Bond gadget kit a mini-water purifier, a high-tech "mixed-oxidant" device no larger than a stack of pencils. It doesn't do much to improve the taste of Cairo tap water, however, so I stick to the admittedly wasteful practice of water bottles. For dinner, I try one of the big boats moored in the middle of the Nile that cater to Western tourists and upscale Egyptians. The heavy hand of America is once more apparent—the place sports a Chili's, which I give a miss in favor of something more local. Again, freshly baked pita. I could get used to this.

After the pharaohs came the Muslims and the Copts, each of whom set up shop at opposite ends of the sprawling city. I walk the mile or so east of the city center to Islamic Cairo; although the streets become narrower and less clean, I don't feel unsafe. For all my tales of would-be scams and swindles, Egypt has very little actual robbery or violent crime: it's a tight-knit culture and thievery is met with ostracism. Consequently, I'm left alone as I wander the narrow alleyways by the Khan el-Khalili, the old Islamic market. Again due to the holiday, the streets are quiet and many shops are shut; still, I find the experience almost more captivating for its tranquility; yesterday Jamil told me that Eid is a family-time sort of holiday. Consequently I see almost exclusively locals here on the streets; the odd pale-skinned Westerner sticks out like a sore thumb.

I turn off here and there onto small laneways where children dart about; from a second-floor window, an activity performed the world over: a woman hangs laundry on a clothesline above the street. Most of us in the West would probably find living here unbearable, the grime and dirt deal-breakers. Still, I find the walkable density to be as welcoming as any medieval quarter back in Europe.

Passing by soaring minarets of various mosques, I reach the Citadel, the sprawling complex built by Saladin. I then bridge the distance between this place and the even-older Coptic sector on a bit of modernity, the Cairo Metro. The only subway in Africa, it seems well-run but heavily used: like the rest of the city, it's dirty and crowded.

The Copts are one of the Middle East's many minorities; they're also the oldest sect of Christianity, dating back to 42 AD—not long after the blood of Christ was dry on the crucifix, it seems. The tiny quarter boasts a number of churches that are completely unlike any in Europe: rounded stone towers and domes that anticipate the minarets of later eras. The intricate floral-styled interior paintings and carvings are equally distinctive: this is early Byzantine architecture and I'm not the only one to be fooled by its resemblance to Islamic over Western flourishes. Even the Crusaders persecuted the Copts, not realizing that they were religious kin. Outgoing U.S. President Bush wasn't the first to say, "I thought they was all Muslims."

It's a splendid evening, my last in the city, as I ascend Cairo Tower. It's a 1960s Nasser-era construct built to showcase the nation's prowess, something of an Islamic Space Needle. The white concrete weave of the exterior is eye-catching, but somebody didn't do their homework on capacity control: a single tiny elevator is the only means of access, which means long lines on both ascent and descent. The views at the top are superb and sweeping: Cairo has precious little in the way of skyscrapers; the few it does have are mostly luxury hotels huddled around the Nile.

I stare out at the monstrous city, a liquid expanse of lights stretching to the horizon, and ponder the paradox: on the one hand, the cafés, street life, and urban chemistry make it one of the most exciting places on Earth—in many respects, it could be London, Paris or New York with a cultural and climatic twist. And yet…it's hobbled, a great beast weakened by time and circumstance. Economically the country has been stagnant for decades, with many residents complaining that resurgent religious extremism threatens to de-cosmopolitanize the city. I hope not. It feels as if Cairo is just lying in wait for Egypt to rise again, so it may once more take its place as one of the great centers of the world.

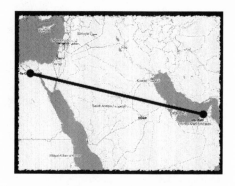

Emir's Playground
Dubai

> In Xanadu did Kubla Khan
> A stately pleasure-dome decree:
> Where Alph, the sacred river, ran
> Through caverns measureless to man
> Down to a sunless sea.
> - Samuel Taylor Coleridge, "Kubla Khan"

*C*oleridge's homilies may fit Dubai well, and I'm arriving at this pleasure-dome of a city in style—another cushy Business Class seat—but still, I'm nervous.

I've eradicated all evidence of my Israeli citizenship and visit to the country...but is that enough? I have a suspiciously large number of visa stamps to and from Jordan from transiting through there to Tel Aviv. I also don't know what immigration computers will say: will authorities here in the United Arab Emirates scan my U.S. passport and instantly know everywhere I've been? Will I be pulled into secondary inspection at an ungodly hour—my flight touches down after midnight local time—and grilled in the hope of revealing my pariah nationality?

The line at the expansive immigration hall moves at a reasonable clip; all immigration officers wear *thawbs*, those full-bodied white garments. I approach the counter, and the somewhat-hefty fellow behind it scans my U.S. passport, then flips through its pages...and flips...and flips. It feels like an eternity. Finally he looks up and placidly asks, "Where are you coming from?"

I answer, truthfully, "Cairo." He nods, stamps my passport, and that's the end of it. Still holding my poker face, I breathe an inward sigh of indescribable relief. Minutes later, luggage claimed, I collapse into a beige Toyota Camry taxi to my hotel.

First order of business in a desert kingdom: snowboarding!

Yes, it's excessive and over-the-top, but I simply *must* experience Dubai's indoor ski slope. In spite of so-so hand-eye coordination I've become something of an avid rider (word to the uninitiated: take lessons). Predictably, most of the clientele here is fair-skinned—something tells me snowsports haven't yet hit it big in these parts. Quite a number of the crowd seem pretty accomplished, partaking of flips and tricks and other acrobatics I'm too fearful to attempt. As ski slopes go, this one's pretty small, though there are some diminutive resorts in the Laurentian mountains near Montréal that aren't a whole lot bigger. A slow-moving chairlift curves around a bend under rows of bright lights built into a sky-tinted ceiling. The place has a familiar odor, of coolants that evoke the hockey rinks of my youth.

"It's like skiing in a refrigerator," says one fellow from France.

The place is kept at an even four degrees below zero Celsius, but without gusts of wind it's almost unsettlingly comfortable; good thing the two-hour ski pass includes clothing. It's an exhilarating novelty—but even hampered by storms, wind-chill, and ice, Mother Nature has little to fear from this place.

A Shell sign midway down the run says it all; without a trace of irony it reads, "HELPING US KEEP THE ENVIRONMENT CLEAN." Interestingly, Dubai's wealth is nowadays only tenuously linked to oil; the Emirate—one of seven that make up this very young nation—mostly ran out of the stuff some years back and made the enterprising decision to diversify. Before coming here I dubbed it the "Las Vegas of the Persian Gulf," thinking I would encounter a place filled with hotels, vacationers, and a party scene quietly tolerated by the otherwise-conservative locals. Instead, as my taxi heads back along the highway-like Sheikh Zayed Road, I spot row upon row of office towers and condominiums. Everything's brand-new or still skeletal and unfinished, but it feels almost more like a business than a recreational center.

Picture-perfect yet sterile; that's Jumeirah Beach Park. Two brightly painted papier-mâché horses flank a colonnaded breezeway. The grass is manicured, not a blade out of place. It's a mild day, a repetition of the weather that's followed me around South Africa and the Middle East for the past month—no complaints there. A sign indicates that one day of the week is ladies only (fortunately for me, not this one); something tells me that, even without the presence of men, the women who come here on such days are as heavily garbed as Puritan settlers in early-American paintings.

The beach itself is uncrowded, but when I try to relax in a lounge chair a fellow with African features hurries up and wags his finger at me. Wordlessly, he draws a dollar sign in the sand: seating is extra even though the park itself charges admission.

I try to swim in the waveless water. It's deep blue and looks inviting, but it's too chilly. Behind the row of palms fringing the sand looms the Burj Dubai, slender and rocketlike, rising in front of clouds that, if you squint, almost resemble the plume of imaginary engines. But this structure, almost complete, is solidly earthbound and record-setting: it's already the tallest structure ever built by human hands; after almost seven centuries, this distinction finally has returned to the Middle East. The previous regional titleholder was the centerpiece of my last stop: the Great Pyramid on the Giza plateau.

I'm about beached-out when an old college chum of mine gives me a ring: it's my friend Marjo, the effects animator whose pals I hung out with back in Cape Town. By utter coincidence we discovered via e-mail exchange that we're in Dubai at the same time: she's here doing some business at the Dubai Film Festival, another of the Emirate's slate of events designed to catapult it onto the world stage.

Marjo and her posse are ensconced at a hotel on the western side of town—what I've begun to dub Dubai's "theme park district" around the ski-resort-bearing mall I'd visited the previous day. But she's yearning for a more authentic experience and wants to come to my corner of town, the old center of Bur Dubai. We meet up across the street from my hotel outside the Al Fahidi Fort, the city's oldest building, now a museum. The fort's sand-colored stone walls surround a fully restored and dry-docked *dhow*, the deep-hued wooden ships that historically plied the waterways of the Persian Gulf—and as we discover, still do.

"I need some spices," she says after a warm embrace and a bit of catching up. She's an avid chef and there's a spice souk nearby, across Dubai Creek in Deira. We board an *abra*, a smallish wooden water taxi that could be a scale model of a full-blown *dhow*. A number of tourists and migrant workers board with us; the boat's buzzing outboard starts up, sending us out on the breezy water.

Calling the waterway a "creek" feels like an insult: it's an expansive saltwater inlet wider than most of Europe's rivers. Although dredged, breakwatered, and lined with concrete banks upon which gleaming skyscrapers sit, it still has the feel of an old harbor: we pass clusters of *dhows* coming and going, or else anchored and bundled together like sheaves of wheat, their decks tightly covered in mangy blue tarps.

"We're still hanging on," she says of the special-effects business. I'm totally out of the loop: the global economic meltdown has pretty much passed me by. "That's why we're here, to follow some leads." Film festivals conjure up images of arty filmmakers in berets checking out oddball indie movies, but really they're conventions like any other.

"So what's going on in your life?" she asks. *What hasn't gone on would be a better question.* I fill her in on the interpersonal ordeals from the past summer, and she delivers the line I so dearly yearned to hear from Steve:

"Oh, *of course* you're angry. You gave Bradley your liver!"

The women in my life get it. Perhaps unsurprising, given that I stem from a family of headstrong women who share with my female friends a pragmatism so often lacking in my male friends and lovers. Marjo may live in hippie Marin County, dye her blonde hair a quirky shade of red, and work in motion pictures, but don't let that fool you: she's a pragmatist, coming off a divorce with a once-high-flying modelmaker, a fellow who collapsed inward into depression and drug addiction.

As we approach the opposite bank, Marjo offers another thought, explaining away the mystery that's dogged me all these months: how the two people in my life who hated each other so found common ground.

"It sounds like they were both rebelling."

Yeah. Heck, both would brag about it, after a fashion: for Steve it meant rejecting *Edward Scissorhands* suburbia and the clutches of a once-abusive mother; for Bradley it was defiance against a lifetime of health-imposed restrictions. Not that I blame either of them, given what they had to face.

I only wish I didn't end up caught in the crossfire.

Siesta time's just ending in the souk. Shops begin to reawaken and crowds are still thin. We encounter a flamboyant, talkative middle-aged American from the Midwest who's shepherding a group of elderly women. He tells us he's lived here for a couple of years and points us in the direction of the best shops with admonishments not to overpay. *Ping.* My gaydar goes off again.

"You should ask him what it's like to live here," Marjo suggests. I almost do but he's in public and in mixed company. The UAE has opened itself up a lot, allowing drinking, pork, and nightlife into Dubai, but is at least as gay-unfriendly as Egypt or Jordan. *No sucking dick in Dubai* runs my mantra. The previous night, after turning on my computer's Wi-Fi, I surfed to one of the fairly innocuous gay news and lifestyle sites—only to find it blocked by the country's servers. The Great Firewall of Arabia. And as with Egypt, nobody seems to suspect *I'm* a homo, at least if the total absence of male solicitations and come-ons are any measure.

Marjo scores me a ticket to a festival event, a tent party for some Italian film. It's at Madinat Jumeirah, another of Dubai's themed hotels. This one's done up like an Arabian citadel: waterways, *abras*, ersatz stone forts. The shopping mall inside offers a modern take on the old souk—though I doubt much haggling takes place here. It's all supposed to resemble a picture-perfect version of Dubai Creek circa fifty years ago, when this place was a dusty pearl-diving outpost. Since it's close to Christmas, the waterways are festooned with lights. A large decorated tree is parked at the base of an open-air amphitheatre. This is perhaps the greatest incongruity of all: I can only imagine Disney-land so festooned for Ramadan.

The tent party is by the water. Just offshore looms the sailboat-shaped Burj al-Arab; it's floodlit, the lighting slowly changing from yellow to green to blue. I can see why this structure has become the icon of the place, its Eiffel Tower or Empire State Building. True to form, it's not that accessible: one can only visit the place with a hotel or restaurant reservation, and the cheapest rooms—all suites, appar-ently—run upward of $1,000 a night.

We get a bit tipsy and chat with other festivalgoers. None are industry heavyweights, which is fine by me: I still recall my days as an aspiring screenwriter, with all the attendant nervousness of a misstep; now it feels good to be an itinerant tourist in show-biz land. A middle-aged fellow next to us is in the midst of setting up a charity to license exhibition of films in poor countries. His business card has that chintzy feel of an industry nobody. Another fellow, a tall drunken Brit with graying blonde hair and leathery skin, tries unsuccessfully to hit on Marjo. Then he gives up and poses for me in front of a large globe-shaped lamp on the beach. He gives me his card and tells me to include him on the e-mail list for my blog; weeks later he sends an irate e-mail complaining I'm a spammer; I think he's just sore he didn't get in Marjo's pants.

The tent is all champagne and backlit bars and minimalism and white, but we get bored and Marjo's business associate offers to whisk us someplace else. James, a handsome young Indian man with blinding bleached-blonde long hair, calls over his limo. We head out to the Palm Jumeirah, a raft of artificial islands that from above form the shape of—what else?—a palm tree. As with much of this city, the structures along the development's central core, the "trunk," are still under construction. An eight-lane road runs up to the development's signature hotel and our destination: Atlantis, modeled on a similar property in the Bahamas.

There's a certain point where themed design crosses over from smartly self-referential to plain-old kitschy, and this place lands a bit over the line: the pillars of the colonnaded main entrance lobby sport bases of white seashells; precast fish scales envelop the columns from base to tip. It looks like a hotel designed by twelve-year-olds—though the Dale Chihuly sculpture, a surreal kaleidoscope of glass in the middle of it all, offers relief.

Also, the place thinks big: three-story aquarium big, a fish tank replete with an ichthyologist's wet dream of under-the-sea life. I shoot some video of sharks and rays for my fish-crazed nephews back home. James tells us he was here when this venue opened in September.

"Dubai punches well above its weight," he explains. The opening gala was attended by Robert de Niro, Michael Jordan, Denzel Washington, Sir Richard Branson…we grow weary hearing him rattle off names. More fireworks were shot off than at the Beijing Olympics. I cannot help wondering, however, with the global economy tipping, if this isn't some sort of swan song for a latter-day gilded age, people partying like it's 1929. Indeed: one year after my visit, the place flirts with insolvency.

But this night, it's just more fruity drinks with friends new and old: James has with him an Arabian fellow with impeccable British accent.

"We're like brothers," he says. Marjo shoots me a look: *brothers?* Ping again.

We order *sheesha*, water pipe with flavored tobacco. It's enjoyable, but a part of me craves something stronger. None of that here, to be sure, though apparently cannabis in one's hookah (as the pipe's more commonly known in the West) was big in Egypt in the 1970s. Then again, wasn't it everywhere?

There's no jet-skiing allowed in Dubai. Not for environmental reasons, to be sure, not in this place. Commerce is behind it: Dubai is in the process of building more Palm Islands and all that dredging and dropping means watercraft restrictions offshore. I do learn of one place that offers it: in the waters off Sharjah, the neighboring Emirate whose central city butts up against Dubai and is only minutes by cab. Good enough for me.

I get the taxi to drop me off at the verdant waterfront park—only to realize after it leaves that I'm still on the Dubai side. The jet-skiers can be seen splashing around the inland waterway that divides the two Emirates—but the walk from one to the other is a 45-minute affair.

No big deal: it's another perfect day and the trek is trifling after all that hoofing about in Europe.

Unlike the Dubai waterfront, the jet-ski spot looks like an abandoned moonscape: an empty spit of sand with a mound of earth in the middle. The purveyors have a fly-by-night feel, but they're pretty on-the-level—this is not a place that tolerates fly-by-nightness. Together with a bunch of other tourists I'm soon bouncing away on the inland lakes surrounding Sharjah's downtown. The water is chilly, and we're warned not to cross to the Dubai side or head out into the Gulf; happily there's enough around here to keep everyone entertained, and by restricting the noisy watercraft to this area the Emiratis manage to retain some semblance of good-neighborliness: jet-skis aren't beloved by boaters. I'm only a casual rider so I savor my afternoon communing with the waves. A bunch of us ride up to the inlet leading to the Gulf, where big waves bounce us nearly skyward; in the distance, supertankers glide south bearing the region's *raison d'être*.

Some months later I have dinner with Renaissance Man. He's since visited Dubai on a work-related trip and returned home with experiences utterly unlike mine.

"I almost didn't recognize them," he says of some expats he went to visit. "They have servants. They order them around, yell at them. It's like they've regressed a hundred years. When I called them on it they said, 'You don't know what these people are *like*.'"

Ever the (straight) dapper playboy, he also managed an interlude with an Emirates Airways flight attendant.

"I went to her flat in Emirates Towers. They used to be the tallest buildings in Dubai." I remember them—twin triangle-topped high-rises on Sheikh Zayed Road.

"They pair up employees to share flats," he recounts. "I walk in, and one of them's getting ready to leave, putting on makeup like she's going to an audition. Then another friend of hers comes in. She's just come back and looks a wreck. Her face is all swollen."

Emirates sets harsh standards for its staff: they need to look perfect at all times. They're even encouraged to flirt, and rumor has it some sex-for-money goes on behind the scenes.

"They can't be married or pregnant. And definitely not gay."

I hear a similar story from a compatriot of Renaissance Man's, a photographer assigned to capture a high-end traditional Muslim wedding out in the desert. Tents are dappled in gold. Men and women are strictly separated—though as foreigner and photographer, this fellow was permitted entry into the women's sanctuary. Covered head-to-toe in Muslim garb, the ladies inject themselves with controlled substances (though I never find out which). The men, meanwhile, off on their own, drink themselves into numbing stupor.

I didn't witness any of this. That's the thing about pleasure domes: ever so deft at concealing what simmers beneath.

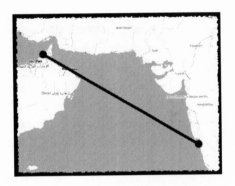

The Beach
Goa

A thicket of palms angles outward over creamy sand, craning their necks for a better view of the sea. It's a total change of pace in Palolem Beach, on the seafront in the southern reaches of India's smallest state.

Say the word "Goa" to Indian nationals and you'll likely encounter a mild smirk: it's not "really" India, it's resortified, overbuilt...you can eat *beef* there, for heaven's sake.

All this only heightened my curiosity: as an inveterate non-globe-trotter—before this journey at least—I find exploring the better-trodden places not merely useful for their touristic convenience, but also to better understand why people think they suck. The best travelers are infinitely adaptable...well, *almost* infinitely; I confess to a princess-like yearning for quiet and comfort. But there's something to be gleaned from nearly every person, place, and circumstance—and on this journey I leave myself open to it all.

Another über-glam Business Class flight—this time care of Cathay Pacific from Dubai to Mumbai, one of the few times I've wished a plane ride was longer. Then an even shorter but surprisingly pleasant hop on one of India's newer carriers; the country's growing range of domestic indie airlines compares favorably in both price and service with the better discounters in America and Europe.

Two gentlemen in a white four-door hatchback meet me at Goa's humble airstrip. From the airport near Panaji to Palolem in the south is a languid, ninety-minute drive down a two-lane road. We rumble in and out of villages, strips of rundown two-story buildings with crumbling, brightly painted concrete terraces. Every now and then, a new glass-and-steel structure emerges. I see peasant farmers tilling terraced, oily-soaked rice paddies with the aid of donkeys and oxen. The soil is a coppery red, the rolling hills dense with jungle foliage. And in ever-increasing numbers, cows wander the side of the road as would errant dogs back home. For "India Lite" it feels awfully authentic.

We pull off the main road, past a sign that reads "Palolem" with a heart next to it. Many of Goa's beaches in the north have become package-tourist heaven, attracting flocks of middle-aged Brits and Russians; at the airport I saw a couple of large planes from these two nations. Yet Palolem in the south remains a place apart, attracting the offbeat backpacker looking to drop out and relax. Christmas is peak season, which doesn't deter me: I'm eager to see what holiday-time is like with backpackers of the world on a beach in southern India.

I booked a hut right on the sand, part of a small cluster painted in colorful pastels. It looks heavenly from the outside, but inside it's a different matter: a large bed covered in mosquito netting inside a very rudimentary wooden shack. The bathroom is exposed plumbing, bare bulb, plastic floor with a drain above which hangs a skinny shower-head. Oh, and no hot water, though there is a communal hot shower nearby. The toilet is of the standard Western variety rather than the squat-style preferred by the locals. Still, it's the most rustic accommodations I've had since enduring summer camp at age twelve.

Nevertheless, I make it a point to stay, if only to test my tolerance for such conditions; looking on a calendar and on a map I discover my journey is about halfway done. Appropriate, then, to spend it under different circumstances than I've enjoyed so far: no museums, no big cities, no air conditioning, nothing significant to do for an entire week. A vacation from a vacation.

The friendly neighbors, mostly Brits, make it easy: I meet Michael, a hunky young twentysomething in a fishing hat, almost right away. Raj, a slight, dark-skinned fellow with shaved head, shows up a little later in the bungalow next to mine. A native of this country, he's lived his whole life in England; his accent bears little trace of his ancestry. Next door to him is Patrick, a tall, richly tanned, soft-spoken sort. But beneath the gentle demeanor slumbers an adventurer's spirit.

"I'm only here a few days," he adds. Most of the rest of the gang are here through the New Year.

"After Christmas I'm going on a tuk-tuk race across the country."

We all head to a seafood place along the beach, perched on the upper terrace of a rather rickety-looking building. The main floor houses a curiously deserted bar. Everything's freshly caught: the waiter brings us a platter with a thick pack of fish on it for us to pick and choose.

"Forty rupees," says the waiter, pointing to one specimen.

"Thirty-five," Michael answers. Apparently haggling is done here even in restaurants. Or maybe not: the waiter offers strained, polite refusals. I agree to pay the posted price for my selection—I hate haggling, and it's still under ten dollars, half what it would be at a comparable place back home.

At dinner I meet Heather. Sweet and fetching, she's sharing a bungalow with Michael. Her utterly different complexion from his— luscious brown hair and skin that tans cocoa—leads me to assume she's his girlfriend.

"No, we're cousins," they laugh. They looked at me kind-of oddly when I implied they hooked up. Personality-wise too their differences are more than skin deep: she's going to work on a cruise ship after this journey is done; he's a former Royal Navy diver who's starting a stint with the London Police. He finds out about me and is utterly, pleasantly unruffled by the gay thing. This might be generational again—he's twenty-two—but the Yankee in me can't help but think *why can't our military be this cool?* Later he busts his toe on some loose metal by some stairs.

"I'm fine!" he says, dipping the toe in the salty ocean as we fuss and fret. More amusing than alpha-dog.

Then the crowd starts talking football—"And don't call it *soccer*," they admonish. *Yeah, I know.* I saw *Green Street Hooligans*, which left a question smoldering in my brain.

"What's up with the violence?" I ask. Americans may be oh-so competitive, but you don't exactly see them beating the crap out of each other when Green Bay trounces Pittsburgh.

"You have to remember where hooligans come from," Patrick offers. "In America, people move around a fair bit, yeah?" *Uhm, sure…*just look who he's talking to. "People in the firms,"—the term for the football gangs—"They've lived in the same part of England, the same city, the same area, sometimes the same street for generations.

"Their team means everything to them."

Food for thought, as is some hash Patrick slips me later that evening; lying in bed under the net, crispy smoke from a mosquito coil swirling nearby, I embark on a mental seventh-inning stretch.

What's this trip doing for me? Museums and beaches aside, how about my inner state? I've distracted myself, pushed the past away in a pageant of cathedrals, boys, family footsteps. But I wonder if this restless, energetic style of travel in fact inhibits self-discovery. I look at the other long-rangers—folks like myself out in the world for six months or more. They're doing it slow and cheap: a smattering of countries, or even just one, stays of many weeks, surface transport even in rougher lands, dormitory hostels and other shared accommodations. I look around my plywood room: *this is typical.*

Backpacker purists insist that the jarring experience of roughing it builds adventures and memories, even nourishes the soul. *Ugh.* I've recoiled from that, tried to find the balance between costly top-tier tourism and bare-bones vagabonding. And yet, I wonder sometimes if I'm simply on an extended business trip, bouncing along the surface of the world both physically and psychologically. A stone skipping on a glassy lake like the ones counselors effortlessly tossed on warm evenings at summer camp.

Again summer camp. This shack is too much like those woodsy bunks from back then.

Or maybe that's just the hash talking.

But I'm not feeling rushed. Either in body or in spirit. Oh sure, there are always places where a traveler thinks *shoulda stayed longer*…but so far I've regretted nothing, have garnered something out of every place I've been. This second-guessing, rather, feels like a habit from back home: the urge of a "maximizer" to tailor, to perfect, to "make the most," whatever that means. I do that a lot, as do many midcareer professionals in North America. Perhaps *this* is the challenge of traveling at this stage of life: one's focus, drive, and skill are in high gear. The wheels are turning. In youth, there is often a feeling of putting off responsibility; later in life, one begins to apply the brakes. But not now. Even for those who are not baldly ambitious there remains, in our society, a sense of relentless thrust toward betterment. Is there not the danger, though, when off the grid, as I am for an extended period, to impulsively follow grid impulses and grid behavior?

Maybe. But then, I've never been one to swim with the stream. On the one hand, this can be great: not too many round-the-world trips mix up a Business Class seat with a Cairene slum, afternoon tea at Fortnum & Mason with MDMA at a Soho discotheque. I suppose every traveler hopes their panoply of experiences will help them answer their own Big Life Questions—in my case, to understand the pattern of unremitting transience in my workaday life.

Is this the right venue to find answers? On the road, connections are necessarily transitory: you meet, form a bond, engage in life-changing discussions, maybe enjoy a sexual romp, move on. But, as I've begun to discover, these bonds can make up in intensity what they lack in duration. Maybe *that's* what I need to focus on during the back nine of the journey: cultivate the richness of travel's encounters, glean as much out of these connections as I can. Only that can make this voyage feel more like enlightenment and less like a skipping stone.

Okay. Enough navel-gazing. The next night I haul myself out. Palolem is nowhere near the party hotspot of Anjuna and Vagator up north, though this winter they're all pretty subdued: it's barely a month since the Mumbai terrorist attacks on a couple of luxury hotels, attacks that deliberately targeted foreign tourists. The Indian authorities have amped up security—tourism accounts for a significant proportion of any number of local economies. Still, it feels like they're making rookie mistakes: they've outlawed all music playing after midnight—ten o'clock between Christmas and New Years. The big parties up north, which I'd hoped to attend, have all been canceled. So much for "keep doing what you're doing or the terrorists have won."

Nevertheless, Café del Mar, the nearby beach bar, is buzzing; earlier I discovered there's one other gay guy on the beach—India in general and Goa in particular is not really a destination for the pink dollar. Alphonse is friendly enough, a dark-haired Frenchman in his early thirties with a gaggle of female friends...but we're not into in each other. I spend the evening hanging with Team Scotland, as my British cohorts have dubbed them, a gang of rowdy fellows staying in our bungalow cluster.

"Now ah see it," one of them says in a burr, commenting on my jeans and fitted black sleeveless top. "Tonight yah'r lookin' *gay*!" *Yeah, that was in case Frenchie was hot.* I'm about to join in the inebriation but for that familiar aroma wafting on the breeze. Two stoners lounge on the terrace made of sandbags: Nikki, an arty South African girl, and Andy, a shaved-headed Englishman, a dead-ringer for Moby.

"No *hashish*," says one of the waitstaff as he cruises by.

"It's just a cigarette," Andy replies.

"You think I'm stupid. I go to school. I smell it. No *hashish*."

So that's what they teach in school out here. The global pervasiveness of the drug war never ceases to amaze me. International treaties ban pretty much the same stuff everywhere, the Netherlands' social experiment be damned. How is it the nations of the world are so good at forging consensus on recreational substances but can't seem to reach it on nuclear weaponry or climate change?

So it's back to the legal stuff. "Here, try this." Michael and Heather hand me a bottle of Kingfisher, the local brew. Normally I'm a beerophobe but this stuff is light and smooth. *I can drink beer again!* My first brewskie in close to a decade. The logo's familiar, an orange-and-white bird with upraised blue-tipped wings, the same as on the tail of my airplane. A beer company with an airline. Am I the only one who finds this strange?

If there's one thing that grates on a traveler most, it's unsavory reminders of home. I try to give Americans the benefit of the doubt, but cliché persists. Over a nice lunch of chicken vindaloo I meet Larry, a TV producer from L.A. who works on one of the dumber American reality shows.

"This place is *pitiful*," he says with a scowl, squinting around. Then he learns about my accommodations.

"You're staying in a beach hut? They're the *worst*."

On and on he rambles, complain, complain. *Please, somebody make him shut up.* Salvation arrives in the form of two Danish lads who want to take a scooter ride. Together we head to the shopping street perpendicular to the beach and hire a couple of motorized steeds. Oliver and Matthias hop on one and I get on another—not that I would have minded either of them riding with me: one's a nerdy/cute blonde, and the other's got rich olive skin and black hair, incongruous for a Dane.

We literally head for the hills, pulling our bikes off the road at a trailhead. We hike for a spell.

"Look," Matthias points to some broad brownish leaves covering the earth. A tree frog sits on one, barely perceptible amid the surrounding foliage. We're interrupted by shrieks. High above, monkeys swing by through the canopy of trees. The acrobatics are spellbinding as they leap from vine to vine with perfect synchronicity. Snagging a photo is impossible: these creatures are too damn fast.

We ride north to Agonda. Just before the beach loom the frothy white spires of a church. A sign in English reads, "Saint Anne's Church." I don't think twice about it until I realize *wait, I'm in India.* But Goa's different: a Portuguese colony until the 1960s, many locals remained Catholic, a tiny enclave in a vast Hindu-Muslim sea.

Agonda is another Palolem, a pretty strip of sand fringed by palms and equally rudimentary—and kaleidoscopic—beach huts. No air-con or hot showers here either. The boys laugh when I grumble.

"The huts are temporary," Oliver says. "Because of the monsoons. They take them down in winter."

He's got one bit of good news when he hears I'm planning to visit Thailand.

"There they have everything. All the hot showers you want. And they're cheaper than here in this crazy high season."

"Why do you want a hot shower anyway?" Matthias asks. He has a point: it's thirty-plus degrees Celsius with sauna-like humidity. A *cool* shower would be great but mine are ice-cold. Where *does* water that cold come from anyway, here in the Indian tropics?

I don't *have* to stay where I am: a short walk through the forest later that day brings me to Patnem Beach, where more permanent structures—wood-capped cinderblock shells, the telltale hum of air-con, the tick-ticking of tall metal cylinders bearing hot water—sit at the edge of the sand. But at this point inertia, engaging company, and strong hash conspire to keep me in place.

America returns, this time sitting at dinner with some of my fellow stoners from the previous night. The improbably named Dhruva, a dark-haired boyish type from Florida, celebrates his twenty-seventh birthday with some cake.

"The other gay guy was hitting on me," he says. "He kept on buying me drinks." He is kind of cute but I get the picture: no straight-boy fantasy hookup from him.

"How'd you get a name like that?" I ask. Not exactly central-Florida standard.

"My parents were Hare Krishna," he says. He fathered a kid in his early twenties; later he did some time in the pen. The guys sitting next to him—three astoundingly cute Swedish boys (Scandinavians: they're *everywhere*)—invite us to finish off the last of their weed. Their hut's up in the hills, by the edge of the beach.

"Where are they taking us?" Dhruva asks. Their secluded compound has that dark and mysterious *Deliverance* feel to it.

"Maybe we'll get gang-raped," I suggest. Dhruva smirks.

"You'd like that."

"Not gonna happen!" cries out one Swede. *Had to try.*

"It's not a cult," Dhruva says about his parents' faith. But talking about it gets him going on a pot-fueled reverie about God and spirituality…it's innocuous and well-intentioned, but I can see the secular Scandinavians' eyes glaze over—and not just because of the weed. In my frame of mind, all I can think is *not another one.*

Sitting at an Internet café the next day, I have my weekly chat with Ryan.

"My new hobby is bagging on America with the Europeans," I say.

"Oh, that's nice," he replies. I can hear the sarcasm crackling across the seas and continents. "You really shouldn't be doing that considering you just got your *citizenship.*"

He doesn't get it. In fairness, none of these folks fit the loud, "Ugly American" stereotype. But they remind me of those elements of my adopted homeland that I dislike. Perhaps this is a byproduct of leaving the country, the continent, behind: the flaws stick out so much more. But Ryan is still back home, probably wondering if my disillusionment suggests stronger stuff about our future together.

Christmas Eve. The sandy courtyard between the semicircle of huts is decorated with a nativity scene, care of the folks who work at our establishment—they too are Catholic. It's also the best weather day of all: hot like the rest, but clearer skies and brisker winds. The normally placid sea offers the best bodysurfing so far; I trudge out to the edge of the shallow sandbar and catch some waves. The water is deliciously warm. At low tide I amble to the northernmost end of our mile-long beach, off of which lies a small island. The tide's made it more of a peninsula: it's ankle-deep water for several hundred feet.

Some beautification is in order in advance of the night's festivities: Michael, my British hut neighbor, recommends a spot toward the main road where a shave can be had for around two dollars. Complete with facial massage, it's enormously invigorating: I'm all aglow. An ayurvedic massage is next—more expensive and not quite as refreshing as the shave. I've never quite gotten the point of massage: I've had a range of different kinds and none seem do much for me. This one too leaves me suspiciously unchanged.

The nighttime festivities are subdued thanks to those music-playing ordinances. Security is further stepped up: at the entrance to the beach by the little shopping lane, some Indian military have set up a makeshift sandbag fort; they leave it unmanned for much of the evening, however, patrolling up and down the sand with automatic rifles. We still don't think they know what they're doing.

At dinner, Whitney and Sam, attractive blondes from Calgary, help me cruise cute guys on the beach. This proves frustrating for all of us, as they've got boyfriends back home and the boys here are all straight. Then TV producer guy from L.A. tries to hit on Sam. She's not biting.

"We should go get dessert!" she says enthusiastically. Translation: *lose this loser.* I've partaken of some hash again so it sounds good to me. We leave TV guy behind and head to an ice-cream shop on the main road…a Baskin Robbins, of all things. *Oh, yes, a milkshake!* Almost as refreshing as the frigid blasts of air-con in the tiny shop. Outside stand some cows, part of the small flock that usually can be found lazing on the sand most afternoons. I offer them thanks for my dairy confection. *Okay, I must be stoned.* The girls giggle.

"They're much friendlier than the ones in Varanasi," Whitney says, petting the beasts. "One practically charged us there."

Beachside living must agree with them too.

It's a bittersweet goodbye at sunup, again an echo of summers at country camp. Of all the places in my journey, here connections ran the deepest. Maybe lack of comfort does breed congeniality. Then again…glancing at the time, I start the countdown in my head until my next hot shower. It's ever a balancing act to find comfy digs, cool people, opportunities for personal insight—and not too many Yankee Doodle Douchebags. Is that even realistic? At the midpoint in my travels I'm still not sure, and Palolem offers no clear answers.

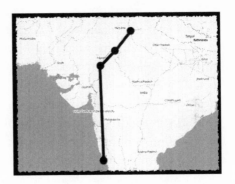

Children of Kings
Jaipur, Udaipur & Delhi

A t three million and change, Jaipur, Rajasthan's state capital, is a minnow among Indian cities. But right away it's clear: this is *not* India Lite.

A slim, tall Indian fellow, handsome and barely student-age, picks me up at the airport in an immaculately restored silver Ambassador taxi. That's about the only thing that's immaculate: Jaipur is a tangle of crowded streets, dirt paths for sidewalks, cluttered open gutters. The bus station near my hotel sits on a tarmac of greasy asphalt where decrepit vehicles belch fumes and disgorge huddled masses. Other hordes squat on the pavement. It feels like a refugee camp; later I learn it was, housing those fleeing the neighboring Sindh province of Pakistan half a century ago.

Then we round the corner behind some half-completed buildings and everything changes: the street is lined with elegant homes and apartments, former *haveli* converted into intimate hotels. Behind greenery and wrought iron gates, I spot my accommodations—a couple of white-stucco buildings surrounding a tiled courtyard. For around $20 a night, my "super-deluxe room" features curlicued dark-wood furnishings, an air-conditioner, and—heaven!—a hot shower.

I'm set to meet my colleague Bill and his partner, Dario, at their hotel for an early day of sights and adventures. As with Marjo in

Dubai, I learned serendipitously that their Christmastime visit to India overlaps mine. They're doing it up American-style: two weeks, a hired car-and-driver, stays at upscale hotels. *Should make them easy to find*, I muse as I set out in the predawn dark. I follow my innkeepers' advice to nab one of the ubiquitous yellow-and-black three-wheel auto-rickshaws from a stand just outside the bus station. As I round the bend, a number of these look eager for my custom. I approach one.

"Can you take me to the Golden Tulip Hotel?"

He stares at me blankly and repeats the last word, "hotel."

"Do you know where that is?"

Another blank look, then a conference with some fellow drivers. Then it dawns on me: *they don't speak English.* I've been good about this, loading up my iPod with phrasebooks in six different languages. But I didn't bother with India, a country where I'd been repeatedly advised, "English widely spoken, especially in tourist-facing industries."

Not so at six a.m. at a Jaipur taxi stand.

My driver at least knows numbers and advises me the fare is fifty rupees. He motions me to climb in the back, then he grabs another fellow to ride shotgun. *Uh-oh.* I'd been advised not to ride these things if there's more than one person up front. But it seems legit: the other guy interacts with people on the street as we stop every few blocks for directions. Then he hops off midway through our journey; the driver continues to stop frequently, as if we were a bus. I think he's more lost than I am.

Finally, we turn off the road onto a lavish ultramodern compound. We pull up the drive, more than a little out-of-place amid the expansive elegance. I hand the driver his fare, only to learn—this much English he does speak—that the fare has nearly doubled. It's a pittance, maybe a dollar extra, but no. I'm not doing it.

"That's what you said, that's what I'm giving you." Why should I pay for the fact he didn't know where it was? The sliding glass doors slide open as I approach. The driver follows me in, growling in the local tongue. I explain it to the front desk, and they dismiss the guy.

"I'm so sorry," I say. I'm flustered and it's not even seven in the morning. The front-desk fellow smiles and replies in crisp Indian-accented English.

"Don't vorry. It's all ovuh now."

Just then Bill and Dario emerge from the elevator; after the usual embraces, I learn the plan has changed: behind Bill's black-rimmed rectangular glasses he's ghostly pallid.

"I was up all night. Food poisoning."

A first in his three trips to India. He's ambulatory, but definitely no sightseeing for him. Dario, a talkative, pale-skinned Cuban, is doing only slightly better.

"My back. We drove for nine hours yesterday from Agra."

So much for riding elephants. On to Plan B.

A bit of Aleve from my medical kit—"You're ready for everything!" Dario remarks—and we're good for a bit of sightseeing. I meet their driver, a Mr. Singh from Delhi, turbaned and a bit taciturn. He suggests a morning amble around town.

"We always do this, a car and driver," Dario explains while Mr. Singh's Nissan negotiates traffic—car, bus, oxen, bovine, and human. "The roads are so bad and there's no signs anywhere."

It feels a bit Little Lord Fauntleroy at first but it's a pleasant change of pace. We buzz past Jaipur's City Hall, a Capitol Building in miniature set on its own imposing hillock; the Palace of the Winds at the edge of the old city, a slender salmon-hued building, parabola-shaped, and scored with intricately carved windows. Its sole purpose: for wives of the Maharaja to watch the world go by. We reach the entrance to the Pink City, the old rectilinear town center laid out by Jai Singh—for whom the city is named—in the early 1700s. The entrance gate's triad of pointed arches are enveloped in lacy, intricate white-painted patterns set upon the pink stone. Just inside, snake charmers wail at cobras so stiffly upright it's almost tempting to shake them to test if they're real (we didn't). And ever-more traffic—clusters of motor scooters dart and weave between bigger vehicles and carts pulled by lumbering beasts; some whiz by scant inches from pedestrians or from the edges of crumbling pink buildings. I conclude that Indian drivers are masterfully coordinated.

Almost everywhere we stop, either in traffic or to get out of the vehicle, we're confronted by beggars—children and old ladies mostly—placing hand to mouth. When we're in the car, they make a beeline for us in the back seat—they know where the money is. Sometimes they rap on the windows if they feel ignored. All those stats about India making strides to reduce rampant poverty feel utterly false; this place feels more like those documentary films of India from several decades ago.

Still, Jaipur captivates: Jai Singh was as much scientist as ruler, Rajasthan's Thomas Jefferson. We visit the Jantar Mantar, an oversized collection of astronomical instruments reminiscent of the diagonals in a De Chirico painting. Massive bronze tablets are set into circular carved stone. The world's largest sundial, almost a hundred feet high, casts a shadow you can see moving—it's that big—on this brilliant morning. I'm reminded of the Medicis half a world away.

Jaipur's City Palace is not quite so striking, though bits of it dazzle: a blindingly colorful doorway in blue, orange, and white, the decorations blending to become the feathers and bodies of peacocks. Nearby sit two Brobdingnagian-scale silver urns, reportedly the largest in existence.

To know the soul of India, one must travel on its railways; to that end, Dario and Mr. Singh drop me off at Jaipur's railway station, a salmon-painted building with an annex bearing a shabby ticket office. Indian trains are always overcrowded, so space is made available to foreign tourists; my plan is to take the night train to Udaipur, then head back north to Delhi to make my flight in a few days. Alas, even with consideration for visitors the trains are oversold: it's the week between Christmas and New Year's, and though neither of these is much of a holiday in India, it's still a busy travel season. Plan B again: do it by plane. Sounds simple, but it takes most of the afternoon as I fight with my hotel's sluggish Internet connection. So much for those Indian tech-support clichés.

There's supposed to be good eating nearby. I try my hand at the auto-rickshaw stand again, offering the drivers a couple of restaurant selections that came recommended. A bunch of them huddle over my list of names and accompanying map but look as perplexed as the fellow from this morning. *I'm not going through* that *again.* I thank them and try walking to the closest eatery, less than a mile away. I pass a few quieter side streets of lit-up apartments and the odd midrange hotel, but for the most part I'm hoofing it down busy main roads, more dirt sidewalks, roaming cows, a cacophony of horn-honking. It's dispiriting enough that I give up partway and head to the larger hotel adjacent mine that features a quiet rooftop eatery. The food's expectedly good and the price is right…though I get the sense, gazing over the manicured lit-up garden and arrays of Christmas lights adorning the balustrades, that I've again stepped through the looking-glass into that other India of comfort and privilege.

Rajasthan means forts: the word *Rajput*, the clan from which Jai Singh was descended, literally translates as "children of kings." Untangling this region's web of petty principalities and fiefdoms bedeviled the framers of Indian independence. The forts are their earliest legacy, basically hilltop towns and palace compounds that predate the cities that now surround them.

The drive to the forts just outside Jaipur passes through the squalid, filthy northern part of town. Pigs, cows, and chickens forage along trash-strewn streets. Women in iridescently tinted saris dodge traffic. A child in a blue shirt and grimy sandals stares at me as we drive away from a spiderweb of bicycle rickshaws.

The city fades away. Mountains surround us, parched and brown—utterly unlike the red-soiled verdant slopes of Goa. Rajasthan lies at the edge of the Thar Desert, the eastern fringe of the world's greatest arid expanse that stretches almost unbroken from Gibraltar in the west to northern India in the east. Ancient fortification walls climb nearby hillsides, a Great Wall of India in miniature. Bastions and archways lie to our left behind a zigzag of walls and walkways. The fort of Amber.

I miss the cutoff time to ride an elephant uphill to the fort but manage to follow on foot the last of them plodding upward. Their ears, faces, and trunks are adorned with colorfully faded patterns in chalk. Hawkers run alongside, harassing tourists riding the beasts. One vendor is especially persistent, even as the flustered fellow on the pachyderm keeps saying "no." The seller is undaunted, lowering his price more and more, until finally the exasperated tourist cries out.

"Even free! NO!"

The seller moves on: three more elephants to go.

At the expansive entry courtyard I dodge the offers of guides— each claiming more expertise than the last—and opt for the recommended audioguide. It's terrific, shedding color and texture on the rambling hilltop palace. The maharajas were polygamists; as with their latter-day counterparts in Utah (at least if the HBO series *Big Love* is to be believed), the first wife ruled the roost. The others spent their days jockeying for position to ensure their sons would inherit enough of their father's wealth. The wives' quarters were designed so that the maharaja could access any one of them without the others knowing.

The melodrama this place must have seen is unimaginable.

I snag another opportunity for an elephant ride after lunch: the beasts end up on the main road leading to the fort, and one of the elephant wranglers, in conference with my driver, negotiates a price. We bounce along the roadway for a spell, and all is well with the world until the elephant jockey grunts at me.

"You give me big tip."

It doesn't sound like a request.

"At least five hundred rupees."

This on top of the already-inflated "after hours" price. I give him half what he asks, suggesting he'd do better with a more subtle approach. Somehow I think that's unlikely.

I'm the only one eating this early in preparation for my crack-of-dawn flight. One of my innkeepers, a Mrs. Dimple, offers company. Her family's lived in Jaipur for generations. A slender, finely attired, bespectacled woman whose English is that gentle lilt common to this country's elite. Talk of travel and far-off locales leads her to show me a collection of National Geographic magazines begun by her grandparents—every issue going back to the 1960s.

"I remember that one!" I exclaim, pulling out a prophetic special from 1980 on the future of energy. Flipping through its pages feels like little has changed; one article on nuclear fission is titled: "Too Hot to Handle?"

"Don't stay in Paharganj," she tells me. It's the backpacker district of Delhi, and my reading about it in guidebooks is giving me flashbacks of Islamic Cairo or the streets of north Jaipur.

"There's a new guesthouse near Connaught Place," she says, writing down the number. Might come in handy as Delhi's like Cairo in another respect: accommodations come very cheap or very pricey. Maternally, Mrs. Dimple bids me goodnight, promising to rouse me early the next morning.

I almost miss my ride to the airport. I keep an eye out for my young driver and his silver Ambassador but they're nowhere in sight. After some increasingly frantic phone calls to my driver James' mobile—which he doesn't answer—the snoozing fellow in a car across the street calls out.

"Airport? James sent me to take you. Too early for him."

Yeah, for me too. I can't help but smile at this bit of extreme local outsourcing.

Udaipur is little. It's said to be India's most romantic city, though as we approach the guesthouse where I'm staying I'm hard-pressed to see how: again trash-strewn gutters lining narrow, crowded streets. The smell of cow urine wafts on the breeze. Given that it's holiday and wedding-time in Udaipur, most of the better midrange accommodations are taken; mine's not bad, though its proximity to Jagdish Temple, the city's large Hindu shrine, means that every evening and morning I am greeted with melodious chants.

I suppose there are worse fates.

The temple's a good place to begin explorations: I remove my shoes at the entrance, as is the custom, tipping the wiry old partly disabled man who places footwear along worn wooden shelves. A fair-haired family, wholesome with plump paterfamilias, does the same. The shoe attendant asks where they're from.

"America," they answer.

"*America!*" the man gleefully exclaims. "*Barack Obama!*"

There it is: restoration of my homeland's overseas rep right before my eyes.

The temple's main structure is a tall pyramidal shape bearing an explosion of intricate carvings. I circle it slowly, taking in the astounding detail. Inside is a statue of Vishnu, the four-armed Hindu deity. Compared with the dour solemnity of human figures in even the most expressive of European cathedrals, the renditions here feel positively giddy.

It may be an arid town, but Udaipur is lake country. Manmade, of course, a long time ago: a number of small inland waterways fed by mountainous streams were enlarged to form Lake Pichola. As I amble through the narrow laneways toward the water, the crowding and shabbiness ease. Here some of the city's nicer hotels are located, yards away from the *ghat*, the wide path of stairs leading into the lake. It looks like those iconic images of the Ganges at Varanasi, but for me, movie buff, a more pop-cultural image springs to mind: this is where they filmed *Octopussy*, the Bond flick from the 1980s. A number of rooftop restaurants make the most of their fifteen minutes of fame, advertising "Octopussy Show" screenings that begin at dusk.

Instead of 007 I opt for a bit of shopping. I wander into one establishment to browse for a small silk painting of Ganesh, the fat elephant-headed deity known as the "remover of obstacles." *I could've used you last summer, Ganesh.* Though truth be told most of my obstacles were directed inward. Still, perhaps the designation for this Hindu potentate is apt: I find he distantly resembles a mob boss.

The shop is empty, and its portly shopkeeper reacts to my entry as if Ganesh himself had walked through the door. Tea is ordered stat, and a number of specimens are taken out of old-style wood-and-glass display cases.

"Okay, this one," I say, and try my hand at haggling, naming a price.

"Oh, sir, you kill me without a knife!" shopkeeper retorts. *I can't do this.* We end up agreeing on a price much closer to what he asked—but really, we're talking about a difference of maybe five dollars.

"No children?" It's not the first time I've been asked this in India.

"Nieces and nephews," I reply, and that seems to satisfy him: for a smidge more he tosses in a few silk-painted birthday cards.

Udaipur's City Palace is five minutes on foot and way more impressive than Jaipur's. Maybe it's a testament to tenacity: the ruling Mewars resisted every ruling imperium to come through here, from the Mughals in the sixteenth century to the British in the nineteenth. Their palace is an imposing jumble of stone buildings, columned breezeways, and—specialty of the region—intricate cut-glass artwork adorning walls and ceilings. As with Amber, it's crowded—at least the parts of it that are priced for locals. The southern half of the palace, part of which is a hotel, features steeper admission (300 rupees versus 25—six dollars instead of fifty cents). Crossing into the higher-priced section, the crowds evaporate; this part of the palace complex sports perfectly manicured grassy lawns fronting cleaner stretches of water. A stone staircase leads down to a boat launch to islands out on the lake.

One island is simply one large building, the ice-cream white Lake Palace; it's a luxury hotel and admittance is for guests only, cash replacing royalty as the exclusionary hegemon. It's a surreal sight, akin to decks of some grand old ocean liner forever marooned offshore. Next to it is Jagmandir, another island palace accessible to visitors. With a number of well-heeled locals and foreigners I board a small ferryboat, a putt-putting canopied affair with a flat bottom designed for the shallow water. Passing the steps of the *ghat*, I see women young and old washing clothes, their feet, even their long hair. In the distance, the Monsoon Palace perches atop a hillside; it too saw big-screen exposure in the Bond film; I remember boyhood days when the words "Monsoon Palace" uttered by Roger Moore evoked a locale impossibly distant. We round the Lake Palace, finally pulling up to the Jagmandir dock. A smiling hostess greets us; I half-expect Mr. Roarke to pop out and say, "Welcome to Fantasy Island." The India of grime and crowds is a memory.

Jagmandir's not that big a place, with much of it given over to a day spa and wedding reception area that looks to be gearing up for a nighttime event. I stroll the grounds, check out the diminutive palace buildings, and enjoy a late-afternoon tandoori snack as the bleary sun sinks behind some palms.

Boats come and go from the island every few minutes; I just miss the regular ferry and am set to wait for another one, until the driver of a smaller tender offers to take me and a German couple back to the mainland in an unusually sleek, handsome craft.

"It's the maharaja's private boat," he tells us as we roar away from the island. "He allows it to be used to transport the public when he's away."

The maharajas kept other motorized vehicles too: throughout the twentieth century, one generation after the next had a thing for cars, and some of these are on display at an old garage a mile or so from the town center. I find myself the only visitor there the next morning. The old caretaker, in terse Indian-accented narration, raises and lowers the garage doors of the semicircular compound while describing specs of the different vehicles.

"Model A Ford, 1930," he says of the beast glinting in red and black. The other cars are beguiling enough but this one's a beauty. Those goofy aphorisms car nuts emote about vehicles calling to them actually resonate for me in front of this squared-off soft-top—yup, it's even a red convertible to boot.

Although the present-day maharajas no longer have any political power, they still possess significant holdings and retain some influence in the region; today's figurehead continues his forebears' vehicular fixation, though his passion is solar vehicles. A few of these low-slung contraptions are on display, their silvered solar cells lining the sleek vehicle bodies.

Across the way is a newly built three-story office building with a Barista Coffee shop at its base. Inside, a smattering of Indian yuppies chat in groups or check e-mail on Blackberries. It looks so incongruous I imagine it was dropped from Milan via an Oz-like tornado. Meanwhile, outside, reminders of the old India press against the glass before the shopkeeper shoos them away: a mother and child beg for change, their hair unkempt, their clothing stained and ragged. The little girl clutches a dirty, naked baby in her arms.

My flight to Delhi is delayed. The cause is familiar, though the season feels all wrong: fog in December? It's Delhi's wacky weather patterns: near-freezing winter nights produce haze for weeks on end. This adds to my trepidation as the city is not known to be the easiest to negotiate. Again and again I read stories of taxi scams targeting unsuspecting foreign tourists, including drivers who only take you to hotels where they earn commissions—whether that's your stated destination or not.

At last we roll to the gate. *Okay, it's not a shithole,* I notice, stepping off the jetway: India's decrepit infrastructure's been targeted for upgrades and the airport looks no worse than many back home. My luggage arrives swiftly. Taxi scams look like a thing of the past care of a pre-paid taxi stand: I'm handed a white slip of paper that the driver is supposed to receive—and hence get paid—only upon arrival at the chosen destination. But then, just as it's all going right…I'm waved over to a beat-up black-and-yellow hatchback housing an irate driver who speaks no English. No worry: I've come prepared with map and directions to my guesthouse. I show these to the driver to no avail: he brusquely waves them away.

Then my bargaining chip is taken: in order to exit the airport, drivers are required to present the pre-paid taxi slip. I ask for it back and the driver blows me off.

"Do you know where the hotel is?" I ask. Fortunately it's in the very heart of the city. It appears he has no clue, and I look out the windows nervously, wondering where in this metropolis of sixteen million people he's taking me.

I see signs that read, "Connaught Place" so at least I know we're on track. He circles around a bit, then stops and yammers and gestures to the door: get out. It's eight o'clock in the evening, in an unfamiliar neighborhood in New Delhi. Typical for India, signage is sparse. I try hailing an auto-rickshaw, going through several until finally I find one where the driver speaks English. The fellow studies my map.

"Atithi Guesthouse. Do you know where it is?" *For fuck's sake, he's got a map in front of him.* He too drives around and around—Connaught

Place is a circle and this is starting to feel like Chevy Chase in *National Lampoon's European Vacation*. Finally the roulette wheel stops at some shabby-looking hotel—not the right one. Then I do what I should have done all along: call my guesthouse.

"Yes," answers the owner, Vinay Kumar. "I'll come by in five minutes to collect you. You're less than half a mile away." He shows up moments later in a late-model black sedan—I know which side of the looking-glass he inhabits. A grandfatherly fellow, he apologizes profusely—it was his suggestion that I take a taxi.

"This is not supposed to happen in Delhi anymore!" he asserts.

Vinay's a retired business-owner who's decided to give innkeeping a whirl. He's done up the expansive bedrooms with stone flooring and mid-century furnishings. The place is newly opened and feels it: adjoining my tidy, expansive stone-floored room is a bathroom with the occasionally misaligned fixture. Vinay is overeager, an Indian-style Jewish mother with motley crew of servants. Upon learning of the malfunctioning toilets he's on the phone to the repairman pronto.

"Have some dinner," he says, ordering around his crew in Hindi to whip up a repast. "Next time, you come back with your girlfriend." He's crestfallen that I'm single and unmarried.

"Nah," I offer. "It's the greatest gig around, being the out-of-town uncle."

"I disagree," he says sweetly. I remain mum on being gay.

Bill and Dario are doing better and have made it to Delhi; they come and fetch me the next morning for a tour of the city. It's said that world capitals often are unrepresentative of the country they command, and in Delhi's case the charge partly sticks: the place has its share of squalid stalls and cacophonically honking horns, to be sure, but for the most part it's pretty clean. Streets are broad, sidewalks are paved, and the air—in spite of lingering haze—is generally clear. There's something of a monumental feel to it all. And nary a lazy bovine in sight.

"We are preparing for the Commonwealth Games in 2010," Mr. Singh explains. He motions to construction scaffolds blocking some streets. "Soon a subway to the airport." *I'll cheer when that day comes.* An end to taxi scams. Meanwhile, those belching two-stroke auto-rickshaws I've seen throughout the land have been replaced by newer models powered by natural gas. And the cows?

"They are no longer permitted in the city," Mr. Singh officiously states. *Humans 1, cowshit 0.*

Most of the tidy midrise downtown apartment blocks are reserved for federal workers. The area immediately to the south is also governmental: it's the actual "New Delhi," a designation often given to the city as a whole but really intended for this 1930s district, once upon a time headquarters for the British Raj.

Then it's one-two-three, sprawling, capacious Delhi landmarks: Qutb Minar, Humayan's Tomb, and the Baha'i Temple. The architecture in each is as monumental as the grounds: in the case of the former two, Islam by way of India care of the reigning Mughals; in the case of the latter, a modern lotus-shaped froth-white structure representing one of the world's newest and most peaceful faiths. Not so peaceful for me, however: halfway in I'm seized by a sudden case of the runs—the only time this happens during my India visit. I just make it to the bathroom—I'm grateful that the serenity of the Baha'i shrine is equaled by its proximity to a commode.

Aside from that, more catching up: office politics, travel in poorer countries—"Some people expect a tip if you so much as look at them," say my friends—and musings on sexuality. For me it's easy to go under the radar in India as a solo backpacker; for Bill and Dario it's another matter. People seem unaware that they're coupled, as they too have gone through the "Married? Children?" rigamarole. Even their driver seems unaware, though I'm not sure how long that will last.

New Year's Eve. We plan a subdued gathering, dinner at one of Delhi's elegant hotels. Breaking with gastronomical type we dine at the hotel's Thai restaurant. Upstairs in the hotel bar a party of expats is brewing; we hear the raucous music but we're digging the mellow vibe too much to venture up there. The clock strikes midnight and we ring it in with an adjacent table. In bed not too long after, which suits me just fine: I hope to expend my celebratory energy on holidays less familiar.

We rise next morning hungry for some local flavor, and Mr. Singh agrees to indulge: he takes us to his home, a modest yet cheerful ground-floor apartment in a neighborhood of well-maintained three-story buildings. Good to see that not everybody in India is either millionaire or pauper. His two young children run around playing while his wife presents us with some sweets. She runs a small garment business nearby, a shop overflowing with patterned saris and such. We thank them profusely for their hospitality, and agree that the visit, for us, was heartening in its banality.

Meanwhile, I still haven't worn out my motivation for the touristic: I hop on the city's subway—the most sparkling piece of infrastructure I've seen in three weeks—and head to the Red Fort, global HQ for the Mughal Empire of ages back. As with Jerusalem, Delhi's been destroyed and rebuilt many times; the Red Fort is totem of only one of its many previous overlordships. I'm not sure if this is indicative of the country's religious tensions, but I find relatively little mention of the Mughal's faith: they were nominally Islamic—which explains the separation of men and women in the forts and palaces of Jaipur—but they borrowed Hindu influences freely. One ruler even made up his own religion.

On that subject, Bill and Dario ask Mr. Singh about faith—or rather, its absence: are there any atheists in the country? His response: a confounded, "Oh no. In India, everybody believes in God."

Old Delhi lies just outside the Red Fort. I wander its narrow streets, mindful of pickpockets who supposedly are everywhere—just in case, I come prepared with my daypack, replete with slashproof interior, mesh webbing, and tamper-proof zippers. No crooks on my watch to test this out, thankfully, just the usual touts shilling for my custom: taxis, rickshaws, and knickknack-sellers. I tell one especially persistent fellow, "No means no." His response: "No means *yes*." I can only hope he never discovers the date-rape drug.

Reaching Connaught Place, I walk halfway around the huge circle and grab a bite at an old-style English pub. I want to visit the park in the circular center, but security in the wake of the Mumbai attacks is hyper-vigilant: my daypack may be safe against thieves but it's not allowed in the park.

My feet are tired but my shoes are more so: four months of trudging halfway around the world have left my black Eccos scuffed and worn; a shoe-shiner offers me the "Indian price" for his services—20 rupees, less than 50 cents. He does such a great job I gladly overpay for some new laces. It's the last thing I do in India.

Bill and Dario's goodbye, which they later recount to me, beats mine by a country mile: when Mr. Singh drops them off at the airport, Bill figures it's time to lay things on the table. While Dario organizes luggage, Bill turns to Mr. Singh.

"Did you know that Dario and I are a couple?"

Mr. Singh smiles and nods.

"And that friend of ours, David, he's also gay?"

Mr. Singh pauses for a long moment, then says to both of them, "I wish all of you the very best in the world, and hope you will return." Then he embraces them farewell.

If that's not a Hollywood ending, I don't know *what* is.[1]

---

[1] Mr. Singh seems to have anticipated current events: on July 2, 2009, India repealed Section 377 of its Penal Code, overturning a 150-year-old ban on "unnatural offences," which included gay sex.

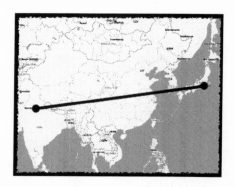

Electric City
Tokyo

*B*usiness Class again for a flight swiping across Asia in the dark: north India to eastern Japan. This one's merely a "lie-flat" seat (as opposed to a full flat-bed) on a Japan Airlines 747, but no complaints from me. I can't get the eighties hits "Mr. Roboto" and "Turning Japanese" out of my head so I dig them up on my iPod and play them incessantly until nodding off. A respectable night's sleep over the Himalayas and the hinterlands of China, breakfast over the Sea of Japan, and an early-morning arrival into Narita.

The airport's far from town: even the smooth and spotless express train into central Tokyo—a delight after all this time in the Middle East and India—takes over an hour. It's got plenty of gee-whizdom to keep me amused, however: a digital map plots the train's progress from the airport all the way into the city while a robotically perky, melodious Japanese woman's voice announces the stops ("SHIN-juku! SHIN-juku!").

The days of $10 orange juice and $400 a night hotel stays are not entirely vanquished, but for the most part the city's much more reasonable than during Japan's go-go 1980s. My hotel lies on a main road right in Shinjuku, one of the mammoth city's five or so downtowns; comparable to a Holiday Inn Express or Days Inn back home and—the real kicker—about the same rate as my Delhi guesthouse. Small but very comfy rooms. In the bathroom, a Toto

Washlet toilet, replete with heated seat and Mission Control-ish instrument panel affording all manner of ablutions.

I lost my electric shaver somewhere in India, which makes for a good excuse to visit this city's electronics stores. A couple of rides on the surprisingly intuitive metro system—the map looks like a tangle of overcooked pasta—lands me in Ginza, the city's upscale shopping district that's also, incongruously enough, home to its most garish electronics store, BIC Camera. Outside it's a black slab, a flatiron monolith with huge-screen display out front. Inside, arrays of carnival-barker salespeople on megaphones call out the latest specials; a narrow atrium reveals several floors of goods piled high, discount store-style. A closer look reveals products unavailable back home: Japan's rep as bleeding-edge-central remains intact. It's geek heaven; I christen this bustling place of flashing gizmos and dubious misspellings—"Bru-Ray?"—my Vatican City. Finding the shaver seems anticlimactic.

For the biggest metropolis in the world—thirty-five million, more than all of Canada—Tokyo's gay scene is relatively small. Japan's still something of a traditional, wife-and-kids country. Most of the gay spots are in Shinjuku Ni-chōme, a modest walk from my hotel. En route, just past the train station, lies a narrow-alleyed district of blazing lights and (straight) sex bars—Shinjuku San-chōme. A wrong turn lands me here, though I linger a bit, finding the rush of crowds and music intoxicating. A muscular Caribbean man comes up to me.

"Someone said to me," he says, "that a handsome fellow is looking to see some girls."

"I think you got the wrong guy," I smile, and ask for directions to Ni-chōme.

"*Oooh*," he says, like I just farted. "You don't want to go there…it's a *gay area.*"

"Yeah, that's what I'm looking for," I reply. He looks incredulous.

"Really? Are you *sure* you're gay?" Yup, pretty sure. I'm wearing mildly flashy jeans and a fitted top—oh, but I forgot: what passes for gay attire in America is *de rigueur* hetero-wear overseas.

Ni-chōme is also a warren of narrow streets, though the vibe is more subdued and the buildings are smaller. They still sport columnar neon signage and those ever-confusing Tokyo addresses, which go by block number rather than street address. I follow a few guys—some Japanese, the rest Aussies and Brits, all definitely gay—into the bar I'd been seeking, the curiously named Arty Farty.

It's friendly inside. The place could be a clone of the George in Dublin or the Bronx in Cape Town. An even mix of locals and *gaijin*. I chat with a blonde beefy Swedish guy, then end up doing some bumpy-grindy dancing with a tall couple from Minnesota. Mario's the more gregarious one, grabbing my crotch and teasing me with bits of make-out between vodka shots. His boyfriend, Matt, is more demure, though he's the stereotypically better-looking one; this is a trend I find all too frequently. Mario's interested in a threesome but Matt isn't. But they're nice—did I mention they're from Minnesota?

"I used to live here," Mario says.

"Yeah, until *Daddy* stopped paying for it," Matt retorts with a smirk. He stayed on, making this a *really* long-distance relationship.

"I teach English," he says, "but in Kyoto." As it gets past five they take me to an all-night Italian place for some pizza. Dashing through the streets, they drunkenly giggle and gab in a mix of English and Japanese. Nothing further happens, and I walk home in time to see the sun come up over the blocks of skyscrapers adjacent to my hotel.

The previous night leaves me frisky, so I hop online and check out the offerings. A promising-looking half-Brazilian, half-Japanese guy answers and agrees to meet me that evening. At the appointed time I reach our rendezvous spot outside some shops. I spot a grungy-looking fellow in track pants looking like he's waiting for someone as well. *Oh no*…but it's not him. Bruno shows up a few minutes later. He's a kind, talkative twentysomething with a killer smile, jet-black hair, deep brown eyes, and tan Brazilian skin. Cute. And he's interested in more than just fucking: our evening has the feel of an honest-to-goodness *date* as he takes me to a nearby *kaiten-zushi*, one of those conveyor-belt sushi joints. Tasty and delicate and under ten dollars. Then, surprised I didn't make it up the Eiffel Tower in Paris, he offers up Japan's variant: Tokyo Tower, a 1960s-era red-and-white replica of sorts of the Paris landmark. We wander around the observation deck as he points out the various facets of the megalopolis. The Rainbow Bridge, its suitably colorful floodlights illuminating its suspension towers, makes for a suitable backdrop as we sneak behind a steel truss and snag a snog, as the Brits call it.

We head back to my hotel; it's too late for the last train so Bruno stays the night and proves those clichés about Brazilian sexuality are right on the money. But it feels like more than wham-bam-thank-you-ma'am: we trade contact information, and his demeanor as he kisses me goodbye—passion coupled with sweetness—suggests it's more than a mere gesture.

Jetlag is my friend here, for it causes me to rise and sleep late. Ideal for a town best viewed after dark when the gigawatts are on show: near the bustling Shinjuku Station—the busiest in the world, more tangle of department stores and malls than rail junction—hang several of the mammoth-screen TVs made famous in the movie *Lost in Translation*. A couple of subway stops away is Shibuya, where gangs of youths prowl *pachinko* parlors astride a plaza of more blazing signs and wall-sized TVs. Young girls in pink outfits make use of grab-a-stuffed-toy machines bubbling with cloying paraphernalia. By the train station, meanwhile, sits a statue of an Akita: Hachikō, a pooch who loyally followed his owner, a Tokyo University professor, to the train station every morning in prewar Japan—then somberly continued to do so every day for a decade after his master died at work.

More romance the next night: I meet Bruno at the tongue-twisting Hamamatsuchō station near Ginza where he works. It's my first experience with the metro at rush hour, and although not quite the storied experience of uniformed men with sticks packing people into trains like sardines, it's still crowded on a scale unseen in North America—even in frenetic New York. Yet a few blocks away the streets are winding, placid, hilly, enveloped by low- and medium-rise buildings that are the norm in this sprawling, earthquake-prone city. We stop in

at a Korean barbecue joint and Bruno grills me an assortment of
meats. Later we do some discount-store shopping where I pick up
some gear for a planned trip to the mountains next week. We go back
to my place for more sex, then, finding ourselves famished, walk down
the block to one of those automat-style noodle joints: punch in your
order then collect your freshly prepared buckwheat noodle soup from
a cook surrounded by a medley of steaming pots. Flavorful, delicious,
and around six bucks.

"So how come your e-mail address is 'ahavasimon'?" I ask. That's
not Portuguese or Japanese and it sounds familiar.

"My best friend, she's Israeli," he replies. He then shows me some
YouTube videos of Israeli hits—hip-hop again. I add some oldies to
his collection, folk tunes from the 1970s that still ring in my ears
though they've long since dropped off the radar in the Holy Land.

Later that night I endure a mild panic when I try downloading my
day's collection of photos: my camera is dead. I check and double-
check, and all batteries are charged and everything is as it should be.
There's no sign of physical damage. Just…*dead*. A prowl online reveals
that this otherwise-splendid machine is prone to power supply failures.
Terrific. Skype to the rescue, with a call to the Canon U.S.A. helpline.

"You need to send it back here, sir."

"But I'm in Japan," I reply. "Your head office is down the street!"

Doesn't matter. Coming on the heels of the loss of a shaver and,
earlier, of a pair of clip-on sunglasses, I'm starting to get upset: the
unforeseen is always a traveler's bugaboo.

I'm not big on the consumerist notion of "retail therapy," but I
admit to falling under its spell for electronics. I bite the bullet and ship
the inert camera back home, arranging to have it sent back to me at a
future stop. Meanwhile, it's a splendid excuse for more shopping. This
time it's the district of Akihabara, Tokyo's original "electric city."
Emerging from the train, I see a number of kiosk-sized shops lining
the road selling mostly components: power supplies, circuit boards,
and capacitors by the armful in brightly colored plastic bins. Down the
road are bigger outlets offering consumer-oriented gear; I pick up an
inexpensive yet decent replacement to tide me over until my baby
comes back from across the Pacific.

The sun's going down as I arrive in Omotesando, a district of narrow laneways, funky shops and high-end boutiques—Rodeo Drive meets Haight-Ashbury. I meet up with yet another friend of my film-effects pal Marjo. Julian used to work in that industry but has given it all up to move here. Ethnically Chinese but all-American by birth and upbringing, he's a recent transplant here with his Japanese wife.

"It's an adjustment," he says. A career in visual effects is tough to leave. But he chose this path, among other reasons, for his wife to be closer to her family. *My ex would love you*, I think: this was precisely the sacrifice Bradley wanted me to make, to stay in Boston and accept more limited career prospects. Still, the shift seems to be working for Julian: when I ask how he feels about his adopted city his face brightens.

"I love this place!" Like me, he's a devotee of science fiction and modern architecture, and Tokyo offers plenty of both. We wander the Omotesando streets, gawking at wildly shaped polygons of buildings housing Fendi and Cartier.

"Ever had *tonkatsu*?" he asks.

It's Japan by way of the West: breaded deep-fried pork cutlets brought to this country a century or so ago and vacuumed into the culture just as the imitative Japanese did with *chocoretto* on Valentine's Day and *basoboru* the sport. Derivative, maybe, but delightful.

Okay, now jetlag *sucks*, as there's one early-morning event I want to witness: the Tsukiji Fish Market, reportedly the biggest in the world. I rise too late for the famed tuna auction, which is just as well: it's recently been closed to the public in the wake of a noisome few disturbing the plump fishies and their would-be buyers. But I'm still early enough to find the place abustle: a cavernous semicircular warehouse by the waterfront uncounted football fields in length. Inside, forklifts wend their way past rows and rows of stalls. All manner of sea life—in various states of disassembly—sits in foam containers or, if still alive, swims in plastic tanks. A scattering of us interlopers prowl the place, but for the most part this is a working wholesale market and we're admonished to keep out of the way.

Best part: breakfast. At the market's fringes lie a few hole-in-the-wall sushi joints. Dodging the light rain that has begun to fall, I pick one more or less at random; inside it's crowded with locals chatting amiably with the sushi chef along with a smattering of bleary-eyed *gaijin*. It's not cheap: my hearty-sized sushi platter nudges thirty dollars. But eminently worthwhile: gossamer-light and fresh, arguably the best I've ever had. Raw fish for brekkie now makes complete sense.

Nearby, the Edo-Tokyo Museum fills a cavernous boxlike structure cantilevered on four massive pillars. It's okay, but heavier on props—re-creations of feudal-era Edo and nineteenth-century Tokyo—than on history-telling. And precious little on the ignoble period of Japanese fascism culminating in the Second World War: after a few references to rising militarism in the 1930s, the exhibits segue straight to Allied bombings in the 1940s. Nothing on Pearl Harbor, Japanese depredations in China, wartime leader Tojo…it's all ignored. This in contrast to Berlin, almost overwrought about its Nazi past. I can see why China remains frustrated: failure to redress for past crimes isn't so neighborly.

Bruno's had his wisdom teeth out the day before so I don't expect to hear from him. But he surprises me after I send him a "get well soon" text message. He's doing great, and invites me to his friend's apartment where he's housesitting while she's away. It's a cramped and rather Spartan space with an overly affectionate Bassett Hound, but my charming Brazilian makes it all work as he cooks us some dinner. We watch a bit of TV then have a final evening's amorous romance. As has become our pattern, we climax simultaneously; afterward, he runs his fingers on my face.

"Such soft lips."

I don't want to go. We hold each other, drifting off for a spell before I have to head out for my train. I cross over the pedestrian walkways of Shinjuku one last time, my mind a reverie of sushi and sinuous skyscrapers and gadgetry and Brazilian romance under the watchful neon-girdled eye of the electric city.

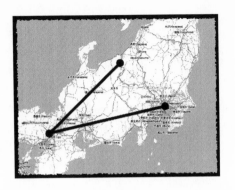

Empire of Sun & Snow
Kyoto & Hakuba

The Nozomi Shinkansen Series 700 glides noiselessly into Tokyo Station. Gleaming and white, squarish porthole-style windows and an incongruous duck-bill nose, it's not yet ready for boarding: first an army of diminutive pink-suited Japanese ladies combs the train, wiping windows and turning around seats so that all face front. It makes Europe's trains almost seem slovenly.

So too the journey: it's not any faster than the TGV or Thalys back on the Continent, but it feels like more of an adrenaline rush as we leave the endless array of Tokyo suburbs behind. Puffy clouds blend seamlessly into the creamy snow-cone that is Mount Fuji, *fuji-san*, a mountain so eye-catchingly iconic I cannot take my eyes off it for many minutes. But at 200 miles per hour, even its great hulk rapidly recedes.

Kyoto. *Why am I here again?* I just left behind the trip's first bona fide romance. Though I'm feeling alright about the decision: the affair ran its course, offering both of us the right amount of physical and emotional nourishment. Any more would feel gratuitous. Besides, there's nothing worse for a traveler than outstaying a welcome, of transitioning from skipping stone to bottom-sinking boulder.

Kyoto is tranquil, linear—against Tokyo's noisome splat of neighborhoods—and chilly. Sequestered in a hilly valley, it's the coldest-weather place for me since Copenhagen. Here I'm anonymous again—those Minnesota boys from the previous weekend, one of whom lives here, never gave me their contact info. There's little gay life and I can't even think of a filmic evocation. Oh wait, there's one: *Lost in Translation* sees one character come here to retreat, just as I'm doing. It's the anti-Tokyo in more than just the anagramic: the place feels like a city-sized incarnation of a Tibetan monastery.

All those temples explain the vibe; my guide lists dozens scattered across town and tucked into the hills, though the biggest of them looks to be mere blocks from the train station: the Higashi Honganji, said to be the largest wooden building in the world...so where is it? Aside from earthen-black entry gate and forebuilding, all I see is a squat, white, barnlike enclosure. Oh, that's why: it's under restoration, a simultaneously heartening and dispiriting prospect for the traveler; the fruits of worthy activities you won't get to witness.

But still, this feels a bit excessive, sealing off the whole complex inside another building. Wouldn't scaffolding suffice? Well...no. Europe's palaces both actual and spiritual are hewn of masonry and stone—hoping, maybe, to remain for eternity. But that wouldn't fly here, in a land fraught with earthquakes. Wood is better, as it flexes and torques more than brick or stone—a fact not lost on builders to-day in California, on the other side of the Pacific Ring of Fire from this island nation. Unfortunately, wood rots and wood burns. This temple was first built in the 1600s, was rebuilt in the 1890s, and is now again being reconstructed. Still, significant parts of the place are open. I follow a smattering of Japanese and remove my shoes, trundling the cool wooden paths in my socks through the complex. A fright-indu-cing bronze dragon fountain spits water from its mouth. Intricate wooden ceiling moldings are encrusted in gold. The main hall is visible through the enclosing maintenance structure: a huge chamber, massive chocolate-brown pillars supporting a high, checkerboard ceiling.

Kyoto's laid out in a rectilinear grid, something I associate with North American rationalist town planning, not with cities 1,200 years old. Well, it turns out the New World wasn't the first to lay out streets this way: the old imperial capitals of China started the trend, and the Japanese, as is their wont, imitated them. But in contrast to New York or Chicago's brawny city blocks, the effect here is subdued, a mix of newer structures—most verging on the dull—slotted in between the *machiya*, traditional wooden townhomes with slatted rice-paper windows on the ground floor and flat bamboo rolling shades on the second. I walk north along the Shirakawa Canal just east of the station, behind the tranquil backs of homes. In spite of the chill, winter-blooming flowers pop from nearby bushes while an onion skin of water in the stone channel flows gingerly northward.

I can't get in to see the old Imperial Palace—there's an arcane process of signing up for an appointment to do so—so instead it's off to Nijō Castle, the real power center of the country for some 250 years. When the Tokugawa clan took over affairs of state and emas-culated the Japanese emperor in the 1600s, they built this place to the chagrin of the Kyoto establishment. *New money*, it was said of the Tokugawa, their headquarters considered gaudy, excessive—vulgar, even. I guess it's all relative, as the place feels tremendously subdued against the Rococo insanity of Europe or the intensely patterned detailing of Islam or the Hindu.

Instead, a thatched wooden entry gate marks a break in horizontally striped dun-colored fortification walls. At each end, white sentry towers with faceless, filled-in windows, all capped by the characteristic Japanese-style upturned double roof. The complex is ringed by a rectangular outer moat and, inside, a square inner moat. The low-slung buildings with arching black roofs seem spare; a few patches of gold trim mark bits of ostentation. The throne room now contains wax dummies—representing the shogun and his court—sitting on tatami mats on the floor. Only the shogun himself is slightly elevated. Louis XIV would have hated it.

Yet another national holiday! It's *seijin shiki*, Coming of Age Day, when the country's youth turn age of majority (presumably not all at once), which in these parts is twenty. Roaming around Higashimaya, the eastern part of the city abutting the foothills, I see crowds of youngsters heading to reception halls. Boys wear suits while girls sport colorfully patterned *furisode* kimonos. Porcelain-doll lookalikes, they yammer on mobile phones while waiting for the festivities to start.

Snow starts to fall as I reach a busy shrine, incongruously garish red with green-tiled roof: it's not that old—1895—and has the feel of a themed restaurant back home. Its fences look coated in snow—wait, that can't be, it's not falling *that* heavily. Up-close it's clearer: legions of small white paper slips tied to the fencing in orderly rows. Homilies left by the faithful. These were, apparently, an inspiration for the inscriptions now found in fortune cookies.

Japan's two religions, Shinto and Zen, have coexisted in the country for eons. The last place was devoted to the former but farther on, up the quiet hills, lie shrines of the latter. Here skies are clear and crowds are gone. One temple is set upon rambling hillside gardens filled with carved stones, like a graveyard outside an old New England church. Beside it, a square three-story pagoda. Inside it's awash with ornament. Some bits are familiar—statues of the Buddha with bulbous bald head—but most are not: a display panel outside holds rows of small wooden pieces, each carved with a few Japanese characters. Inside is an altar, supported by two gilded beams in front of which hangs a colorful arrangement of paperlike cutouts. Somewhere in the distance flute music plays. It accompanies me throughout my walk around these near-deserted temples and the quiet residential neighborhoods nearby. Its volume is steady, never growing louder or fainter until I leave this district altogether. I was never able to place its source here in the still, dry, cool mountain air.

I haven't read *Memoirs of a Geisha*, and yet Gion, the old geisha district, feels familiar like some phantasmagoric old movie set: narrow streets flanked by brick walkways along which wooden *machiya* overhang slightly as if leaning into the street. No geisha are about, though their talents are still available, if hard to come by. Apparently their services were not sexual...though I suspect some were pressed into such activities. In any case, I make do with a more pedestrian spot for a Kyoto dinner. My middle-aged male waiter is uncharacteristically gruff; I doubt *he'd* make the cut for geisha.

Nearby lies Kyoto's bustling shopping district; a maze of pedestrian shopping arcades stretches for hundreds of yards, bearing shops both traditional and modern. Hordes of Coming of Age youth are shopping away, kimonoed girls enjoying their newfound adulthood browsing the racks at Benetton.

The snow may have only dusted Kyoto, but in the mountains to the northeast a blizzard was brewing, dumping over a meter of snow over the holiday weekend. Or so it seems as the train pulls into Nagano, a drab, gunmetal-gray Japanese town that hosted the Olympics in 1998. The real action during the Games, however, was at Hakuba, an hour's bus ride to the north. As we head along the winding two-lane highway, I see tree branches heavily dappled in white. A promising sign for my intended couple of days snowboarding in these parts.

It's getting dark as I get off the bus and am met by Albert Kikstra, a tall New Zealander with thinning blonde hair. He runs the bed & breakfast where I'll be staying, a short walk to the base of one of the region's "ski fields," as the Aussies and Kiwis call them. The B & B's a predictably cozy alpine sort of place: high wooden beams, ski apparel drying on the upstairs banister, smallish rooms with gas-fired heaters. In the common room a family watches a Hollywood action flick on a large flat-screen TV.

Japan seems an improbable place for snowsports, but its combination of craggy peaks and heavy snows from the Sea of Japan renders it just as conducive as Colorado or Chamonix. I remember documentaries with newsreels of prewar Meiji-era Japan, scratchy black-and-whites of lithe women on old-style wooden skis. The sport is still popular nowadays but it feels like North America a generation ago, all sleepy base lodges and surprisingly reasonable lift tickets.

But the snow! Acres and acres of soft, fluffy, wondrous powder, set against picture-perfect mountain vistas. Hard to believe the region isn't as well-known or well-publicized as Squaw Valley or Switzerland: I'm one of the few people from my part of the world, the remainder mostly folks from Down Under enjoying the reversal of the seasons. It's midweek and the place is otherwise deserted.

No complaints about that: the second day I'm here is quieter, colder, and windier, but it imparts a deliciously lonely boreal quality to the mountain. Snowsports are where I connect with nature, bundled up against the elements, gliding down a trail of moderate pitch (anything more threatens to swamp my abilities), sprawling vistas of mountains and valleys stretching for miles and miles. It's a pastime I could never share with my two closest: Steve's flat feet and Bradley's enlarged spleen—a byproduct of his liver condition—meant no alpine snowsports for either of them. Too bad: I think they both could have benefited from the elemental wonder of the mountains.

My B & B doesn't have a hot tub, but something even better bubbles nearby. Seismically active Japan is riddled with hot springs; consequently, the Japanese have made a near-ritual of the act of visiting hot-spring baths; these *onsen* dot the landscape, water pumped from deep underground wherever it doesn't bubble up naturally. The mineral-rich soaking is said to be good for the skin, to say nothing of muscles aching from two days of bent knees aimed downhill on a slab of fiberglass.

It's dinnertime when I arrive at the facility. A smattering of Japanese guests take a meal in the dining room. The changing area, the showers—where one must cleanse oneself beforehand—and the baths themselves are deserted, their woodsy planks and lockers antiseptically spotless. The water is near-scalding hot—almost too much to handle in the indoor pool but just right in the outdoor. It's a perfect meditational bookend to a week of Buddhist temples and sugar-white mountain trails. The crisp, cold air—outside it's around five below Celsius—coerces waves of steam to swirl over the torrid waters and up into the starry, snowy black.

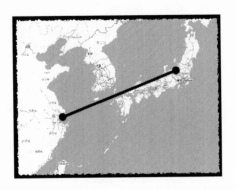

Yesterday & Tomorrow
Shanghai

*I*t's hard to get excited about taxiing to a gate. Oh sure, the eagerness of arrival and all that...but the approach itself, something I've seen a million times, is usually about as compelling as watching paint dry. But not here. Shanghai Pudong looks and feels like a spaceport. Cue the Vangelis music from *Blade Runner*.

More transit geekery beckons on arrival: skipping the taxi line, I follow signs that read "MAGLEV TRAIN," a sleek airport-to-city conveyance that hovers, care of electromagnets, above a special track at 300 miles an hour. It's a short ride so it reaches that velocity for only a minute or two. The low hum makes the blur outside almost abstract. And yet, I'm entranced, nose pressed against the glass like a ten-year-old. As during my Eurostar ride under the English Channel, I cannot fathom how passengers around me can be so nonplussed.

Maglev technology isn't yet cost-effective, and this is more a vanity project to showcase Chinese economic prowess than a practical means of arriving in town: I need to catch two more conventional Shanghai Metro trains before being let out on the street at Huaihai Road, the main shopping street in the old French Concession formerly known as Avenue Joffre.

Avenue Joffre. I've heard that street name my whole life. My grand-folks lived it up here during the city's decadent heyday in the 1930s...then endured the austerity of Japanese occupation during much of the Second World War. When a young Christian Bale salutes

Japanese fighter pilots in Steven Spielberg's 1987 film adaptation of
J.G. Ballard's *Empire of the Sun*, he does so in uniforms modeled on the
school my father attended.

The hotel is fantastic—and amazingly inexpensive. An online
search lands me at the Donghu, a complex of former French
Concession mansions. The main building was once the home of
gangster Du Yuesheng. In later years it saw life as a U.S. Consulate.
From behind the tall fence and wrought-iron gates, green floodlights
illuminate magnolia and bamboo trees framing a terraced stone
building. The lobby is a pastiche of chandeliers, dark-wooden Chinese
furniture, and front-desk staff who speak pretty respectable English.
My room is tremendous, with king-sized bed and ornate writing desk.

At almost twenty-two million people this is one of Earth's largest
metropolises. But the city proper is surprisingly inviting, strollable,
safe. I head east, down Huaihai Road, dodging knockoff-watch touts
clustered around the metro station—they're surprisingly persistent,
though pretending I don't speak English or Chinese seems to shake
them off.

I emerge on Nanjing Road. The once-elegant shopping street is
now pedestrianized and working to recapture its former glory: a blend
of upscale and discount stores; a cloying trolley-type train ferrying
tourists across its mile-long expanse. Skyscrapers loom on either end
while the brilliant cavalcade of signs assaults the senses like an Asiatic
Times Square. I love it immediately.

At the end of Nanjing Road I come to Shanghai's most famous
roadway, this one fronting the Huangpu River. Nowadays it's known
as East Zhongshan Road but is forever familiar to Westerners by its
old Anglo-Indian name, the Bund.

It's massive—some ten lanes wide. It was the city's main commercial thoroughfare in the days when British, French, and Americans
carved the metropolis into zones of influence, mini-colonial enclaves.
After the Revolution the Communists held the place in stasis; only
when the country began to assert itself as a world power did the city
reawaken. Mercifully, the powers-that-be took their cue from

preservationists the world over and left the old city core intact. The Bund is perhaps the proverbial star atop the Christmas tree of that effort: its midrise edifices are brilliantly floodlit, a banner-wall pastiche of ornate neoclassicism along the riverbank.

On the other side, meanwhile, lies Pudong, once a no-man's land of warehouses and gangster dens, now a photogenic collage of skyscrapers. The promenade that abuts the river is busy with Chinese on holiday, snapping photos of their country's entrant in that unending game of Great Skylines of the World.

Gentrification is rampant. Ground Zero for this is Xintiandi, a pedestrianized district of restored *shikumen*—three-story terraced townhomes of gray/brown brick—integrating a mix of shopping, dining, housing, and entertainment to form a "lifestyle center." True to form, it features a Starbucks—nope, not going in there. Instead I meet an old Chicago pal for dim sum. Adam's a yuppie-ish late-twenties SoCal transplant out here as a techie team lead, part of Microsoft's operations in China.

"You don't really save on headcount," he explains as he fills me in on the details of outsourcing. "But we're not doing it for the cost-savings." Like most multinationals, Microsoft wants in on the monstrous, morphing Chinese market. *Yeah, yeah.* Normally I'm keen on all this but the vagaries of the technology industry right now feels like another life. Happily, Adam's got more to offer than that: I've often steered clear of yuppie manager types, but his demeanor is genuine, earnest, bereft of the brashness that he agrees can be grating about the crowd back home. Perhaps that's partly what motivated him to shift his life 6,000 miles; makes my relocations seem almost sedate.

"It's not all that different here," he says. "Some things took getting used to. I stood in line for four hours to pay my cable bill. They said it's the only place you can pay it. Then I heard you can pay a guy to stand in line for you."

"How's the gay life?" I'm always curious about that one.

"Yeah…" he mulls over that one. "For a regime that's usually intolerant, they're surprisingly not too bad about it." Shanghai's scene is still small but growing fast. I ask if he's into the local citizenry.

"Not really," he replies. *Translation: not a rice queen.* It's one reason why white boys settle in these parts. Instead, Adam contents himself with long-distance affairs with myriad Europeans.

Where Xintiandi ends, Old Shanghai begins—the once-walled, oval-shaped district squeezed in between the Bund and the Western concession districts. Nine hundred years old, it's all of what was the city before the colonials came; in their time they kept it a fetid slum. It still has a grimy feel but its narrow streets are cleaner than Old Delhi or Islamic Cairo. Elderly Chinese play mahjong in front of curio shops where lie clutters of picture frames, old gramophones, statues of the Buddha and Chairman Mao. Hanging on a clothesline is a dried-out whole chicken, head intact, next to towels and sheets. In the hazy background loom residential skyscrapers, some still under construction, threatening to encroach on the tangle of the old.

It's a similar scene in Honkou, a district of two- and three-story tenements across muddy Suzhou Creek northeast of the Bund. This was once the old Jewish ghetto, home to tens of thousands of European refugees from Hitler's Germany. They're all gone, of course, but it's still a bustling zone of bicycles, motor scooters, and shop-keepers pushing two-wheeled carts laden with sacks of goods. Some streets are a mess of dirt and gravel, but it isn't the filth of neglect: holding court over the pile of earth is a white canvas sign with neatly stenciled lettering in English and Chinese: "THE PENINSULA, SHANGHAI. OPENING 2009."

I'm eager to explore my family's old haunts but I don't know where they are: my septuagenarian father and his older cousin Joe were children back in those days. All my grandparents—indeed anyone in my family from that generation—are long gone. Before my journey I photocopied an old map of Shanghai and pored over it with my dad, but he was hard-pressed to point out particulars. I'm rescued from a fruitless wander by a latter-day expat, a pal of my elderly relatives:

Patrick's out of town the week of my visit but he sends me a plethora of e-mails, cross-referencing Joe's and my father's memories with present-day places. I park myself at a trendy café with Wi-Fi Internet, spread out my maps on the creamy modern coffee table, and figure out my route.

My forebears lived in the western corner of the old French Concession, about a mile or so from my hotel. I hop off the metro at the corner of Huashan and Hengshan roads—once known as Avenue Haig and Avenue Petain. The vista is one of big-box shopping malls and towering glass skyscrapers, unrecognizable to Shanghailanders of yore.

Fortunately, side streets are unchanged: rows of mini-villa homes in a variety of styles—Tudor, Mediterranean, lots of Art Deco—hide behind high stone fences. Signs in English and Chinese denote "HERITAGE ARCHITECTURE" with building description and date—most of them from the 1920s and 1930s. Some of the grander mansions are now consulates, as in Cairo's Garden District or Newlands in Cape Town. It feels a bit unreal, walking the heart of China's biggest city engulfed by structures straight out of Kent or Marseilles.

I soon come upon the first of my family's former homes: the almond-colored Art Deco Picardie Apartments, now a four-star hotel; so too is the former Haig Court Apartments, a white-stucco and red-roofed midrise with large green front lawn. Once my father and aunt played here under the watchful eye of the family's numerous servants. Inside, the lobby is small but inviting, tiled floors and beige travertine running halfway up the walls. I forward a picture to my father and he's overcome: it's exactly as he remembers it as a boy of nine. He's equally spellbound by photos of a nearby red-brick cupola-topped building looming behind wrought-iron fencing: the original Shanghai American School. The building is now a naval academy, but the school itself has reopened for business nearby to handle the tide of expats again calling Shanghai home. No servants for these folk, I imagine, unless you count the ones standing in line to pay your cable bill.

The most inspiring place is also the most down-market: at the prow of a triangular intersection lies the former ISS Apartments, a red-brick and stone flatiron affair with Parisian-style neoclassical balustrades. This was where my family lived when the Japanese marched into the city on December 8, 1941, the day after Pearl Harbor.

"We woke up to a big commotion," my grandmother used to recount. They were out at a late-night party the night before. "Japanese soldiers were sitting in a tank, and a policeman on the street was very angry. He kept on screaming, 'Thees eez *Frahnce*! Thees eez *Frahnce*!' But they didn't care. They just laughed at him." One set of colonials replacing another.

My father's wartime stories also bubble up in my brain: one day, he recollected, as he was walking home from school, a pair of P-51 fighter aircraft roared overhead, out of the clouds, just over the tops of these buildings at the leafy intersection where I now stand.

Surreal.

My grandfather worked on the Bund, at the Hongkong and Shanghai Banking Corporation building. The eponymous bank is still around—HSBC—though the building is now in the hands of a local concern. It's still grand and still all business, with a flotilla of humorless guards forbidding me from snapping photos of the elegant lobby and the dazzling ceiling mosaic. Instead I content myself with snaps of the bronze lions out front, one sleepy, the other in mid roar. These too have a storied past, having been taken by the Japanese during the war to be melted down then later restored and replaced. Somewhat totemic of the city as a whole.

From yesterday back to tomorrow—specifically, Tomorrow Square, the pencil-shaped office tower overlooking sprawling People's Square in the heart of the city. A shoeshine vendor tries to coerce me into his services by squirting polish onto my shoe. I move my foot away just in time and hurry across the street, losing him in the crowd like a character in a spy film. I duck into the nearest building, which happens to be the imposing modern flat-topped slab of the Shanghai Urban Planning Exhibition Hall. It sounds like something out of Communist central-planning hell but it's actually one of the better urban history museums I've visited: one massive floor dedicated to the city's past, then three more on recent development and plans for the future—including the biggest thing set to hit Shanghai in decades, a world's fair in 2010. On the top floor lies the most extensive city model I've ever seen of any place, past or present, complete with in-depth plans for infrastructure and neighborhood growth in the coming decades.

There's a bridge missing. I know because I try in vain to cross it. The century-old steel-truss Waibaidu Bridge—formerly the Garden Bridge between Hongkou and the Bund—has been taken down for restoration. The garden next to it is still there, built by the Western powers and formerly barred to native Chinese. Appropriately, there's now a soaring modern sculpture commemorating the country's liberation from foreign occupation.

The park also offers a fun, if kitschy, way to cross the Huangpu: a theme-parky ride in slow-moving rail cars inside a tunnel under the river. During the crossing, a light show flashes on black tunnel walls while electronic music plays in fitful syncopation. Yet another spot where a dollop of *hashish* would come in handy.

Pudong looks dazzling from a distance but once within its confines it's yet another bland, contemporary skyscraper district, L.A.'s Century City revisited. Interestingly, its main thoroughfare is called Century Avenue. Size queen that I am, I skip the multi-ovoid, Oriental Pearl tower and the more polygonal Jin Mao building for the newly completed—and tallest—World Financial Center. From up at the top, some 1,400 feet, the Bund's stately strand of edifices resemble the urban model in the museum. The observation deck itself, straddling both sides of the square cut-out "carry-handle" top of the building, is sleek, white, modern, and otherwise nothing much to write home about aside from the view. I sit on a white-cushioned stool, sip some sparkling water, and watch the lights come on in the dusky haze.

Wujiang Road is a small, pedestrianized street packed with food vendors, and on Adam and Patrick's recommendations I stop at the busiest of them all: Yangs Fry Dumplings, a crowded hole-in-the-wall with a line of people out front. I start with an order of four dumplings and sit myself at a table crowded with Chinese young and old. I precariously lift one dumpling with chopsticks—I've always had trouble using them—and *splat!* Hot liquid explodes in my face. My tablemates laugh, indicating in gestures and broken English that the dumplings are filled with broth; typically one eats them in one mouthful. I figure it out quickly enough and go back for four more.

Dessert calls for something more in keeping with my obsessions: Adam's bogged down at work but sends me to Whisk, an Italian place on Huaihai Road. A dessert display case is a jewel box of chocolate delicacies...so precious, apparently, that they forbid me from photographing it. Instead I order an upside-down chocolate cake, basically a dense pot of the stuff flanked by vanilla ice cream resting atop surreal swirls of dark chocolate sauce. Furtively glancing about to ensure no waitstaff is present, I snap a picture of this concoction before devouring it like a cobra swallowing a hapless rodent.

Thus sated, I happen upon one final family history stop: my father used to swim at the pool of the French Club; the palatial three-story French Renaissance structure is now the most spiffed up of all, repurposed as a high-rent Leading Hotels of the World.

It's dark and the boutiques of Changle Road are closing for the night in the old French Concession. China has been on Western radar of late for its relentless, aggressive push into First World-dom: support for brutal regimes in Burma and Sudan; environmental chaos unleashed on water and air; heavy-handed censorship of media and information. As its biggest city, Shanghai is both representative and unrepresentative of that, just as New York is and is not America. Critics no doubt look at the Starbucks and McDonald's and see a latter-day wave of imperialism and greed. But I can't help thinking it's different this time: now the Chinese dictate the terms. This is their prosperity, their expansion, their enrichment. The mistakes they're making, the greed that underlies it all...it's all too familiar to students of British and American and French and Spanish expansion of previous centuries. I hope they learn from our mistakes—and theirs— to the same extent as this revived metropolis has the power to dazzle.

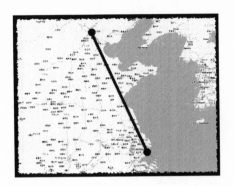

Alley, Palace, Wall
Beijing

T he night train from Shanghai to Beijing begins with a crowd of people outside the Shanghai Railway Station. It's a scene reminiscent of India, impoverished migrant workers camping out or milling about the station courtyard. But then, the gates open to the spanking-new express "Z" train that makes the nightly run between the two cities. It's a lot more crowded than my last overnight rail voyage back in Europe, but the four-person "soft-sleeper" cabin is at least as comfortable. The Chinese students sharing the room with me are unfailingly polite and quiet as mice.

Most other passengers have packed their dinner, but since I didn't I amble on over to the dining car. Out the windows, city lights melt away to dark countryside while at my table arrives a respectable meal of cashew chicken. A sound overnight rest—this train travels the 600 miles between the two cities nonstop—precedes a predawn arrival into Beijing. I glance at the time as I disembark: the train is punctual to the minute. It's a changed world when German trains are an hour late and Chinese ones arrive on time.

Dengcao Hutong, one of the Chinese capital's storied alleyways, is quiet in the early morning; the shops that abut it on the main road are shuttered. My little courtyard hotel lines the alleyway and it's a delight, the room punctuated by a tall canopied bed and a yellow silken settee—and as in Shanghai, for an impressively modest sum. It's also walking distance to the Forbidden City and Tiananmen Square, an achievement in itself in this sprawling metropolis of wide boulevards, spread-out apartment blocks, and Moscow-like Ring Roads. After a few days in the city I dub it the Chinese Dallas.

It's a cool, damp, misty evening as I set out in search of duck—Peking Duck. A cheap-and-cheerful eatery in the nearby shopping area, Wangfujing, looks hopeful. An appetizer of steamed broccoli, tightly packed like a floral arrangement, comes with the duck itself which sits on a porcelain platter capped with a duck's head. It's a bit greasy. Best of all is the introductory page of the menu, where the restaurant reveals its *raison d'être* in glorious translation:

> Our warmhearted service looks like and is
> that the cool breeze in summer affect people deeply.
> It seems that our crystal sweat is in winter
> chafing dish warm the bottom of the heart;
> When our tasty good food and the graceful environment
> is that you are out, often think of the home returning;
> Your is that we with satisfaction think if the result reaching;
> Yours again presence is to us best affirm.

I couldn't make this up if I tried.

Dessert is easy—the adjacent night market stretches over a city block, a steamy cavalcade of vendors offering up cooked starfish, meats on a skewer, and gigantic strawberries. The latter make for a nice break from my choco-frenzy.

Beijing may share latitude with the American Northeast, but its winters are dry: the city sits near the steppes of the Gobi Desert. That doesn't mean it dodges the cold, however, in its case brought on by Arctic blasts from Siberia. The next morning I'm raring to go visit the Forbidden City. It's one of those "pretend-nice days," the sky a rich blue, the sun sparkling, the normally hazy air glassy-clear. But when I step out of the *hutong* onto the main road, *ka-pow!* A knifelike blast of wind. The gates of the Forbidden City are a mere fifteen-minute walk, but by the time I reach them my eyes literally are tearing from twenty-below-Celsius-plus-windchill.

No problem, I figure: weather like this should be perfect for exploring a palace, like a rainy museum day back home. Well, think again: the Forbidden City's complex of buildings are scattered across an enormous expanse, capacious open plazas and lengthy breezeways throughout. Most of my visit is a game of dodgeball with the wind, in and out of drafty building after drafty building. Most are made of wood—as with Kyoto's temples, this complex is the largest collection of timber structures on Earth.

Nevertheless, the place captivates, and arctic blasts mean thin crowds. The vistas through doors and archways at upturned gold rooflines are beguiling. The plaza outside the Hall of Supreme Harmony is a pageant of symmetry. In the center of every monumental stairway, giant dragon carvings of solid stone angle downward—it was here where the emperor's palanquin descended during ceremonial occasions. All very staged, very regimented, very hierarchical…and, of course, full of intrigue. Scores of concubines and even more eunuchs ran the joint to varying degrees of disgruntlement; one of them once set the wooden buildings ablaze. Meanwhile, I could use a concuboy or two right about now: call it one way to keep warm.

One pavilion affords an exhibit of historic clocks used by the various emperors: elegant, ornate, hewn of wood and brass, freestanding devices and diminutive golden varieties shaped like stagecoaches and elephants. I'm looking for the historical irony here and I don't find it: China was an early leader in clockmaking with the invention of the water clock; these, however, had problems with accuracy as water-based movements become clogged with minerals. Mechanical movements were the answer…but it wasn't the then-xenophobic Chinese who developed them. They relegated this task to the Europeans, and it was through such innovations that the acquisitive powers of Europe technologically leapfrogged the Celestial Kingdom, eventually subjugating it altogether.

Time for some KFC. Yes, really. The fast-food chicken chain has taken China by storm, and I'm out to continue testing my anecdotal theory that overseas fast food—in some places, at least—is better than the swill we get back home.

A sign on the Tiananmen Square eatery indicates it was the first one in the country, remodeled with "CAESIOUS BRICKS OF BEIJING-STYLED TRADITIONAL QUADRANGLE COURT-YARD." The menu is all chicken sandwiches...and I daresay it does seem tastier than North American offerings. The ambience surely helps, tasteful décor and respectably garbed Beijingers chowing down on this bit of Americana.

The square itself, largely empty thanks to the shiver-inducing Gobi wind, is a controlled-entry space: underground pedestrian entrances—the only way to get in or out—feature airport-style X-ray machines and armed soldiers. Clearly a reprise of the 1989 riots is unlikely. It's a gargantuan space: at one-sixth of a square mile about triple the size of Red Square in Moscow. It even has a mausoleum of Mao at its center. I arrive too late to see the guy but circle the becolumned modern structure, flanked at every corner with heroic Communist-era statues of workers of the world uniting.

South of Tiananmen it's another story: Qianmen Street was given a makeover in preparation for the Olympics, and the effect is somewhat Main Street P.R.C. Imperial-era China has been resurrected, complete with gaily painted entrance gate, clanging trolley cars, and rows of townhomes bearing shops.

The wind eases up some so I keep at it, taking a couple of subway rides south to another sprawling, expansive space: the Temple of Heaven. Once the official prayer grounds of the Ming and Qing emperors, its buildings are in the same style as those in the Forbidden City: red base, layered roof gables in shades of blue, red, and gold. But it's so much more than that. It's the roundness that does it, lending the imperial style yet more elegance and grace.

Social life beckons: some correspondence on Gaydar with a cute Colombian boy snags me an invite to a going-away party. The guy's an embassy brat living in Sanlitun, Beijing's trendy northeastern district. Arriving by taxi, I discover an area newly glitzed-up, complete with

Apple and Adidas stores. My guidebooks make scant mention of it: it enjoyed a raucous trade of expat nightlife before the Olympics, but its prettification is so recent that even current-year guides are out of date. It's the second time that's happened today: earlier I had a lengthy walk to find a subway station half a mile north of where the map said it would be.

I meet Christjin and his posse, including his Indian friend, Bakhti, who's headed home the next morning. I'm handed a margarita and introduced to the rest of the gang, a bunch of expats including two other gay guys and a girl from Toronto. The drinks keep flowing, and people start dancing. Christjin's pretty friendly, the paragon of the gay social butterfly, putting his arm around me, making flirtatious comments, all that. But when I try responding in kind, he recoils.

"*You're* getting very touchie touchie!"

It gets worse: I learn that most of these people were other gays he invited on Gaydar to compete for his attentions. Meanwhile, Toronto boy, drunker than me, comes onto me a lot less gentlemanly than I did to Christjin earlier. So much for Canadian reserve. I'm not interested, but he doesn't get it. We're set to go to another place, but screw that: I lose the crowd en route, hop in a cab, and go home.

You win a few, you lose a few. Though after that romance in Tokyo, the evening felt barren—and not just because I didn't get laid. Maybe I've upped the ante *too* much, not simply hoping for but demanding that my travel liaisons be fulfilling, deep, and revelatory; this cannot be expected of everyone, everywhere. And yet…the crowd I was with fell so far short of the mark that it almost felt like a step backward in my quest to better understand the world and myself.

Or maybe I'm just missing hot Brazilian sex.

For now, however, more edifice-gawking will have to suffice. My theme today: the modern. In the city's spread-out business district, wide boulevards fronting boxy office buildings, I reach the CCTV building, the M.C. Escher-esque trapezoid set to be the headquarters of the state television agency. George Orwell never looked so fab. A couple more subway rides to the north lies the Olympic Green. In spite of the lingering frost, it's actually pretty busy here in the days before Chinese New Year: an array of street vendors sells drinks and snacks in the chilly plaza.

"One water?" I ask, using the Chinese word for it. The lady smiles, shakes her head, and holds up a bottle of Dasani: it's frozen solid. Nearby soars the "Birds Nest" stadium, a tangle of asymmetry that a breathless public address system proclaims—in English and Chinese— is the "largest steel structure in the world!" Next door, the cube of the Aquatic Center is a bit of a disappointment—it looked so dazzling all lit up at night for the Games, but in the harsh light of day it's a squat pile of bluish plastic. In spite of the cheerful red-and-gold lantern-like New Year's decorations and the gaggle of tourists, I learn the facility has no expected future use.

I haven't tried Sichuan food yet and decide I'm up for the challenge: the eatery I plan to patronize isn't near any subways. Cabbies don't do much better: two cannot figure out where the place is from a map and directions in Chinese given to me by the hotel. The third gets the neighborhood right but gets the main street wrong. Fortunately, my sense of direction is better than theirs, so I disembark and walk the short rest of the way. Luckily dinner's worth it: spice and more spice. I shall rue the day when my stomach can no longer handle the fiery.

Still no luck with any more Gaydar boys, so I rise early and head back to Tiananmen Square for my one extra-urban jaunt: a sign marks the "BEIJING HUB OF TOUR DISPATCH," where I purchase a ticket for a bus trip to the Great Wall. I've eschewed both my hotel's foreigner-oriented coach tour and the option of spending a mint on a private taxi out there to experience it this way, the local Chinese way. But as I look around, I fear I may be the only one: the shabby bus depot is deserted in the early morning hours.

That soon changes as a bunch of local tourists come loping in. We board a newish white bus and are off before nine in the morning. The guide speaks only Chinese but two fellows sitting across from me help out—wouldn't you know it, they're a gay couple from California. Jimmy's Vietnamese by descent but a U.S. native; Stan's from China so he is anointed translator. Right next to me, meanwhile, is an initially quiet Chinese high school student going by the name of Silver, be-spectacled and stocky in a Michelin Man orange jacket.

"Computer programming?" he exclaims upon learning my profession. "I study that in school! Object-oriented design!"

It's probably too early to talk Java and C++ but somehow I get drawn into it once more.

"The Great Wall" is really many walls, a series of unconnected fortifications built at different eras and nowadays in various states of restoration and repair. The stretch at Badaling is the most touristed, but at this time of year it's the only one easily accessed. When we pull up we discover its normally carnival-like space quiet, the array of chintzy shops at the entrance shuttered. We climb the hill to the deserted battlements. We stroll through guard towers like sentries of the past guarding the Chinese empire from invaders to the north...that is, when we aren't freezing our asses off.

One thing helps with the cold: I always pictured the Great Wall as a gently undulating structure stretching across the hillsides. This is true, but what the photographs miss is the fact that the wall doesn't flatten out the contours of the terrain: when it goes up a steep hill, the battlements become a steep staircase. Ninety minutes of up and down makes for some serious calf-burning. So *that's* how the locals stay thin.

The crowds materialize toward the end of our walk where the touristier portions reassert themselves: there's a gondola from an adjacent valley running up to the hilltop. Another option is more appealing: I hop on an alpine slide running down a sinuous steel track. A couple of minutes of gentle exhilaration—I think this ride's more for kids—and I'm back where we started.

On the bus ride home, we drive through the portion of the wall where the Ming Dynasty was defeated in the 1600s, and the country was taken over by the last of the noble families, the Qing.

"It was a great barrier," Silver says, citing the oft-repeated mistake that you can see the thing from space. "But it also represent our mistakes."

"Really?" I'm intrigued by this bit of teen philosophizing.

"We close ourselves off from the world. We fall behind."

I consider those clocks back in the Forbidden City. No xeno-phobic anti-technologist here: Silver plans to study computer science in America after high school, then come back here and put his skills to good use in the burgeoning economy.

I'm anticipating a quiet night in preparation for a predawn flight the next day, but fate has other plans: a fetching blonde exchange student from Eastern Europe, whom I'd been fruitlessly messaging for the past days, pops online and suggests we meet up at a pre-New Year's party. *Oh, not another one.* I'm fearing another debacle, but something about this guy feels different. Two subway rides to the high-rise student ghetto in the northwest and I wait for Marius to show up. Lucky me, he's even cuter in person: lanky, slightly bookish, nattily attired in black coat, with thin aquiline nose and sweet smile. Half-Russian, half-Lithuanian, he's a poli-sci student at People's University. We hit it off right away.

We hop in a cab to a friend's apartment: Craig's a fiftysomething gay EFL (English as a Foreign Language) instructor. He's been here three years, hailing originally from Southern California. His two roommates are two cute, young Chinese boys.

"They're a couple," he says, "but nobody else knows."

On TV is the annual Chinese New Year special, this country's answer to Dick Clark's Rockin' Eve.

"Here. For good luck," one of the roommates says.

I'm handed some dough and ground pork. Dumpling-making is a New Year's ritual intended to bring good fortune.

"Here's how you do it." Craig, Marius, and the gang show me the ropes, folding soft dough over spiced meat. They're actually not too tough to assemble. Off to the kitchen to the deep fryer, and soon after it's a splendid late dinner. Marius and I use the opportunity to start holding hands—after washing them of dumpling goo, of course.

On TV, meanwhile, floats a colorful array of ethnic dances.

"They make it look like everything's hunky-dory between all the minorities," Craig says. "It's not true." He motions to his Chinese roomies. "But they don't care."

It gets noisier outside as people shoot off firecrackers in the street. I don't think much of it until Marius hauls me to the balcony shortly before midnight. As the clock strikes twelve, the city explodes: fire-works—the professional-looking kind, umbrella cascades of color—shoot off from everywhere. Up, down, all around our fifth-floor perch. It's dazzling, deafening, completely impromptu, utterly amazing. When no one's looking, I sneak Marius a kiss…and he reciprocates with equal passion.

Gung hay fat choy indeed.

We stay until two, talking politics, the world, America. Craig echoes my frustrations; it seems to be the recurring theme among expats I meet: they're far from home for a reason.

Time to go. We get in a cab. "Come with me," I whisper to Marius and he shrugs. Then his stop comes up.

"It's okay, you can keep going," he tells the driver. We drop off a couple of other friends then head back to the *hutong*. He seems hesitant at first, but only at first: this palatial four-poster bed gets put to good use. In the middle of it all, he looks into my eyes.

"You're a really nice guy."

I smile, but I'm really tearing up inside: my past conflicts some-times leave me wondering if I'm the coldhearted one, standing in judgment, pushing people away. But I know warmth and sincerity when I see it; here it is, lying next to me on our only night together in the fading crackle of New Year's in Beijing.

City on a Hill
Hong Kong

*Y**ou got big shoes to fill,* I muse at the high-rises of Hong Kong as I ride the MTR from the airport into the city. Shanghai was a wonder and Beijing a come-from-behind surprise. But I'm not worried; this city's reputation precedes it and I almost feel like I've been here already: prior to the 1997 handover, hundreds of thousands of Hong Kongers emigrated to Canada in fear of the Communist behemoth swallowing this bastion of Western capitalism. Instead, at least from what I've seen, the opposite happened: Hong Kong's free-market frenzy seems to have infected the mainland.

The streets of Tsim Sha Tsui, the waterfront district of Kowloon, immediately feel different: double-decker buses, vehicles driving on the left, and density...lots of density: this city is said to be the most skyscraper-laden of any on Earth. After Beijing's sprawl and Shanghai's colonial spread, it feels like a tin of sardines.

The next morning offers up a most unexpected challenge: it's holiday time and the multitude of laundry places—I suppose calling them "Chinese" would be redundant—are shuttered. Evading my hotel's pricey full-serve offerings, I sneak into the nearby YMCA and run a couple of loads there. Next door bask green Rolls Royces outside the Peninsula Hotel adjacent a waiting red Ferrari. The movie Rolodex again conjures up an association, a 007 film from decades ago.

Nightfall brings more New Year's spectacle: the fireworks display to be shot off over Hong Kong Harbor, a more officially sanctioned—

and, I imagine, even more impressive—spectacle than what greeted me in Beijing.

I wander the narrow side roads of Tsim Sha Tsui until I reach the waterfront, where crowds have begun to gather some three-quarters of an hour before blast-off. It's a mild, foggy night and the urban thicket of Hong Kong Island lies before us, brilliantly illuminated. I realize, however, that I'm rather far from the action and that my view will be partly obstructed, so I walk down the cordoned-off roadway to try to get a closer view.

I don't get far before I encounter barricades and police redirecting the flow of the crowds. My intended destination—where I was earlier in the day, in front of the Peninsula Hotel—is mere yards away. I duck around another narrow side street…only to find it blocked off too. I try another. Same deal. And another. Ditto. The police here seem to have thought of everything. I even try working my way through a block-long shopping mall…but its exit on the other end is likewise cordoned off.

"All full. Everything!" says a harried police officer. Meanwhile, I hear familiar thunder: the show's already begun. I race outside, but can't see a thing. I dart and dart and dart, finally reaching a main road near the waterfront; there I catch a smidge of color reflected in the glass of some tall buildings—the only bit of the show I manage to see.

Sometimes being a "maximizer" isn't so smart.

I reach my target area for the fireworks the next morning, this time to catch the fabled Star Ferry across the harbor. Unlike the night before, at this hour there's just me and a smattering of early-risers at this bit of waterfront, awaiting the battered, oval-shaped green-and-white boat groaning its way across the water.

After the unprepossessing blend of banal glass boxes and grimy cinderblock towers of Kowloon, I'm expecting Central, the downtown part of Hong Kong Island, to offer a positive contrast. A Manhattan to Tsim Sha Tsui's Newark. No such luck: aside from a few eye-catching edifices and cutely clanging double-decked trams plying the streets…well, Central is *ugly*. I've come to expect great world cities to

blend history and modernity in wondrous, furious synergy. There's
none of that here: just row upon row of blandness.

Okay, maybe uphill: the escalator to the Mid-Levels is a half-mile
series of covered moving steps rising 400 feet out of Central and into
the residential districts above. Victoria Peak dominates the landscape
of the island, and living on its slopes is much coveted. The escalator
provides a leisurely segue from downtown's bustle—significantly
muted this holiday morning—to trendy shopping streets and high-rise
apartment districts.

This is not any better. I cast my eye upon the Mid-Levels, an agglo-
meration of some of the ugliest high-end apartment blocks I've seen.
Unlike mainland China, which went into economic stasis during the
Communist era, Hong Kong kept growing…and growing…and
growing. Weedlike, I'd say, judging from these structures. No wonder
all those Hong Kongers found a new home and happiness in Toronto—which in spite of its size and sophistication has to be one of
the most architecturally flaccid big cities on Earth: they didn't have a
terribly comely urban benchmark to start with.

To get to the top of the Peak, another motorized conveyance: the
Peak Tram, a red-painted historic funicular. Now I see where all the
crowds, conspicuously absent most of the day, are hiding: it's almost
an hour's wait to get on. Once onboard, the chattering passengers
settle down to view the spectacle outside: a thicket of green
punctuated by the occasional building. At the top sits the misnamed
Peak Tower, a flying-wok-shaped contraption housing touristy shops,
cafés, and eateries. But the real draw is the view: that incredible vista of
cheek-by-jowl skyscrapers. The clouds have lifted and blue sky renders
the scene even more spectacular. *Of course.* These buildings look amazing as a collage, a cubist homage to urbanity. Up-close, however, they
give drabness a new meaning.

Escaping the crowds reveals the real splendor of this place: instead
of taking the crowded tram back I wander down side streets. Here
tourism gives way to natural splendor, urban grime to lush subtropical
hillside. There's really nothing quite like this back in America: mountainous, urban subtropical jungle. The most interesting topography lies
in the parched West while the verdant Florida tropics are flat as a
pancake. The quiet roadway feels like a jungle trek, until I reach an old

stone obelisk on which is carved, "City Boundary, 1903." I'm not ready to face city life just yet, so I duck into the splendid Zoological and Botanical Gardens and commune with birds, primates, and a cluster of Chinese banyan trees whose broad trunks and ropelike roots feel like something out of a fairy tale.

The train west, toward the gondola to the giant statue of the Buddha at Po Lin, is again crowded—but this time I'm not too worried: most of them alight at the transfer stop to Hong Kong's variant of Disneyland. But my relief is short-lived: when I reach my destination and round the bend of a shopping mall...*ugh*. More hordes waiting in line to see the Buddha. I stand in the slow-moving queue for almost an hour, then, realizing I'm barely halfway through, give up and go home.

I have better luck at the night market on Temple Street, an inviting array of gift, doodad, and electronics vendors. Part flea market, part Oriental bazaar, a wander down the narrow lane provides the perfect antidote to the endless queues. The tangle of people feels alluring rather than oppressive, and the food offers a pleasant respite: I sit on a painted wooden picnic table with a cluster of locals and muddle through an order of deep-fried spicy crab. It arrives soon after, drowning in hot chilies.

I've got barely enough time for a jaunt to Macau, the former Portuguese colony just across the Pearl River delta. The speedy, sleek jetfoil seems to compensate for clunky border formalities: as part of China's rigorous "one country, two systems," both Hong Kong and Macau continue to be treated as foreign nations, not only to the motherland and the rest of the world but to each other. Consequently, it's a passport-stamping, customs-and-immigration-resplendent episode to get on and off. One would think they'd take a lesson from Schengen-era Europe.

Macau is grand: it was one of the first European colonial possessions (dating back to the 1500s) and one of the last to be relinquished (in December, 1999, more than two years after Hong Kong itself). Although it possesses some of the same boring sky-rises and crumbling older apartment blocks, beyond them lies the historic quarter: here it's a pageant of curving streets, of gabled European façades, of mustards and ochres and cream-colored buildings climbing up hillsides. History at last!

I'm no gambler, so I give the new part of Macau a miss: two of its islands have been landfilled together to create Cotai, a Las Vegas Strip here on the Pearl River. Still, the town's kitsch calls for a nod so I stop in at the Grand Lisboa, a ludicrous, floral-shaped skyscraper done up in gold reflective windows. Yes, really. Inside is equally gaudy: thick pale-blue pillars, more gold, and modernist crystal chandeliers descending from the ceiling like rain. It's lunchtime, so I head upstairs and enjoy a club sandwich above the casino floor. I even sneak a photo before the ever-mindful security guard wags his finger.

The ride back is quieter: most people are still gambling or sightseeing but I've got a plane to catch. As with the previous day, skies have cleared by afternoon. The wind whips up spray outside the speeding ship's windows, streaking the scene like a Turner or Wyeth painting. My iPod, set to random, flips to the haunting rendition of "Mad World" from the film *Donnie Darko*. Forested peaks lurk behind blurry water as the jetfoil races back to its nest on the shores of the urban thicket.

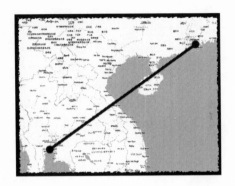

(The Other) City of Angels
Bangkok

Soaring over the Gulf of Tonkin, I'm a bit anxious—though not for a reprise of Vietnam War hostilities.

Another developing-world megacity. On the one hand, I'm dreaming up golden temples shimmering in the tropical heat, rivers and canals teeming with ferries and longtail boats...and on the other the memory of Cairo, Delhi, Jaipur—to say nothing of a recent viewing of *Brokedown Palace*. Additionally, Thailand is coming off a near-coup d'état a couple of months back when protesters shut down the airport—the very one I'm set to arrive at in an hour's time.

The protesters are long gone and Bangkok's Suvarnabhumi Airport is a spotless wonder of industrial concrete, steel, and glass—a worthy rival for the palaces of flight back in China. My cabbie is friendly and kind, and consults with my map—yes, they're of use here, unlike India—to find my little hotel. The inn itself is just right, a budget-boutique deal with modern minimalist lobby, cellblock-style corridors, and rooms whose air conditioning feels more like refrigeration after the humid outside. It is *hot*—at a mere thirteen degrees north of the Equator, Bangkok is the sultriest capital city on Earth. Lush greenery explodes into hotel breezeways as if eavesdropping on guests. And to think: barely a week ago my teeth were chattering in frigid Beijing.

I'm staying in Sathon, a short walk from the nightspots of Silom. Wandering outside for an exploratory nighttime stroll, I blink a few times to ensure I landed in the right place: those scuzzy byways of touts and fleabag hotels made infamous by *The Beach* and *Brokedown Palace* are nowhere apparent; instead, Sathon (both the name of the district and the main road) is a broad boulevard of speeding vehicles, leafy gardens, and modern high-rises—almost disappointingly a dead-ringer for Wilshire Boulevard or Collins Avenue back home.

Well, not exactly: Bangkok is a blend of broad thoroughfares and small, skinny alleys—*thanon* and *soi*. The former carry the city's hectic traffic but the latter are where life happens. Silom's crowded pavements are transformed into a lively night market underneath the concrete canopy of the Skytrain—yes, Bangkok, land of tuk-tuks and crushing traffic has jumped on the urban-rail bandwagon and boasts a fledgling system, both above- and below-ground. I cruise by Patpong, a couple of *soi* dedicated to sex shows. I'm not interested, of course, but simply need to verify that places advertising "Pussy eat banana!" really exist. Oh, yes they do.

Silom's other *soi* are gaytown: a raft of passageways about a hundred yards deep filled with nightspots of all kind. The most popular watering hole at this hour—it's approaching midnight, early in this town—is Telephone, though when I walk in I find the crowd on the older side for my tastes.

Actually, scratch that. There *are* younger guys, but I see the pattern: young paired with old, another young one paired with old, young/old, young/old…it's May/September romance central. Not an uncommon occurrence in both gay and straight worlds—to wit: Michael Douglas and Catherine Zeta-Jones—but here it feels like the only game in town. Predictably, many of the older fellows are Caucasian, the younger ones local.

I do see one younger fellow who isn't already spoken for, a tall, slim local boy with faux-hawk, chocolate-brown eyes, patterned sleeveless shirt, and Diesel jeans. His name's White and he invites me to meet his friends. It's tempting, but at this point my second wind is starting to expire; we trade numbers, a brief kiss, and a promise to meet up tomorrow.

For one (brief) night in Bangkok, things are looking up.

The Thai are compulsive snackers. Hence the presence of food carts everywhere: on major streets, lesser roadways, *soi*, even in front of restaurants. I'm more a three-squares-a-day type and am still unsure about street food, so a more conventional eatery is my first stop. Walking along Sathon I see, in the middle of the roadway between the speeding cars, stagnant brown water—so stagnant I'd mistaken it for concrete. It's a *khlong*, one of the city's many canals that have been swallowed up by the forces of change.

I reach the broad Chao Phraya River and find it's met a happier fate: the broad, muddy waterway is still very much a working river, lumbering ferries making way for zippy longtail boats. These are flat-bottomed skinny craft with upturned prows, powered by hulking car engines connected to long metal shafts sitting squatly in the stern. Their propellers churn river water like a giant hand blender mixing up a milkshake.

I hop on a canopied ferryboat north to Rattanakosin, the old historic part of the city. As we head up the curl in the waterway the modern high-rises of Sathon give way to more traditional river life: canopied wooden docks backing onto ramshackle, uneven structures; ever-more-colorful longtails bearing produce for the floating market upriver. The tapering stone tower of Wat Arun, the Temple of the Dawn, looms on the opposite bank.

For a harried Asian metropolis of twelve million, Bangkok is endowed richly with temples. Appropriate, perhaps, for a city whose ludicrously long ceremonial name begins with "City of Angels." The faith here is primarily Theravada Buddhism, a hodgepodge of Buddhist and Hindu practices that seems to lend itself to the grandiose: at the temple of Wat Pho lies an enormous Buddha in recline, over a hundred feet of dazzling gold arms, legs, body, capped by an inscrutably placid countenance. Intended to represent the Buddha at the final stage of life before attaining Nirvana, I half-expect Strauss' Zarathustra theme from *2001* to come on in the background. Instead, there's a gentle tinkling sound: behind the great statue is a row of copper-colored pots into which old women drop coins. Given my penchant for lie-flat seating I dub him "Business-Class Buddha."

The temple complex is equally impressive, jeweled spires rising like puffs of soft-serve ice cream into the hazy sky. Massages are offered—apparently this is where Thai-style massage began, and I suspect not of the same variety one sees in Patpong. I'm more captivated by expressive stone statuary, all flowing beards and dragon-head belts that feel distinctly Chinese. They are, in fact, and date back centuries. So too do the Chinese in this land, who have been migrating here for a millennium and were the forebears of present-day ethnic Thais.

The Thai have an odd relationship to their king—at least it seems weird to Westerners like myself accustomed to the slings and arrows hurled at our leaders. They *adore* the guy. Unconditionally. Through and through. Although Thailand is a constitutional monarchy, you'd think it was of the absolute variety: derogatory comments are anathema, prosecutable under *lèse majesté* if not met by the threat of violence at the hands of a local. Pictures of His Majesty are everywhere—adorning tiny shrines on major streets, in taxicabs, on billboards; often festooned in yellow, the color of the monarch's birth month. Attempts to look up more information on the guy on Wikipedia are met by a "PAGE BLOCKED" response while in this country. Apparently the adulation is deserved: King Bhumibol Adulyadej, Rama IX, has meddled in politics at the right times. I've read stories about his facilitating the country's rise out of military dictatorship, mediating between squabbling factions, and working to improve living standards. Normally, I would corroborate this with locals, but *lèse majesté* gives me pause.

Instead I visit the palace. Good thing I came appropriately attired—long pants required—as the kiosk that lets you borrow a pair was out...not that the prospect of wandering about the palace grounds wearing borrowed trousers was so appealing to begin with. The grounds are immaculate, carpetlike grass leading to Wat Phra Kaew, Temple of the Emerald Buddha. This one is a ramble of distinctive Thai rooflines, their tips angling upward with a flourish. One of its three towers is a huge conical bell, gold from base to tip.

All this buildup, yet the eponymous statue inside is a mere half-meter tall. And not even emerald but jade. It's got a solid Indiana

Jones pedigree, though: carved 2,000 years ago in India, it ended up in the hands of the Cambodian Khmer before the Thai snatched it several centuries ago. I find this saga more entrancing than the spectacle outside, where the faithful are bowing and praying. This could be Saint Peter's in the Vatican or the Western Wall in Jerusalem or a Cairene mosque; just replace the brand names. I should feel more reverent toward this display of faith, but once again I find myself unable.

Emerging back on the street, I come across Bangkok's backpacker palace, Khao San Road. It's a clusterfuck of garish signage, cheap hotels, girls having hair braided at outdoor stalls, even a full-sized tuk-tuk hanging self-referentially above an oversized road sign. All backpacker nationalities are represented: I see Israeli signage on a travel shop, and lingering for more than a moment out front I'm greeted in Hebrew by its shopkeepers.

I meet White that evening for a bit of late dinner before hooking up with his gang back at Telephone: Niran, a talkative pint-sized local and his *farang* (foreigner) boyfriend Philip, a teacher from Toronto. White is pretty subdued and, perhaps fittingly for his chosen English name, a bit bland once I get to know him. Niran is more forward.

"You like top or bottom?" he asks. The number-one gay sex question.

"Versatile," I reply.

"I'm a top," he says, beaming, then ogles a passing guy with an "*oil,*" an expression that sounds like a cross between an old Jewish man and a duck.

"He a rich boy," Niran says of his friend White, a Bangkok native. Niran's from the countryside, here in the big city to date Canadians and party with impunity. Not too different from back home.

We head to our next venue, the aptly named DJ Station. Here the Ecstasy tabs come out, and I find myself unprepared as I came with relatively limited cash and no ATM card. This means the rest of the gang blitzes through the night and I find myself running out of steam as we head to venue number three, the even more glitzy G.O.D.— Guys on Display. White's giving off mixed signals: on the one hand, he's aloof as a poker queen; on the other, whenever I suggest heading home he insists on just a bit longer. We take a taxi to one final spot—a hetero after-hours place housed in a former theatre—then finally I cajole him to come home as I'm about ready to fall flat on my face. On the ride back he keeps me lively with a bit of make-out. We doze for a spell after reaching my hotel room, then have the usual fun under the sheets while the sun rises behind the curtains.

It's midafternoon by the time we get up and go, this time for a ride on the Skytrain to Siam Square. Bangkok's multi-story shopping mall is glassy and modern—there's an Au Bon Pain, for Pete's sake—but White steers me away from all that to a section patronized by locals.

"This is better than street food," he offers. It's the same noodles and curry, but he's right: it looks a lot more appetizing. Predictably, my dish makes me lunge for water. *Hot! Hot!* White shakes his head as he samples my dish. "This is not spicy," he says.

"You want to try good street food, go to Chinatown," he offers, as we say goodbye and he heads home on the Skytrain.

I don't know what to make of this one. It all felt so businesslike, even though no money changed hands—I've never had to do *that*, thank goodness. But here again, the less-than-satisfying encounters only serve to highlight the richer ones. Maybe there's something to that: it signals that I'm *not* fit to become a professional nomad. That I will return home as I've more-or-less planned. That I'm somehow working through the parameters and limits of transience.

After dark I take White's advice and hop over to Chinatown, street-food central. Its garishly lit streets are choked with kiosks and paint-faded wooden tables stretching for blocks and blocks. In a reprise of Hong Kong I crowd onto a bench and eat with a gang of locals. As we dig into our noodles, randomness asserts itself in the form of a man leading a small elephant. The honking, hurrying tuk-tuks and cars miraculously avoid colliding with the beast, as if it were one of the angels for which the city is named.

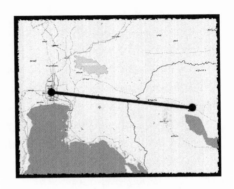

Dominion of the Khmer
Siem Reap & Angkor

*H*istory doesn't offer a ringing endorsement of Cambodia: when I hear the name I think of skulls—all those atrocities committed barely a generation ago by the Khmer Rouge. I consider Israel, Germany, and the Holocaust and wonder how a country with wounds so fresh can open itself to foreign tourists and still feel whole.

Siem Reap, the gateway to Angkor, the principal city of the Khmer Empire centuries ago, offers hope: driving in from the airport, new hotel construction is everywhere apparent. The former French colonial resort that once played host to Charlie Chaplin and Jackie Kennedy seems as determined as Shanghai to reclaim its luster. Happily, it remains affordable—even more so than Bangkok or mainland China—and warmly welcoming. As I settle in, the courteous staff at my little hotel suggests visiting Angkor now, in the fading light of afternoon when it's at its best. They hook me up with Wei, the driver of a "motodop," a rickshaw pulled by a motorbike. No scams or funny business here: it's all a standard price, fifteen dollars a day. The motodop is a delight: the smells, sights, and bustle of the place are up-close and personal instead of behind the glass of an air-conditioned car.

Rose-red Petra, Jerusalem's City of David, and Rajasthan's fort at Amber may have been impressive, but Angkor beats them all in sheer scale: sprawling over an area the size of the City of Los Angeles, at its peak in the 1200s it housed over a million souls—rivaling ancient Rome as the largest pre-industrial settlement in the world. Its best-known temple, Angkor Wat, is only the foremost of many ruins scattered around the jungle.

We turn left at the end of the main road, beyond which lies a perfectly even waterway dividing the jungle thicket: the square moat of Angkor Wat. At 600 feet it's wider than most rivers I've seen, its deep green waters looking surprisingly fresh. I cross the stone-paved causeway into the entrance gate where a mix of Cambodians and foreigners wander in and out. A skinny old woman with a walking stick, bell-shaped wide-brimmed hat on her head, and large plastic sack slung over her shoulder, hobbles past. Two young monks, barely out of their teens, pose for me. I hear a lot of French spoken. As with the Brits in India, it's interesting to watch the interaction between these tourists, descendents of local colonial masters, and their now-independent former subjects. Everyone gets along, eager to leave the past behind—especially if the visitors bring dollars or euros with them.

The passageways are lined with stone guardrails that terminate in a flourish, a shell-shaped serpent-headed form, a "talk to the hand" gesture. They're *naga*, mythical serpentine beasts that are among the many expressive creations here chiseled in stone. The Khmer were a creative lot, which perhaps explains why Hollywood has used this place more than once: as a location for *Lara Croft: Tomb Raider* and as inspiration for Disney's Jungle Cruise ride.

Cambodia's on an "anything goes" kick—at least when it come to tourism. While party-hearty Thailand cracks down on drugs and unsavory behaviors, in this country you can, apparently, fire an AK-47, hook up with a prostitute for three dollars, or sample weed-infused pizza. The first two choices aren't my thing, but the third one sounds promising, if unlikely: it's listed in a *Lonely Planet* guidebook.

The pizza place is humble enough, wood beams and tropical décor, typical banana-pancake-trail feel with smatterings of hippie Westerners seated at a half-dozen tables. I order my pizza "extra happy"—yes, this really is a selection on the menu, though it doesn't spell out exactly what that implies. As pizza goes, it's pretty tasty. I don't feel anything immediately though that's not atypical for cannabis consumed via the stomach. Ignoring the taxi touts I walk back past the elegantly lit Hotel de la Paix, down a more humble local shopping street, and across the river, its tall trees festooned with tiny white lights. I might be feeling something, but it's still too early to say.

It hits me harder as I return to the hotel, coming in ever-increasing waves as I read, watch a couple of videos on my netbook, and eventually pass out, still relatively early, in a happy herb haze.

I awaken at dawn. *Shitfaced.* I can barely stumble to the bathroom. Extra happy indeed...I call down to the front desk and ask them to tell Wei to come back at one in the afternoon; I simply *cannot* tromp through jungle temples in this state. It's almost as strong as the mushroom trip back in Amsterdam. I go with it, drifting in and out of sleep. Every couple of hours I try walking, but it's not until noon that I'm actually able to cross my smallish room in a straight line.

I apologize to Wei, telling him I was feeling a bit under the weather. He's all smiles, probably wise to what really went down. No problem, he says: he's taking a computer course and the morning off gave him some time to study. I still gladly pay him the day rate, of course.

Heading back to Angkor, the warm breeze out the motodop does me good. We pull into a parking area where a number of other drivers are sprawled out on their vehicles, slumbering in wait for their day hires. But no rest for Wei: he's brought a couple of books along.

I head up a long path enveloped by greenery. Every so often a child approaches, trying to sell bracelets or other souvenirs. Likewise I hear the call from vendors lining the path, wares neatly laid out on colorful blankets. Telltale signs that yes, this place is on the developing-world tourist trail just like the Giza pyramids or the forts of Rajasthan. And yet, if the tenor of hawkers reveals anything about national character...these people feel softer, kinder, less inclined to price unfairly or treat every "no thanks" as an opening to an unwelcome negotiation. The Khmer seem above that.

This in spite of their horribly bleak past, of which I'm reminded as I hear traditional music—haunting and twangy on stringed or percussive instruments—played by victims of land mines. Some are missing limbs, others cannot see. All are neatly dressed in white shirts, seated on low wooden risers on the dirt path. Cynical urbanites like myself are often hardened to this scene, yet the pathos does not feel exploitative or forced. I give them some money.

Finally I reach the ruins of Ta Prohm. This temple has been left by restorers in a state of carefully managed decay, an exemplar for all those books and TV shows about Life After People. Dozens of giant banyan trees have overgrown walls and buildings, their octopoid roots seemingly devouring manmade piles of stone. Creeping and corpuscular, the tree roots almost seem to move—or maybe that's just remnants of extra-happy pizza. Actually, my stoner trip is fortuitous: this part of Angkor gets busy in the morning, and now in the midafternoon I'm all alone with the stone walls and the trees.

Bayon, the mountainlike temple at the heart of the park, is the place to catch those enigmatic, blank-eyed smiling faces. They're so large they're made up of many stone pieces fitted together like a jigsaw. No one knows who exactly these faces represent: a king, fragments of the Buddha, or some other exalted figure. Like the "Mona Lisa", the countenances are at once soothing and inscrutable. And again, I thank my timing: I'm alone here with the great faces.

Okay, not quite: a young Cambodian in plaid shirt and thin strand of mustache pops out of a temple chamber and offers to show me around. He's sweet and disarming, typically Khmer. He doesn't tell me much I don't already know but I play along.

"Can you give me something for school?" he asks sweetly. *Sure, why not?*

"You're very handsome," he says provocatively. *Oh, geez. I'm being propositioned.* Too bad he's not my type, though I suspect even if he was I might have passed: recent romances leave me trending away from quickies. I bid him my thanks and move on.

Another night's sleep cures the lingering hangover and I manage an early start the next day. I explore some of the lesser sites in the fresh morning light, serendipitously happening across the most enchanting spot of all: the Terrace of the Leper King.

Although rumor has it one or more Khmer rulers may have had leprosy, I learn this site really is a tribute to the Hindu god Yama. Atop the pediment, a simple statue, enigmatically smiling like those Bayon faces, greets the dawn garbed in orange robes. The air is perfumed by incense sticks burning around the monument. But the most compelling sights lie below, in a mazelike complex of passageways thick with stone relief carvings. Blank-eyed, crowned figures stare downward; others, more expressive, dance bewitchingly or carry ancient weapons. The expressiveness of the faces, the melding of real and supernatural…it's every bit as articulate, as profound, as entrancing as anything by Donatello, da Vinci, or Michelangelo in the palaces and cathedrals of Europe.

The columns of a nearby temple culminate in a flourish, but it's not an abstract shape: this is the Terrace of the Elephants, and the caps of its pillars are in the form of pachyderm heads and ears. It's a good setup for my next adventure, which begins at the end of a queue ending on a wooden staircase nailed to a tree: here we tourists clamber aboard elephants for a ride around Bayon. The setup here is, consistent with Khmer hospitality, refreshingly straightforward. A standard price, elephants that seem happier in these moist tropics than they did in arid Rajasthan, and the subtlest of all suggestions for offering jockeys a tip: pockets at the back of their green jerseys. I try striking up a conversation with mine, but his polite nods and repetition of the same half-dozen English words suggests that's all he knows. I try French, thinking lingering colonial memory might help, but no luck there either. Instead, I enjoy the view high above the humans, donkeys, and motor vehicles; the SUV of the ancients. Judging by how much they eat and shit, similar issues with fuel economy and emissions.

I return to Angkor Wat for a look at its innards that I missed the other day. It began life in the Hindu faith, then was reconsecrated when the Khmer switched to Buddhism. One room, the Gallery of a Thousand Buddhas, is testament to this, though relatively few of the eponymous likenesses are around: they were destroyed by the Khmer Rouge in their bid to annihilate the past. Fortunately they stopped short of going all the way: psychotic and genocidal, Pol Pot's regime still placed a likeness of the iconic temple on their flag; a more ornate variant graces the present-day national standard.

Aside from its bulbous domes, the Wat's most distinctive feature lies along its perimeter: bas reliefs some six feet in height and hundreds of feet long depict Hindu epics and historical battles. It is said that all the atrocities of the Khmer Rouge can be found here, on these carvings of ancient savagery…but then, this could probably be said of most ancient civilizations; our reverence and nostalgia often obscures blood-drenched reality. Echoes of the Colosseum in Rome.

Driving back reveals modern realities: we pass rows of shanties on slender wooden stilts piled precariously above sickly green water. As with the townships of the Western Cape, these buildings are made of scraps and leftovers, wood and corrugated metal. *So here's where the other half lives.* And yet, though perhaps it's my bias toward these gentle people, it feels less squalid than Egypt's Memphis or India's Jaipur; I'm hopeful that as Cambodia continues to emerge onto the world stage, its inhabitants will see their lives improve.

Out for a meal after dark, I happen upon Siem Reap's bar street, filled with young backpackers. The elegant terraced blocks of buildings are perhaps the strongest moniker of the town's former colonial status I've seen. I chat with a British foursome seated next to me who've just arrived in town, full of energy.

"So what's fun around here?" they ask, and I tell them about Happy Herb Pizza. Just plan on some extra days if ordering it extra happy.

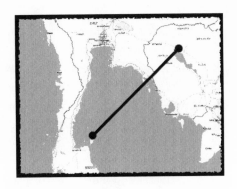

The Beach, Redux
Koh Phangan

"Hey, what's up?"

I look up from my in-flight magazine to see a slim, Dumbo-eared, redheaded teenage boy plop down next to me. More shy but equally affable is his dishwater-blonde girlfriend who finishes stowing her pack above. Chatty airplane seatmates can be a blessing or a curse, but the vibe I get from Taylor and Kaily seems positive. They're both from Vancouver, visiting Thailand for the first time; like me, they're headed to Koh Phangan, the backpacker-centric tropical island off Thailand's eastern coast that's become famous—perhaps too famous—for its rave-like Full Moon Party on the beach.

"We saved up most of last year to come here," they say, working as tree-planters in the British Columbia wilderness.

"So how're you liking it?" They seem so bubbly the question hardly seems necessary.

"We got sick in the north, up near Chiang Mai. We spent most of it in the hospital."

Ugh. Guess I should count my blessings. This hasn't happened to me yet, at least not really.

"Yeah, I've had a bit of the runs since coming here," I offer. That much is true. Bradley again pops into my mind: his up-and-down liver condition meant all manner of bathroom issues, prompting a whole new language of euphemisms.

"We called them 'heavy-flow days,'" I explain. "And when it all came out, 'emotionally satisfying.'" Bradley had some trips to the john that seemed to last hours. My seatmates seem amused.

We land in Koh Samui, the neighboring island whose airport has transformed it from backpacker haunt into haven for the package-tourist set. A fortyish German fellow shares a minivan with us: he's been here many times, and offers up jaded grins in response to Taylor and Kaily's cheery enthusiasm.

"We don't know where we're staying yet. Just gonna hit the beach and find a place."

German guy chortles. "I'm staying clear of Haad Rin," he says. The party beach. It's such a cliché: the giddy flourish of youth played against the world-weariness of age.

The ferry leaves from Big Buddha Pier, so named for a large golden statue that faces away from us as we chug out of the blue bay. It's an old white ship, blue trim, streaks of rust emanating from bolts in the hull. On board are piles of backpacks and their owners—all of them really, really young. None are particularly chatty and neither is Taylor, whose skinny frame hangs off the back of the boat, white T-shirt flapping in the breeze: he had trouble with his ATM card back at the pier and he's feeling frustrated. I can't say I blame him: I may be a generation older, but stuff like that throws me for a loop as well.

"Here." Kaily shows me a parasol she picked up at a nearby shop: brown rice paper, intricate calligraphy, and a wooden handle, it looks like a supersized version of the garnishes that come with fruity drinks.

We separate at the ferry dock on Koh Phangan, my teenaged pals off to find a place on the noisy party beach while I jump in a *songthaew*—pickup trucks whose rears have been fitted with wooden bench seats and a canvas roof—for the drive to my resort on Ban Tai. When I booked online they indicated it's barely ten minutes away, but the drive feels much longer. The *songthaew* bobs and weaves over winding mountain roads until reaching the long flat plain that sprawls over the island's southeast. Assorted shops and restaurants are scattered along the roadside, a bit more built up than Goa. Looks promising so far. My accommodations are in a cluster of bungalows run by a weathered, tan German fellow with pale hair and faint body odor. He takes my passport and asks for all remaining monies up front. This is not entirely unprecedented in Haad Rin at Full Moon Party time, but it's a first for me on this trip.

Then he shows me the bungalow: a spacious whitewashed structure with red-tiled roof, wrap-around balcony, air conditioning, and—wait for it—bona fide hot shower. It's easily triple the size of my digs in Palolem, and cheaper to boot.

I soon learn why: Ban Tai Beach is narrow, waveless, shallow, cluttered with seaweed. I want to spend no time on it, unable to swim in its waters without feeling like I'm in the world's biggest wading pool. The eateries and nightspots on the main road are equally flaccid: they have the feel of strip-mall establishments in some faded inner-ring suburb back home. Maywood, New Jersey with palm trees. One establishment, recommended by my hotelier, looks good at first: multilevel, dun-colored painted woods, a large bar at the center. Only no one's there at mealtime and the hostess is asleep when I call. Across the way it's a bit busier, but the food's so-so and the waitresses, garbed in tight-fitting short-shorts and halter tops, seem almost more interested in picking me up than in serving me dinner. One of them puts her arm around me and says, "You want massage?"

Haad Rin'll be different, I determinedly assert, climbing into a *songthaew* for another motion-sickness-inducing ride over the hills—*this* situation is going to need fixing tomorrow with some wheels of my own.

What's known as the Full Moon Party beach is in fact two strips of sand on opposite sides of a narrow peninsula. In between them lies a dense clot of narrow, concrete-paved shopping streets geared at the young foreigner crowd: Internet cafés; Israeli, Italian, and American eateries; travel agencies; bars and more bars and still more bars. Definitely not the sleepy place it once was. Still, unlike those authenticity-chasing purists, I'm not bothered: with the right entertainment and friendly crowd, this could do me fine.

I test the waters at a surprisingly good Mexican restaurant—Thai food merits a break this evening—where I sit at a corner two-top tapping away on my netbook. The foursome at the next table—American from their accents—ignores me until one of the group, a husky fellow in a baggy orange T-shirt, pipes up.

"Hey, you a *Lonely Planet* writer?"

"No," I reply, smiling. "Just working on my blog."

"*Oh*," he says, and turns away. Conversation ended. A waiter brings the brunette sitting diagonally across from him a chocolate dessert.

"Looks good," I say. She smiles weakly with that *why are you talking to me?* look in her eye.

Off to the beach, a furious press of bars and nightclubs blaring a cacophony of tunes. A crowd is gathered around a huge flaming jump rope; beefy muscular guys dodge the flames. It's Spring Break in Cancún, two months early and 10,000 miles away. People party in close-knit packs of threes and fours. No one mingles.

I find a vacant seat next to a fire twirler, a wiry muscular fellow spinning his flaming baton in front of a semicircular cluster of white plastic lawn chairs. I'm there for maybe ten seconds before some curly-haired frat-boy type approaches and points to his friends.

"Dude, this is my chair." Apologizing, I move to get up. He motions me to stay. "No, no, take your picture." Angling my camera, I sit back down—and tumble backward, sprawling onto the surf: one of Curly's female friends has territorially pulled back the seat.

"Oh, sorry," the girl says with a weak smile. At least they didn't laugh.

Then it hits. *I'm actually lonely*, here amid all these hundreds of people. This feels like the closing days of high school. The scene here is so big, the crowd so callow and so closed-off that I feel like a fool for having come to this place alone. From what I can tell, *no one* is here by themselves—and unlike in the gay scene, where lone wolves frequently are welcomed into the pack, no one's looking to meet anyone new. I head back early and dispirited. I can't believe I surrendered my passport and paid in advance for my lodgings: *I'm stuck here.* I was warned that this place had been overrun, lost its original charm. A part of me was curious to see what that meant. But nothing had prepared me for a reception this frosty.

Making lemonade out of lemons, I rent a motor scooter against the advice of my research: many an unscrupulous shop in these parts scrutinize for cosmetic damage to their equipment upon return, leading to exorbitant fees. I inspect the bike carefully before driving off. Looks okay.

In spite of its raver reputation, most of the island is quiet and unspoiled, a bramble of isolated beaches and rolling tropical hills. I cross the southwestern corner of the island to Thong Sala, its main built-up area before the kids took over Haad Rin on the other side. It's a conventional town with outposts of the British drugstore chain Boots and grocery chain Tesco. Relatively untouristed outside of its long concrete ferry pier and the odd *farang* eatery nearby.

I head north, up the western coast of the roughly square-shaped isle. Unlike Ban Tai—a miles-long stretch of charmless, skinny sand—most of the spots here are smallish crescent-shaped spurts of sugary-white. They're quiet, but hardly secluded: bungalow-style accommodations line every one. The demographic is completely different from Haad Rin, however: mostly older European vacationers, their otherwise-pale skin glowing copper or hot pink in the beating sun. It's pretty but not beautiful, not as much as Palolem: those incredible Thai beaches one sees in travel brochures, long stretches of iridescent white meeting waters of angel-blue, mostly are in Krabi and Koh Phi Phi, off Thailand's other coast.

Still, there are enchantments: off Mae Haad, the undulating bit of seafront at the very northwest tip of the island—diagonally opposite Haad Rin in both geography and mindset—lies Koh Ma. It's a hump-back-shaped island that at low tide is connected to the bigger island by a spit of sand. This time, unlike in Goa, it's not low tide, and I wade out on the submerged sandbar with a number of families—yes, actual *children*, a first after the unrelenting march of the eighteen-to-twenty-four demographic.

I'm still not feeling it. Maybe it's the sting of being alone after all those enriching connections in Goa, Tokyo, Shanghai, Beijing. Or perhaps because, as cliché suggests, the expected fails to offer uplift.

And then, as I turn inland, about to give up on the place, the transcendence I've been seeking at last emerges.

Literature and film are redolent with depictions of mountainous tropical islands; many travelers probably feel as if they've visited one already. I move off paved road and onto a brown earthen track...and it's glorious. Every bit and then some what I've been trained to expect. The rough road is equally a blessing: travel is often equated with movement—particularly for a speed junkie like me. But travel is also about slowing down, stopping to notice the splendor you've journeyed to experience. Here it is: thickly forested hillsides; animal creaks and squawks from all directions; two piles of coconuts—one bunch rough and brown, the other smooth and greenish-yellow—stacked beneath a parasol at a sleepy outdoor stand. Nearby is an elephant camp; used for jungle safaris, the beasts now stand idle like motorcars at a rest stop, trunks swinging rhythmically in the heat of day.

And then nature of a more prosaic variety calls. *Damn those runny bowels.* Thank heavens for small mercies, in this case a small shop across the way. Its owner, a sleepy-looking elderly man, points me to a dodgy little outhouse where I have my first encounter with an Asian-style squat toilet. No time to be choosy now. The relief of voiding myself trumps the minor discomfort of the deep-knee-bend position, and I find the nearby hose's stream of fresh water, used to tidy up afterward, to be more cleansing than toilet paper.

Ignoring all those "rough road" admonishments, I turn off the larger dirt thoroughfare onto a smaller one. This one is especially worthwhile, undulating through palm-fringed hills with numerous turnoffs: it's Than Sadet, a series of waterfalls running down to the sea. A short walk through the thicket reveals gentle cascades tumbling over coffee-colored rocks. A knot of other visitors is enjoying the place, lounging on rocks or swimming in the cool waters. They're young and not the friendliest either: one girl almost looks affronted when I ask her to snap a photo of me. Paradise beset by adolescence.

The waveless, shallow waters of Ban Tai may be unsuited for swimming, but I spy a sign at a local convenience store that reads "ONE2KITE: SAIL & JET-SKI." It's just down the way by a small pier bereft of the hordes at Spring Break Central. Unlike Dubai, the water here is bathwater-warm and I have the entire stretch of open sea to myself. I roar off, passing longtail fishing boats and larger, gaily-colored booze-cruise craft ferrying youths from Haad Rin. The island's mountain peaks rise dramatically, the busy fronds of palms by the shore giving way to broad-leaf vegetation climbing the slopes. Two islanders paddle a small rowboat laden with plump red fruit. I cut the engine several times, taking the sun or splashing in the cobalt sea. Suddenly solitude feels right, and the inviting calm of the tropics seeps into my soul at last. I keep the vibe going onshore in my hotel's pool, half of which is a wading-height section for partial—and lengthy—immersion as dusk turns the sky pink behind a cluster of palms.

I'm not expecting much for the climactic event, the Full Moon Party itself. Nevertheless, I've come all this way and it deserves at least a nod. After an early-evening nap I finish my primping and hear a hub-bub outside my window. Three *songthaews* are parked in the drive between my bungalows and an adjacent property. They're filling up with drunken youths, who when they see me call out—friendly for the first time—"Hey, you wanna come?"

Sure, why not? Two of the *songthaews* start to pull away and the last one is full too, but they're quite fine with me standing on the open rear of the thing.

"Dude, you're crazy!" In fact it's exhilarating: I can see everything on the road ahead, and these vehicles aren't moving fast enough for anything bad to happen. As we pull away, dancing waitresses at local nightspots cheer us on. En route, people in neighboring vehicles whoop at us and each other. It's festive, electric, and fun. Sitting in front of me are two seriously cute lads from Great Britain, sweaty in their striped button-down shirts, exuberant, their faces half-covered in body paint.

"We're from Saskatchewan!" cry out a gaggle of Canadians deeper in the vehicle. We pull into Haad Rin and the place feels transformed, festooned with bright neon signage with arrows pointing to "FULL MOON PARTY BEACH." Before we step out, however, the local authorities frisk us all: drugs. This once-narco-fueled event is nowa-days less so.

I'm actually alright with that for a change: normally I prefer the kick of stimulants to the barbiturate effect of alcohol, but I'd rather not deal with Thailand's harsh penalties and reputation for laced substances. My alcohol tolerance is pitiable, a cocktail or two equaling fifteen minutes of giddiness…then time for bed. This time, however, a combination of admittedly dubious health benefit does the trick: a (legal) Sudafed tab, then carefully controlled intake the rest of the evening from liter-sized buckets of vodka accompanied by Red Bull. These are labeled prominently at the many beachside vendors, "ME LOVE YOU LONGTIME."

The Full Moon Party is in fact many parties, a clutter of dance floors set up by the various bars, restaurants, and bungalows along the beach. The music's lively and fun, and I find myself getting a groove on in the sand while watching fire twirlers and scantily-clad youths of both genders. In the middle of one floor, a lone fiddler, white-shirted with shaved head, plays his own tune amid the din. A flaming sign behind dancing girls spells out "AMAZING THAILAND," and for the first time on this island, the pronouncement rings true.

What makes it sing, however, is the crowd: I don't know if it's the alcohol, or other still-available substances, or simply the aura of this event that began as a small gathering of intimate friends…but defenses and inhibitions melt away and people converse, chat, share, even make out—though none of that for me as this is a decidedly hetero affair. I run into the Saskatchewan clan and one of the pack, a beefy fellow, asks in earnest, "So, are you gay?"

He's not, of course, but takes pains to tell me he's cool with it. "We're getting body-painted," he adds, motioning me to come. I follow them to the body-painting booths, where middle-aged ladies paint colorful shapes on young skin. The paint glows amid the wash of black lights all over the beach. We Canadians get the flags of our country on our arms—except they've run out of red. My maple leaf glows orange.

I stay until dawn, watching the round orb of the moon give way to the pink and blue of early morning. As I board a *songthaew* back to Ban Tai, the dance stages are still full, raver kids bopping their slender bodies, silhouetted cutouts against the orange of the rising sun.

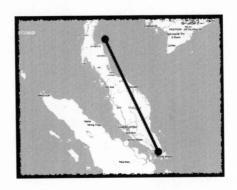

Beyond the Straitjacket
Singapore

T hey said I'd hate this place.

Oh sure, it's a big city, clean, well-run, all that…but random facts and figures mean little to the traveler if unaccompanied by other stuff: congeniality, geographic or architectural appeal, a sense of the unexpected, a love of fun. Singapore is supposed to be the *opposite* of all that, a place those seeking the extraordinary profess to despise.

I pledge to look deeper.

On arrival it could be Hong Kong: a modern, well-run airport, a subway into town (just reverse the letters: MTR versus MRT)…and, dispiritingly, the same bland, boxy high-rises out the train windows. *Uh-oh.* Are the detractors right?

Then I emerge from the subway in Chinatown, where I'll be staying. Cleaner than Hong Kong, to be sure…and more inviting, historic, the traffic even-tempered. Rows of restored shophouses line gently curving roads; my small, mildly elegant hotel is housed inside a couple of the remodeled old buildings.

"I've got a surprise for you," says the front-desk clerk shortly after he sets off my gaydar. He hands me the keys to an upgraded room, old-world furnishings and two queen-sized beds. Maybe he hopes I'll invite him up later, though he's not really my type.

If you put Copenhagen and Shanghai in a blender, I suppose the result would be Orchard Road: boxy malls, glossy high-rises, chain stores. *Where's the fascism, dammit?* I half-expected to see soldiers marching in the streets and police on every corner. Oh wait…there it is, more subtle than that: signage plastered on large, circular green tubs reads, "SINGAPORE: LITTER FREE," while every subway barks out in bold red lettering, "NO SMOKING: FINE $1000." For me, however, attempting a leisurely stroll from Orchard Road to the old city center runs me afoul of a more banal impediment.

It's really, really, really hot.

At one degree north of the Equator this has to be the most scorching, sticky place on my travels—sorry Bangkok, this town has you beat—and after a few short blocks I'm positively wilting. Salvation lies ahead: a palatial, cream-white domed colonial building—already a grander structure than anything I'd seen in congested Hong Kong. But never mind that: it's *air conditioned.* It's also the National Museum, an ideal spot to hide from the elements.

Predictably, the museum is pitch-perfect, with a cheerful introductory film montage leading into richly interactive exhibits re-telling the place's history. Factoids galore: a surprisingly new settlement—1819—established by the beavering Brits to rival the Dutch for control of the Straits of Malacca; attracted people from everywhere as it lies, well, at the crossroads of everywhere; world's largest container port, handling, among other things, one-quarter of the world's oil.

The reason—or is it excuse?—given in these exhibits for the country's crypto-authoritarianism is the challenge inherent in melding and integrating many different peoples at the tip of a continent not exactly known for harmony and peace. What's unexplained is why such heavy-handedness must also extend to all manner of recreational pursuits…though I suppose answering *that* question could fill another book and then some. This island is said to be devoid of fun; only recently has it begun to open up to the arts and nightlife. The Disembarkation Document, meanwhile, stapled into my passport, reads in bold red letters, "DEATH FOR DRUG TRAFFICKERS UNDER SINGAPORE LAW."

With these notions I test out the city's after-dark scene. The place is schizoid in its attitudes toward gays: grudgingly accepted in statements by government officials—but only recently, within the past decade; meanwhile, anti-sodomy laws remain on the books. It's no Tehran, but neither is it Berlin; Houston maybe?

Well, if nothing else, the action's close by: this is probably the only city in the world where the gay district is located in its Chinatown. Around the corner from my hotel lies Tantric: a large courtyard crowded with guys outside complements an equally buzzing scene inside— where I discover a space done up in colorful accents against velvety black. A couple of attractive blonde Norwegian guys catch my attention, but they're a couple and a bit shy. Their friend, Dharmesh, an Indian fellow, starts me talking.

"Oh!" he says about my thoughts on the near-nonexistence of gay life in his homeland. "It's not true. Delhi has many gay bars." *Now he tells me. Where were you two months ago?*

Meanwhile, a tipsy Chinese lad with cute triangular face, tinted hair and melt-in-your-mouth smile distracts—perhaps deliberately, judging by the number of times he bumps into me.

"Oh, sorry!" he laughs. We introduce ourselves. His name's Will.

"So are you from China originally?" I ask, and get a filthy look in exchange.

"No, not Chinese!" I look to Dharmesh: *what did I say?*

"Never ask a Singaporean their ethnic origin," he explains. "They're from *Singapore*, nowhere else."

Well, it probably wasn't much of a faux-pas judging by what comes next: Will drags us across the road to Taboo, another in my world tour of bar/club hybrids; this one's all black, red, and sequins, a fitting backdrop for dancing Asian boys both skinny and muscular. Will and I separate from the others on the matte black of the dance floor; this leads to some grinding and making out. There's a feel of surprise about it all: later we both discover neither had thought of the other as a sexual possibility, but in the heat of thumping disco beats it clicked into place. Sometimes it just happens that way, as does a most random sensation for me at one in the morning.

"I'm starving!" I say to him. "Is there anywhere we can go eat?"

Turns out he was thinking the same thing; he corrals his friend Yan, a darker, hunkier fellow in need of rescue: he's trying to evade an obnoxiously drunk Brit—muscles, pale skin, wifebeater top, whiskers, sketchy for a homo. We all trundle down the block to one of the city's "hawker centers," enclosed ramshackle food courts that seem the unlikeliest places for good eats. But appearances are deceiving: this is some of the best Chinese street food—or non-street food—I've had yet: silky fishball soup and aromatic steamed dumplings.

Yan manages to lose his drunken stalker but Will has different notions in mind: we head back to my oversized hotel room and put it to good use. The hotel clerk from last night is on duty, and he gives us a broad grin as we say goodnight and slide upstairs. As we head out of earshot, Will turns to me and says, "He *hate* me. I steal his man!"

I got me a talker. Just as much in bed as in public. Not just sex talk…I mean full-on *conversations.* In the middle of a pretty good blow job, he looks up at me, incredulous, and exclaims in Chinese-accented English:

"Oh! Yo' cock so *big*!"

I can't help it. I burst out laughing. It becomes our running joke for the weekend.

He may look eighteen, but Will's actually in his thirties, an art director at a local ad agency. He's got work to finish up this weekend so I let myself loose in the city once more. I've adapted a bit to the heat, though only a bit: upon exiting the air-conditioned interior for the sauna of the outdoors, my glasses immediately fog up. Nevertheless, I wander across the city's ho-hum CBD to its Colonial District, an elegant mishmash of low-rise masonry structures, immaculately restored and carefully marked: "VANGUARD BUILDING." "STAMFORD HOUSE." Stuffy and dictatorial maybe, but at least they know how to treat their old buildings. Take a lesson, Hong Kong.

The fairest maiden of them all, of course, is Raffles Hotel. It's a surprisingly diminutive affair—four stories at most—a triptych of colonial whitewash and red-tiled roof that seems ready to fold shut and swallow the parked Mercedes in the driveway. I walk in for a view of the splendid interior but am politely ushered out, Singapore-style, shunted to the shopping arcade around the corner. Here can be found the Long Bar, or at least a reconstruction of it, as the original was once in the main building. I have this place to thank for the tipples of my youth, as do many others put off by alcohol's harshness: it's where the Singapore Sling was invented.

The London Eye was too crowded—and too touristy—for my tastes back in the U.K., but its even larger cousin, the Singapore Flyer, is more tempting. I've long maintained that the Ferris wheel is the scariest ride at an amusement park, what with rickety seats swaying menacingly in the wind. The Prater in Vienna elevated this to relaxed adult-style entertainment, and nowadays cities are engaging in a mini-Olympics for "World's Largest Observation Wheel." This behemoth on the Singapore waterfront, the Flyer, is set to be upstaged later this year by—where else?—a competitor in Beijing. Perhaps it's to compensate for all those Chinese Singaporeans decrying their ethnic roots.

In any case, the ride on the Flyer is splendid, in an enclosed and—thank heavens—air-conditioned cylindrical glass-and-steel capsule straight off the USS Enterprise. Some forty stories tall, at the top we're eye-level with some CBD skyscrapers. But the real view is out in the water: through the equatorial haze, hundreds of ships sit offshore, an ant colony of oceangoing steel that rams home all those breathless shipping statistics. Economic strength embodied in a traffic jam at sea.

A final bit of fancy awaits me near my hotel in Chinatown: a red-ochre castle of a Buddhist shrine, the Temple of the Buddha Tooth Relic. Ostensibly one of Siddhartha's dental remains lies here, as do a few others scattered throughout Asia. The place is about to close, so I miss this Eastern variant on the Ark of the Covenant, contenting myself with the traditional-looking interior and soothing drum bells that usher us out. In spite of its traditional appearance, I learn the building only dates to 2002.

Will *must* like me, because he texts me throughout the day, then meets me for dinner at a pricey but forgettable Thai place around the corner. I'm feeling low-energy but he's having none of it, insisting we go out at least for a little bit. I agree, then after a couple of drinks realize my still-unlearned mistake when partying with a drinker: "A couple" is never enough; it only perks them up more. Will is flushed and raring to go.

"Why don't you stay out and meet me later at the hotel?" I offer.

"No. I come with you," he insists. His desire to drink and dance hasn't affected his interest in *that* activity.

This time it's not so swell, as his intra-coital conversations border on the bitchy:

"You don't like me," he says, more-or-less out of nowhere. Later in the evening, he's still wired and I'm ready to pass out.

"I make you sleep on the floor."

Okay, that's enough. "You need to stop," I say with some firmness. Surprisingly, he pays heed—and apologizes. The rest of the evening is nice, filled with the sort of conversation that usually only takes place after several dates. *Good.* This resumes my pattern of ever-more-intimate romances. It's also good to give back, as Will recounts developmental details about himself that could have been my life a bunch of years back.

"I not out to my parents," he says. This in spite of living with them, Italian mama's-boy style. I can't imagine being thirty-three with a flourishing career and still living a double life with my folks in a Singapore-sized apartment. *Kill me now.*

We head to Little India the next day, another downtown-adjacent shophouse district, this one busier and more hectic than Chinatown. Over lunch in a second-story restaurant of polychromatic buildings, we continue our conversation.

"So what about boyfriends?" I ask him.

"I single for ten years," he says. He fell for a guy early in his coming-out days, but the relationship flamed out and the fellow later married a girl.

"But I still love him," he says. Straitjacket indeed.

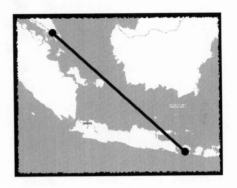

Heavenly Isle
Bali

"*T*axi? Taxi? Transport? Transport?"

Back in the developing world again, I muse, after hearing these cries in the ten seconds after I step out of my guesthouse in the beach city of Legian. A far cry from Singapore's voice-of-Lee-Kwan-Yew signage at taxi stands: "IT IS ILLEGAL FOR TAXI OPERATORS TO TOUT OR OVERCHARGE."

At least the guesthouse offers refuge: from the outside, a modest, low-rise affair; from the inside, a primly modern travertine courtyard whose centerpiece is a shallow pool straight out of *Architectural Digest*.

Legian is supposed to be the quieter cousin of the raucous Aussie-dominated beach town to its south, Kuta, but it and the more elegant Seminyak pretty much all look the same: alleylike streets flanked with small hotels, arts-and-crafts stores, and moneychangers offering a better rate than the official exchange. Outside pint-sized temples lie intricately woven banana leaves filled with floral accents: offerings. Bali literally is a Hindu island in the Muslim Indonesian archipelago. Perhaps for that reason, its people practice its faith with a flourish—though, I'm happy to learn, with an easygoing flourish. Apparently they're pretty sexually liberated too: a smattering of gay bars and clubs dot the landscape in Legian, and here and there I see the odd older gay couple strolling the streets and beaches.

For me, this island's pleasures are more elemental, especially since I did enough partying at my last stop. Double Six Beach offers, for the first time on this trip, an ocean with bona fide *waves*. Not the measly two-foot curls of the Med or the Bay of Bengal: these roll and tumble and break and send me a hundred feet back to shore. It's the surfing that brought people here, starting with American beach-hut pioneers Robert Koke and Louise Garret in the 1930s. Now this part of the island is tourist central, and catering to holidaymakers has upstaged agriculture as Bali's biggest industry.

The results of that are mixed: bodysurfing the big waves is grand, but the ocean isn't that clean, bits of plastic hurrying past on the big breakers. Onshore, it's tough to relax as vendors make the rounds from person to person offering myriad cheap trinkets. Seeking quiet I walk north, to Pura Petitenget, one of the island's many sea temples. Intricately carved wooden doors painted in red and gold leaf open to an elaborate stone edifice, an overgrown sandcastle just steps from palms and sand. But it's the statues that do it: fabulously expressive stone carvings of beasts, demons—and Ganesh, my favorite elephant-headed hero, remover of obstacles.

A spot of dinner and a quiet walk through the *gangs*, the diminutive back alleyways of Kuta near the ocean. There's little crime here, but other temptations instead: two ladies on a motorbike drive up. With a completely straight face one of them delivers the line, "Suckee suckee two hundred rupiah!"

Again difficulty believing I'm gay. *Do I need a sign?* Finally she relents, though the incident almost spurs me to purchase, shaman-like, one of those carved wooden penises for sale at a boutique around the corner to brandish in the faces of future come-ons.

With this on the brain I give Ryan back home a Skype call. He's been incommunicado for some time, and I've been left wondering if my previous rant about traveling Yankees didn't sit so well. *Do I tell him about my hookups?* Hell no: before I left we had an open-relationship with full-disclosure clause, but he made clear he doesn't want to know what goes on out here around the world. Oddly enough, my recent mini-romances have made me hanker for him more. I'm still unsure if I'm the monogamous kind—"like pigeons or Catholics," Woody Allen once quipped—but I know a good thing when I see one; he's a goodhearted fellow with his head screwed on right, which might be the ideal thing to pursue once back home.

He sounds a little shaky, but it's not for want of hearing from me.

"I had food poisoning," he says.

"You mean I'm the one in Thailand and Indonesia and *you're* the one getting the shits?"

Ha ha, he responds. Happily, he's doing better.

"I went away over the holidays." *That explains the radio silence.* Months later I'd learn he'd gone to visit his ex in Boston, to see if anything remained between them (answer: no). I don't know that yet, but my spider sense suspects something.

"So," I begin, a bit nervously, "I don't know what's going to happen when I get back...but I kinda was wondering if you've moved on."

A long pause. I can almost see him smile on the other end.

"I'm still single."

Well *that's* a good sign. Overall, he sounds more pleased to hear from me than he has in a while. We chat about more life details and travel minutiae, but the conversation has served its purpose. It's almost two months before I'm slated to return to San Francisco, and now there's something tangible drawing me back.

It's a reprise of past visits to driver-recommended locales: Nyoman, the fellow who'd picked me up from the airport, fetches me the next morning. Youngish, coffee-colored skin, laidback as a hammock—is there any other kind in these parts? He's set to drive me to Ubud, my next stop, but recommends we go there via a meandering trek around the island. Sounds appealing and the price is right, so no objection from me.

We head north through Denpasar, the island's principal city, though you'd barely know it from passing through: a moderate build-up of two-story shops and homes and slightly heavier scooter traffic is all that separates city from country. The scene quickly turns bucolic once more. We stop at a famed postcard spot—it's on the cover of my guidebook—a steep hillside stairstepped by rice terraces. Their fringes are a riot of green bordering the murky flooding of the paddies themselves. Palm trees poke up on the hillside, then erupt in a mess of forestry at the crest of the hill. Nyoman tells me that the Balinese name for their home translates into "heavenly island." This vista gives the nomenclature the ring of truth.

But only for a moment: soon the cavalcade of sellers descends; they have this spot staked out. One woman sells brightly hued, patterned sarongs for something like four dollars. I buy one, prompting a rash of others to congregate around me in a feeding frenzy. It's an almost embarrassing spectacle. Fending them off, I get back in the car and we continue on our way. I ask Nyoman if this is par for the course and he shrugs. *Yes.*

We head higher into the hills, somewhere to put my sarong to good use. Nyoman fastens it on me with a yellow sash and I feel like I'm wearing Hindu drag. Thus attired, I head through the towering split gate of the Tirta Empul temple, 1,000 years old. In the middle of the grounds lies the main attraction: a large pool, stone-lined, ornately fountained spouts pouring water onto the heads of bathers. Most are Balinese, though a few hippie Westerners are in the water as well. It's said to be sacred, the spring that feeds this long watercourse.

"Created by the god Indra," says Nyoman. There are carved statues bearing incredibly expressive faces, Ganesh once more, and thick schools of fat orange koi in an adjacent pool no longer used by human bathers. The grounds are serene, the green of the surrounding foliage echoed in the mossy, blackened stone carvings. Less serene is the parking area: a row of untidy stalls hawking cheesy souvenirs. It may be the Heavenly Isle but the temple of commerce is never far away.

I'm thus skeptical when Nyoman suggests a stop at a coffee plantation. *Great*—another place where he'll get a commission and I'll have to endure high-pressure sales over beans of arabica. But he tells me a bit more, and I sense it might be different: he knows the owners, and they make a very unique kind of coffee.

Entering the plantation, we come across bushy trees bearing chunky, tapered, burgundy seedpods. These aren't coffee beans but rather my One True God—cacao. I've never seen them growing on trees before, their shiny, mottled, burgundy-colored surfaces offering no hint of the delicacy they will become.

The main plantation compound is just a series of wood huts. A couple of young ladies greet us with warm smiles. A toothless old man sits cross-legged on the ground, stirring some beans roasting in a clay pot. Frenetic brown skunk-sized rodents pace nervously in wire cages: civets.

"For Kopi Luwak," they explain, the super-pricey coffee popularized in the Morgan Freeman-Jack Nicholson picture *The Bucket List*. I'm intrigued: what do these critters have to do with coffee-making?

"Civet eat the beans. It pass through their stomach, taking away bitterness. Then they come out and from that we make the coffee!"

It's supposed to be sinuous and delicate, but the prospect of drinking something manufactured from the anal excretions of another creature is a bit more than I can handle. Instead I browse their shop; they're so low-pressure about me buying anything that I do it almost on principle—not that purchasing their bricks of chocolate takes much cajoling.

Higher and higher into the mountains. Nyoman's got the car radio tuned to some contemporary station; the lush greenery of the Balinese highlands offset by the raunchy tunes of Simple Plan. We pass an old woman balancing a cord of wood on her head. It begins to rain, but this deters no one: I see a scooter rider heavily laden with parcels covered in clear-plastic sheeting. He almost looks like another parcel himself but for his beige rain slicker and round white helmet keeping out the pounding drops. The skies clear as we round the bend—and come upon a broad gorge ringing the towering black cone of the Gunung Batur volcano.

"Many volcanoes in Indonesia," Nyoman says, "more than any other country." Bali alone contains three, and this one, its caldera perfectly formed, encircles the island's biggest lake. Rain clouds ominously hang at its fringes. Finally the skies open up again, just as we reach a lunch spot with a view of green expanse tumbling into volcanic valley.

"Are you married?" I ask Nyoman. For once it's *me* asking the question. Surprisingly, he isn't. Okay, time to try the atheist query. I get the same befuddled response as my friends in India got from their Sikh driver: "No, everyone has religion," he says. For emphasis, we visit one more holy site, Goa Gajah, the Temple of the Elephant Cave.

It's also 1,000 years old, but was lost to the forest until modern times. A huge ruined statue of the Buddha lies in a gully while a misty thin strand of waterfall tumbles into a stream below. This temple is a mix of Buddhist and Hindu, and as the name suggests, devoted partly to Ganesh: a yawning stone opening evoking a monster in a children's book leads to a small, dark cavern where various elephant-head statues lie. Outside, by the gnarled roots of a banyan tree sits an old man, hands together in a meditative state. Religion may not be my thing but there's something elemental, mystical almost, in this place. Heavenly Isle indeed.

My previous accommodations were stellar, but this one—the improbably named Honeymoon Guesthouse in Ubud—leapfrogs beyond: palatial Balinese décor, rose petals on the bed, intricately carved red-and-gold doors not only to the outside but into the bathroom as well. It also snatches the crown for Most Fabulous Place to Perform Ablutions: a gargantuan shower, Jacuzzi-style tub flanked by plants, glass blocks casting soft, Vermeer-like natural light, designer copper sink. All for the price of a Motel 6 back home. I wonder if the name scares away the unsuspecting, fearing a tacky retreat out of Niagara Falls. Interestingly, I see no couples the entire time I'm here.

Ubud, the island's cultural haven in the hills, is only slightly less overrun by tourists than the towns on the coast—at least if the number of cries for "taxi" are any barometer. I ignore these and hoof it a mile or so to the Sacred Monkey Forest. Inside its gates lies tropical splendor, densely wooded thicket, a temple, mossy stone carvings, and Tarzan-esque liana vines. Bali lies at the edge of the Wallace Line—the vegetative divide between the flora of Asia and those of Australia and New Zealand. One small statue coated in bright green moss breaks the majesty: it's a stone monkey covering his eyes while stroking his outsized and very human-looking erect penis.

The real monkeys—long-tailed macaques, actually—are engaged in more family-friendly pursuits. Supposedly aggressive, they're on their best behavior when I visit, sitting in clusters, swinging through trees, their too-cute young playing games of tag. One elder ruminates like Rodin's Thinker, smoothly matted fur surrounding a remarkably humanoid countenance of pink. Below him, a small creek wends its way through the thicket. As with the Elephant Cave temple the other day, I'm overcome with wonder. *Do places like this really exist?*

Culture beckons: after dark I attend a performance of the Kecak. A cluster of men, thirty or so, sit in a semicircle wearing black-and-white striped sarongs. Over an hour-and-a-half of clicks, chirps and animated arm-waving they re-create a fragment of the Hindu Ramayana. Colorfully attired female dancers in gold headdresses, a masked king, a white-costumed monkey spirit...all participate in this interpretive bit of theatre. It feels like a surreal, tribal blend of *Beowulf*, Snow White, and *A Midsummer Nights Dream*. I leave more befuddled than when I arrived.

I walk back flanked by three European backpacker gals—two Brits and an Austrian. We stop for dinner nearby, sharing the requisite where-are-you-from-where-have-you-been-where-are-you-going chat. It's the first bit of company I've had in awhile, and it's pleasant.

More of that takes place the following morning: I wander the lush grounds of my lodgings and happen upon a kidney-shaped pool. Two more Europeans—a fetching female from Amsterdam by way of Morocco and a cute German fellow—sit talking in lounge chairs. They seem to be hitting it off. I don't want to be a cock-blocker but they don't seem to mind. Sofia, the Amsterdamer, delivers a surprising bit of news.

"They've banned mushrooms again."

Oh, say it ain't so...this made up a key part of my journey there. Apparently, she tells me, some French tourist, high on more than just psilocybin, jumped in a canal and drowned. The ruling conservative party—for Holland—now in power seized upon the opportunity.

"We'll see how long it lasts," she offers.

Talk shifts to Australia, my next stop, and a heavyset woman who hails from there chimes in. Hunched in a nearby lounger over a hardcover bestseller, she bears the demeanor of an old man trying to throw errant kids off his lawn.

"I *never* travel in Australia," she proclaims. "What's the point?"

We move on to what we agree is the bane of our travels in the developing world: touting, scams, rampant tourist commerce.

"I think for my next trip I want to go to places where that doesn't exist," I say. I've begun to grow weary of the beaten path.

"Well what do you *expect* if you travel in poor countries?" weighs in Aussie grouch. Sofia disagrees: there are places still untainted, she offers—though like undiscovered restaurants, it's a chore to dig them up before the hordes do. Down Under sniffs and returns to her book.

I've still got the whole day before an overnight flight, so I wander Ubud aimlessly, leaving Janosch and Sofia to continue whatever they've begun. Temples, temples…Ubud is thick with them like flies on a carcass. The Lotus Temple offers, predictably, two stone pools choked with lily pads with the occasional lotus flower poking through black waters. A gold-leafed cornice on the pyramidal stone has at its center a golden swastika. Although it's of the Hindu variety, inverted and not angled like the Nazi variant, it's still a bit jarring to a Westerner, a Jew. The place is empty, aside from a few local laborers setting up for the evening's dance performance.

Rice terraces surround Ubud, though they slope far more modestly than the better-known hillsides from the other day. Nevertheless, a long walk through these is rewarding: I'm the only visitor around, and old paddy farmers male and female offer friendly waves as they go about their afternoon work. The fields are long and broad, stretching for thousands of feet before terminating in tropical thicket.

It's dusk when I return, fading bits of orange sky silhouetting palms and thicket. *My last sunset in Asia.* Sofia lets me use her shower— she and Janosch are sitting in shorts and tees on his terrace; looks like *they've* had a splendid afternoon. Nyoman's coming soon, to drive me back to the airport and new possibilities on the other side of the Wallace Line.

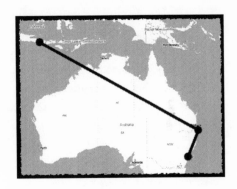

Over the Rainbow
Nimbin, Byron Bay & Sydney

B *oy, this flight sucks.*
I've long since blown my wad, as it were, of Princess Class frequent flyer awards, and now it's back to steerage. I haven't become *so* spoiled as to spurn discount flying altogether, but this outing on JetStar, the Aussie low-fare carrier, is another matter. A too-small plane packed to the gills with a surly lot of Australians heading home, serviced by equally supercilious flight crew: on one leg they refuse to provide me with water when I step onboard.

"We'll be selling it later."

For reasons equally baffling, the flight makes a middle-of-the-night stop in Darwin, where we sit in the small terminal in the tropical darkness for two hours. Meanwhile, my back experiences the effects of that morning by the pool in Ubud, where I'd unwisely forgotten to don sunscreen: it's red and sunburned, and at the airport in Denpasar I'm able to find lots of useless aromatherapy products but no honest-to-goodness aloe Vera. I settle for Tiger Balm, and its tingly heating effects do the trick, though I'm not sure if my fellow passengers appreciate me odorizing the cabin with the balm's minty essence.

At long last, arrival in Brisbane. Well, not quite: since this is once more the First World, I'm set to rent a car…and so, it seems, is half the airport. Two hours later, I'm headed south, on the left side of the road through the coastal hillsides of extreme northern New South Wales. First stop: Nimbin.

Where?

My Sydneysider seatmate Sarah on that delayed flight back in the Middle East talked it up. Nestled between fecund rolling hills with only a hint of crag—more Appalachia than Sierra Nevada—Nimbin's an old dairy farming town that's taken off with the backpacker set thanks to some rather different agriculture. From Wikitravel's "Eat" section: "Best cookies are from the older lady on the 'BringaBong' side of the street..."

With appeal to hippie travelers, the town's accommodations are concomitantly rustic. My shiny Nissan rent-a-car looks out of place as I rumble up a dirt road, cross a small wooden bridge over a stream— longhaired youths bathing within—and reach my hostel. No one's around in the main office when I show up; in the courtyard between the cluster of low wooden buildings, an array of young folk watch TV in the glassed-in common room. Finally the manager of the place— dirty blue T-shirt and dreadlocks—spies me and motions to the office. He puts me in a respectable room with a queen bed—though it's the first spot since Moscow with a shared bathroom. Oh, and no Internet or mobile phone reception. Outside, lounging on a picnic table overlooking a valley is a friendly pair who helps steer me toward the town's best-known commodity.

"You're probably too liyte," says the long-haired fellow in laidback Aussie English. "They mostly sell in the mornings. But you can still try."

I'm sunburned, haven't showered in thirty-six hours, just got off a 2,500 mile cramped overnight flight and completed a two-hour drive...and my first order of business is scoring weed. Priorities.

Having hosted a Woodstock-like festival in the early seventies, Nimbin remains Oz's counterculture hotspot. Although cannabis is no more legal in New South Wales than it is back home, authorities look the other way—more or less—on the trade in this town. Oh, I mean *literally* look the other way: the police station is barely a hundred yards from the rainbow-colored shopfronts on the main drag.

As promised, the street's pretty quiet, though there are a few scraggly looking Aborigines—the country's silent minority—yam- mering away under the awning of a closed-up storefront. I'm not the only one who thinks this is a good place to start: a weathered-looking beefy fellow with muddy hands is walking in the same direction.

"Just got off wohk at the fahm," he says to one of the fellows. "What you got?"

"Sit down, sit down," the dark-skinned Aborigine motions to us. "What's your hurry?" Pot dealers the world over operate at a different pace. Farm boy and I sit on the concrete pavement as dealer dude pulls out a small bag of weed, divides it in two, and charges us each twenty Aussie dollars. The exchange rate—for once, the U.S. dollar is in my favor—makes it a good deal. One shower and pizza later, and I settle in for a mellow evening of cannabis and rest amid the bleating nocturnal wildlife of the east Australian bush.

For a hippie hostel, it's not too social: breakfast sees everyone wordlessly prepare their food. I head back to town—a lot livelier now with several older gentlemen offering to sell me additional herb. I check out the Nimbin Museum, a storefront-sized collection of rooms, dark and cluttered. Predictably scattershot, it's festooned with posters and memorabilia from alterna-fests—from this town's annual "Mardi Grass" to its Aquarius Festival all those years ago. On the poster promoting this year's event: U.S. President Barack Obama, with the quotation: "I inhaled frequently—that was the point."

The drive back to the coast is glorious, but for me it's a bit anticlimactic: Australia's flora is unique, but feels downright pedestrian after all those rice terraces, coffee plantations, banyans, and liana vines.

Nevertheless, Byron Bay pulls off "beach town" better than anywhere I've been—and beach towns are my specialty—managing an unlikely blend of upscale and downscale just right: surfers and backpackers commingle with the odd BMW.

And the ocean! Just as the climate in Nice or Santa Barbara is an ethereal blend of cool and warm, so here the water: smooth, large rolling waves like curls of ice cream off a scoop; blue, clean, and uncrowded waters; a just-right surf temperature—for me, at least—approaching the mid-twenties Celsius. This is the eighth beach I've visited in my six months on the road, and it's the Goldilocks one.

Ditto my bed & breakfast, a cheerful, converted home of pale-blue siding enveloped by a tangle of greenery. This is one place where a shared bathroom isn't a liability: it's across a high-ceilinged wooden hallway, spotless, its only other users two polite Japanese ladies in an adjacent room. Anny, the owner of the place, shows up later that day. A slim, fair-skinned lady approaching middle age, she offers a hand-drawn map with see-and-do recommendations of the town. Hand-painted crafts and wall hangings suggest she's either well-traveled or well-shopped; happily it's the former: Mexico is her passion.

"You live in California and are going around the world and have never been to Mexico?" she laughs. Swapping traveler's tales, we corroborate: JetStar is indeed awful ("I think Qantas started them just to encourage people to avoid low-fare airlines," she offers), and *Lonely Planet* isn't what it once was ("They sometimes read like a Chamber of Commerce advert.").

But never mind all that. Once she learns I'm in computer software, out it comes.

"Can you help me with my Internet connection?"

Byron Bay—named by Captain Cook himself for the Romantic poet—is home to a geographic extreme. This intrigues me as the last such spot, back in South Africa, offered enough romance-inducing vistas to keep Lord Byron busy for several lifetimes. Cape Byron lies on a coastal bluff a short drive from town. Its walking track ambles over green rolling hills. Scenes of beach and blue water—a deeper blue than Cape Point in South Africa—pop in and out of view as I come upon the Cape Byron lighthouse. Still very much in operation—unlike its too-high Cape Point cousin—it's a handsome pillar of white flanked by two Mediterranean-style clay-tile-roofed outbuildings. The lighthouse straddles a rocky hillock where signage—interestingly, in the same earthy brown style as in Cape Point—denotes, "THE MOST EASTERLY POINT OF THE AUSTRALIAN MAINLAND."

The walk down the cliffs is equally beguiling, culminating in a couple of isolated scoop-shaped beaches. A team of sea kayakers is just arriving, all helmets and swimwear and day-glow orange boats. Nearby, someone's piled a series of small stones in a perfect column, Wicca-like, beside the crashing surf.

Just then my cell phone rings, interrupting the reverie. Though the voice on the other end couldn't be more welcome: it's Miri, my youngest sister in Los Angeles. Although she's more than 7,000 miles across the sea and almost a day behind, if you ignore the Date Line the time difference is only a scant few hours.

"I don't know if I'm ready to come home yet," I say. Looking out at the familiar Pacific surf, I'm starting to wonder what else awaits me besides Ryan the fetching swim coach.

"I hear ya," she says. She knows the Bradley/Steve story all too well, and like me is unsure what's going to play out upon my return. Interestingly, she's had a rocky year of her own, coping with a traumatic divorce and lingering immigration uncertainty.

"Maybe somebody up there's trying to tell us something," she offers, given our respective rocky recent pasts. *I wonder.* I may be bereft of religiosity—and I'm mostly out of touch with the economic turmoil back home—but part of me looks on the circumstances that precipitated this voyage and wonders whether I want to face all that music once more.

It's gloomy as my flight makes its final approach into Sydney—though the clouds look to be hurrying away, revealing the skyscrapers of the city's CBD, cubistic in their non-grid misalignment. On the ground we park next to a Singapore Airlines A380; my first peek at the world's largest airliner. Although I'm awed by the technical achievement of the fully two-story plane, its appearance is uninspiring: it's too squat, its cockpit so low it makes the thing seem hunchbacked. *Oh, but imagine First Class!* I fantasize about that private-suite bed I've only glimpsed in photos.

A cab ride into town lands me at Sullivan's Hotel, an austere white box of a building, one of those charmless mid-rise 1960s affairs where the addition of frosted-glass balconies and a sleek, curving blonde-wood front desk qualifies it as "budget boutique."

I have just enough time to freshen up, however, in advance of my big night on the town. First stop: one of the "Hotels" on lively Oxford

Street, two-story establishments with dark-wood pub seating and strong drinks.

"Hi!" It's all hugs and kisses and a joyful reunion with two gals collected during my travels to date: Whitney, one of the Canucks from Goa who's here in Sydney to meet her California boyfriend; and Sarah, my seatmate from that delayed flight out of Tel Aviv. If this isn't proof positive that solo travel need not be lonely, I don't know what is.

"I rode horses in Petra and fell head over heels with the man who taught me," Sarah says. *Hey, at least someone got lucky in the Middle East.* Looks like the same is holding true in Palolem.

"Sam's still there," Whitney says of her other friend. "She met somebody." I guess that might compensate for the lack of air-con over three months.

"*Please* tell me it wasn't that Larry character," I say. It wasn't. *That's a relief.* Guys like him don't need further encouragement.

The gals head home after a couple of drinks—it's a work night for Sarah, and Whitney's in prep mode for the boyfriend's arrival the next morning. For me, however, the evening's just getting started: this is Mardi Gras week in Sydney. Taking place around the same time as its New Orleans counterpart—and Carnaval in Rio—this one's the city's Gay Pride. The main event's still a few nights off but the bars in Darlinghurst, the city's rainbow district, fill up as the night deepens. I start at the Stonewall Inn, much larger and more glam than its New York counterpart, and—surprise—another bar/club hybrid.

Things here move fast: a boy of medium build, slight stoop, curly hair in a blonde dye-job, begins eyeing me, smiling. *I know that look.* A dash nerdy like my first fling back in Dublin, and the coincidence is more than skin deep: his name's Michael and he too is a "uni" (college) student. Making out ensues, as does a trip back to Sullivan's, where he stays the night.

He's really nice, but it hits me as he heads out the door the next morning: *something's missing.* He's a down-to-earth kid going through his "slutty" phase. (Which for me has lasted far too long. Oh well.) But here again, the grander romances underscore what's lacking in the lesser ones. *I know, I know,* you can't meet the love of your life at a club. Or thus goes the received opinion. Then again, that's where

Bradley and I met—and in spite of everything that went down I do not regret the ensuing relationship or the liver donation. Not one iota.

But I'm here in one of the world's gay meccas, might as well give the roulette wheel another spin. Out late the next night, I reach the broad plaza where Oxford and Flinders streets intersect. I notice revelers hurrying into clubs like high schoolers rushing to class after the bell rings. This is part of yet another drug-prevention ploy: the Sydney police have imposed an odd sort of curfew, prohibiting entry to any nightspot between the hours of two and five—though the establishments themselves remain open. *Another pointless gesture.* I head into Arq, a glitzy club hosting an underwear party on its upper level. The high-ceilinged dance floor is awash with laser lights and disco bulbs and crowded with fetching young men clad in 2$^{(x)}$ists or Calvins. Through the large glass revolving entry door I spot a cute guy trying to withdraw cash from an ATM. Playing it a bit coy, I chat with a straight couple nearby. Soon ATM boy floats over.

"Do you know if the machine's working?"

I know a good excuse to make conversation when I see it. His name's Guy and he's a carpenter by trade, quieter and hunkier than most of the gay boys I encounter. Dark brown hair, tight-fitting black satin singlet, and expensive blue denims—he may work in construction but he's still a homo. He spouts random, stream-of-consciousness sentences in something of a monotone, suggesting he's high.

"No I'm not," he says when I ask, but he wants to be. He takes my hand and leads me to Arq's outdoor space, a narrow corridor squeezed between two buildings. We approach a sketchy-looking fellow, pockmarked face and mess of facial hair. He sells Guy two Ecstasy tablets and me a couple more. I plan to conserve mine for the big party, but Guy pops his right away. Then he kisses me and agrees to come back to my hotel. Round two.

Our chunky black shoes thud on the blue-carpeted stairway. I enter the room, stick the keycard in its slot to activate the lights and air conditioning, then continue the proceedings. We're partway into our under-the-sheets activities when Guy stops me. More stream-of-consciousness conversation leads to a drug-fueled confessional.

"My father beat me until I was nineteen," he says, his eyes dry but on the verge of welling up. "Finally I got large enough and broke his ribs." On and on he rambles. *Oh boy.* I try to be empathetic but it's tough to deliver psychiatric insights to a hunky naked guy in my bed at four o'clock in the morning. Then, in mid sentence, Guy interrupts himself.

"I want more pills."

I don't—I'm set for the festivities in a couple of nights and have no desire to overdo things. Okay then, he says. He gets up, puts clothes back on his beefy frame, and bids me adieu.

The ferry dock at Circular Quay buzzes with activity. It's a glorious sunny afternoon, perfect for an outing to one of the city's many beaches. Last time I was here I took a languid bus trip to the clifftops of Bondi and Tamarama. This time it's a ferry to Manly, on the other side of Sydney Harbour in the northwest.

Although it's missing a grand anchor structure like San Francisco's Ferry Building, Sydney's waterborne transit network still puts its counterparts in harborfront North American cities to shame. Digital readouts indicate departures—dozens in a given hour. Boats glide in and out with the efficiency of Japanese trains. It makes sense: for a metropolis draped around the coves and inlets of a drowned river valley, this is a key facet of its public transportation network.

Our boat backs up and turns east, leaving behind the cluster of CBD skyscrapers and the Harbour Bridge. We come upon the Opera House, a structure whose iconic status is even grander in person: its curves and points must be witnessed in three dimensions for the full effect. Up close, the million-plus tiles that form its smooth contours of frilly white reveal themselves. The grit and imperfection of the actual building contrasts, sometimes jarringly, with its formal beauty. But the illusion persists. I maintain that this structure will be remembered as one of the greats in the history of human building.

Onboard are other distractions: two British gay guys named Paul seem friendly enough, and one of them—the better looking one, bronzed skin and brown eyes—seems to take an interest in me. Next to him are some females and a chatty straight boy—a fellow Canuck, I hear from his accent, also traveling the world solo. Then the strangest thing happens: the minute I start to speak to Canada boy—Kyle's his name—the Pauls turn icy.

I lose track of them as the ferry docks, and I wander around Manly for a spell. Perched on a narrow isthmus, it feels like my old Boston neighborhood crash-landed in beachfront New South Wales: four-story brick apartments surround verdant parks and tennis courts. Its main pedestrian drag, the Corso, has more of a beach town feel, surf shops and ice-cream parlors and eateries with my favorite Aussie snack food, barramundi fish & chips. Finally I reach the beach itself, where the gals are burying Kyle in the sand while the Pauls look on, aloof.

"It's Mardi Gras. I want a guy to kiss me!" Kyle exclaims. The British boys smile and do nothing, so I step up. I go easy on him: just a peck on the cheek. I stand up and turn around; maybe the Pauls are in a chattier mood now. I ask them what we're doing later and one replies with a voice that would freeze the sun.

"We're meeting *friends*."

Okay, maybe not. I still have no idea what I did to irk them so.

Parade day at last.

I must admit, Gay Pride events have long befuddled me, odd blend as they are of activist rally and hedonist hoedown. But the Sydney variant sets itself apart: the march runs after dark, allowing the city's drag queens—a stellar lot even before *The Adventures of Priscilla, Queen of the Desert* made them famous—to flaunt rampant, wildly illuminated outfits. It's still late afternoon when I arrive but the crowds are out, some decked out in attire to complement the parade. A bored-looking fellow, shirtless and in black angel wings, withdraws cash from an ATM while his impossibly slender friend in pink shorts dances and twirls to music from a nearby bar. His black T-shirt, cut off at the midriff, says it all: "PARTY PRINCESS."

I purchase a plastic stool for seven Aussie dollars—a wise investment to see over the throng—and park myself next to a crowd of backpackers seated on blankets. They're all straight, save for one: Koen, a tall, blonde, eighteen-year-old from Amsterdam.

"You deserve a medal!" I exclaim. He's the first bona fide gay backpacker I've encountered in all my travels.

Dark at last. The crowd is seven deep. Pre-show entertainers roam the street, though this ebullient throng needs no warming up. As the strains of Bob Sinclair's "World, Hold On" pump out over megawatts of loudspeakers, the parade's first contingent, Dykes on Bikes, roars past, a blur of lesbian leather and exhaust. The crowd goes bananas, the mass of human energy washing over me in a contact high.

After that it's the usual cavalcade of activist groups, radio stations, dancing boys…and Joan Rivers. The septuagenarian comic looks about the same as she did in my youth, when she was a dead-ringer for my manic-depressive seventh-grade biology teacher. Surrounded by men in pompadours, she delivers shtick out of a face spread tighter than a trampoline. But I can't stay for the whole act: it's time to primp and prime for the afterparty, the biggest gay dance shindig in the world at Fox Studios Australia.

An old fairgrounds turned movie studio turned shopping and entertainment complex, this venue hosts the gargantuan affair out of three different buildings. Walking through the expansive park, a middle-aged mom and her daughter—both a bit tipsy—begin chatting me up. Where are you from, how long are you here—usual questions. She's excited to hear I'm from Canada as her daughter's going to Banff to work. Then her mobile phone rings.

"I'm walking in with an adorable gay boy."

Hopefully one of the males this evening will think the same.

A mess of security at the entrance gates, where shirtless guys are checked—very cursorily, more to satisfy the authorities, I suspect—for contraband. I've already downed mine, though as the evening progresses I make a not-so-astonishing realization:

Nothing's happening.

I was never a hard-core user so "brain burnout" is an unlikely explanation. My regimen of antidepressants is a likelier cause, as is my supposition that the quality of this illicit substance has declined over the past few years. The party too, is anticlimactic: I dance and chat up a range of folks—and even have one cosmic encounter, running into a fellow with whom I'd had a fling at this very event six years before.

But surveying the crowd, dancing at all the different spots, it hits me: *I'm kind of over this scene.*

It's a rainy, moody afternoon as I walk down Oxford Street to meet Sarah one last time. She was out of town the past couple of days but her tween son—remarkably precocious—attended the parade with his father. Sarah's happily divorced, and somehow her range of life experiences and perspective makes her a wise confidante. Again I blurt out my life saga, which has been on my mind more of late. To her my angst comes as no surprise.

"You're barely a month from coming home. You're probably scared to death!"

No shit. I recount the misadventure with Guy the other night...and a realization hits me like a speeding locomotive.

That's it. That's the pattern.

How could I have missed it? I leap back through the years of bouncing from town to town, reliving the cycle of expectation and disappointment. At the center of every maelstrom lay a friend—or lover—in jeopardy. Not small-fry, last-picked-in-P.E. sort of jeopardy. I mean addiction, substance abuse, bipolar disorder, sexual mo-lestation...and, of course, liver disease, problem drinking, a downward spiral of self-destructive behavior. Many had trouble holding down employment, or else endlessly tried on careers, never sticking to one for very long. Next to them I seemed like the solid citizen, my own transient existence notwithstanding.

"You think you were trying to save them?" Sarah asks.

Is it that simple? It feels at once grander and subtler than Florence Nightingale Syndrome: it was never my intention to act as nursemaid. And in spite of hardships, these lost souls weren't *completely* lost: they functioned, lived their lives, stumbled and fell, but only to a point. And, to be fair, they were decent, decent folk; their many positive traits obscured the demons within. It was their decency, in fact, that drew me to them, comforted me during those transitions to places new and unfamiliar. I hoped, wished, yearned that by palliating their discomfort

I'd enable them to live up to their best traits, spur them to walk the path of their potential.

Okay, maybe a *little* Florence Nightingale.

"But, you know, you can't insist people do what you think they should," Sarah offers, "even if you go about giving them pieces of your anatomy."

Yeah. These grand gestures were for me always commingled with such great expectations. Steve may have spoken about spirituality and compassion but it was I who put myself on the line, physically and emotionally. I can't say I'll never do it again—that sounds so mean-spirited, like those Republicans back home complaining about their hard-earned tax dollars funding welfare queens. But my choices of lovers and friends will no doubt change. Actually, I think that's already underway: I consider the people I've met on this trip—or levelheaded Ryan back home—and see the sands beginning to shift.

I give Sarah a warm hug. *Oprah, meet your match.* "Come visit me soon," I say. "I'm not that far away." Just on the other end of that puddle called the Pacific.

I wander back through streets equally puddly. Over shopfront loudspeakers warble the mournful strains of Israel Kamakawiwo'ole's cover of "Somewhere Over the Rainbow." *Flow my tears, wind, rain, and song.* It's a baptism of sorts. A goodbye to a former lover, to a once-close friend, to all those old ties that ended in conflict and sorrow. Although I'm sure to encounter other lost souls in life's mean-derings—how can one not?—it is now I, eternal transient, world nomad, who has changed course.

The surroundings echo my mood. Paddington, if not Sydney overall, is a temple of the familiar: brightly painted rowhomes, trendy clothing boutiques, Thai noodle joints sitting stride secondhand bookshops. I feel the tendrils of home starting to reassert their grasp—and, for the first time, the feeling doesn't stifle.

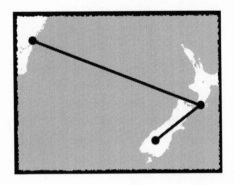

Adventures in Middle Earth
New Zealand

*E*motional breakthroughs notwithstanding, it's still not quite time to go home yet. A few more adventures await…perfect in a country where adventure's the thing.

New Zealand's status as backpacker haven doesn't hurt either: at Wellington's scrupulously tidy airport a kindly middle-aged woman changes my currency, gives me a preferred "backpacker rate," offers me a city map, even takes on bits of the maternal.

"Do you need a hostel for the night?"

Fortunately, I don't—Wellington's standard YHA hostel came highly recommended, and I'm already booked. After she points me in the direction of the airport bus ("much less expensive than a taxi"), I pass a row of brochures geared at the independent traveler. One of them reads "FLASHPACKER" on its face.

Like Little Orphan Annie, I think I'm gonna like it here.

The YHA is nicer than many hotels where I've stayed: a spotless private room with simple floral-print blanket; a view out the curtained window of the city's Art Deco fire station fronting a forested hillside dotted with homes. On the small Formica desk—I blink for a moment in disbelief—some chocolates lie nestled on a small tablecloth.

I *know* I'm gonna like it here.

I'm only in Wellington for the day before hopping on a tour of scenic hinterlands. Too bad: one afternoon is enough to catapult this capital city, population a diminutive 400,000, to near the top of my Favorite Cities list.

By the waterfront, next to the angular slate-gray hulk of the national Te Papa museum, kayakers row in deep blue waters. The city's compact core is a surprisingly bustling kaleidoscope of historic structures tucked beside modest high-rises. I pass an array of eateries, music shops, and bars where indie bands prep for evening performances. Restaurants of all stripes abound, including an I'm-not-sure-if-they-get-the-double-entendre Indian joint whose sign, in green-and-purple letters over a trumpeting elephant, reads "MONSOON POON."

Tucked away in a downtown alleyway is the Wellington Cable Car, a near-clone of its cousin in Hong Kong—though happily this one's mostly empty as it climbs smoothly to the city's Botanic Gardens and neighboring residential district of Kelburn.

A quick stroll around the gardens reveals gently sloping paved pathways, spiky bushes surrounding gnarled trees...and a couple of men in close-cropped hairdos loitering about, eyeing each other lasciviously. *Oh, this looks familiar.* I've stumbled onto the city's gay cruising spot. I'd stay—two of the guys look promising—but my urge to explore overrides my libido. I head out of the gardens and down the hill. I trot down quiet, winding streets lined with Victorians painted in subdued pastels, harbor views of blue commingled with trees of emerald green. It's glorious, an urban love child of Vancouver and San Francisco on the opposite fringe of the Pacific.

The hostel front desk insists I show up by seven for its shuttle ride to the ferry dock. It seems unreasonably early until I arrive in the lobby to find it crawling with more backpacker-laden folk than I've ever seen in one place. The school-bus-style shuttle is standing-room-only. One hunky blonde American, all agrotude and opaque sunglasses, mutters disdainfully to no one in particular, "Fucking *backpackers.*"

It's high season at the end of the New Zealand summer and the line for the ferry looks daunting. We shuffle up the weathered gangplank, the crowds fanning out inside the belly of the ship. This one evokes the vessel on which I crossed the Irish Sea many months ago, and the resemblance is more than skin deep: it used to do the run from Portsmouth to Cherbourg.

Cook Strait divides New Zealand's two islands, and, like other bodies of water in moody, temperate locales—the English Channel comes to mind—it has a reputation for chop. But not today, when the water bears little more than ripples, small waves transforming the glassy surface to a dull matte. As we pull away from Wellington a number of backpackers sprawl out on sofas and sleep, no doubt recovering from a night at bars I spotted the previous afternoon.

I'm glad I made it an early one, though, as this is one of the world's most splendid crossings. Upon reaching the South Island, the ship wends its way through the Marlborough Sounds. The lumbering craft feels too large for the narrow passage of lush, forested hills yet navigates turns with balletic grace. The scenery beside us unspools smoothly, like a movie reel.

We land in the harbor town of Picton, a small arc of white wooden buildings etched into green coastal hills. I'm set to board a bus to connect me with my semi-guided tour the next day…but not so fast: the bus leaving for Nelson, where my tour departs, is full. Just as I'm feeling I'll be stranded in the picturesque but relatively dead hamlet, the driver of my bus points to a rival company.

"Try theeym," he says in that Kiwi accent. Points for offering business to a rival. Sure enough, they're not full, and the driver on this other vehicle is the chatty, grandfatherly type we all imagine we had on school bus trips as children.

Picton to Nelson is only forty or so miles as the crow flies, but the ride is two hours long and dense with scenery: orchards of green stretch to mountainous horizons topped by skies of marching-band blue. We pass over mountains, where familiar-looking trees climb up and down in orderly rows, giant soldiers protecting the slopes.

"Theey're Douglas firs, brought from Ceenada." Apparently they thrive in the mild Kiwi climate, and these plantations can grow, log, and replant at a faster pace than in their native land. More Canadian transplants escaping the winter.

Nelson's a bit of a letdown. It's deserted in the midafternoon, though its cathedral offers an oddball respite: scaled down in magnitude due to World War II, the front spires were never finished and its bell tower is a skeletal hulk. It evokes that old *Star Trek* episode where an alien civilization incompletely resurrects the Wild West, parts of buildings and furnishings missing.

It's a quiet, cloudy morning as a large white bus, its side a blend of tinted windows and photographic adornments, rolls to a halt. The driver-cum-guide, Rick, has the laidback yet hardworking demeanor of a travel-industry insider, the sort of vibe that emanates from ski instructors and tennis coaches. On board, it's mostly youngsters again, which may seem surprising for a bus tour. Come to think of it, what am *I*, consummate indie-traveler, doing on one of these? Both the backpacking set and the high-tone crowd tend to mock guided bus travel, considered the purview of sheltered Midwestern Americans for whom Western Europe counts as exotic.

New Zealand, however, offers something different: three different bus lines target their offerings at backpackers, as I find out almost immediately from driver Rick on the PA.

"You need to leet me know your choice of hostel before the neext stop," he advises.

Here on the Magic Bus, it's all handled for you…though even here I buck the trend, having made my own accommodation arrangements. I'm not on this thing for the all-inclusive experience but rather to meet folks and make my way to the bottom of the South Island via its West Coast.

The morning's sleepy but in the afternoon things liven up: the road slices through the mountains past Buller Gorge, at some spots barely wide enough for our chunky black-and-white conveyance to fit. In one spot the sheer wall of a cliff is notched by the roadway, the rock arcing above and below the pavement, as if cut by a tube. Greenery parts to reveal the steel gray of the Tasman Sea. A small town's Main Street wraps itself around the bus windows: Westport, whose gaily painted flat-fronted Victorians seem too much like Santa Cruz or Placerville or Bodega Bay. The resemblance is more than skin deep: this part of New Zealand was once gold country, though unlike California, this West Coast remains mostly empty.

A thick, beefy blonde Scottish fellow, hair in a faux-hawk, plays cards on the bus with a couple of Danish girls. They're all doing round-the-world Gap Years. Beefcake, however, is doing it at the more customary stage than I: he's nineteen. The ladies are only a bit older. They all lay down their cards, however, once our driver reminds us to look out the window: it's a spectacular coastline of emerald green hills, rocky shorelines, and ocean water that glowers a pale blue within the overweening gray that reflects the moody skies.

"It's really a nice day," Rick says. "The Weest Coast geets up to 3,000 millimeters of rain every yeae," he adds. Some quick math to convert to familiar measures: 120 inches...ten *feet*. All those mountains squeeze it out of the sea like a wet cloth.

Jamie, the hunky blonde, seems to be hitting it off with the girls, but he chooses to accompany me on our next stop. "Don't want to look too eager," he says. We trundle down the shore to see "pancake rocks," so named for layers of erosion that have made the formations resemble a stack fresh off the griddle. The sea swirls in and out of rocky openings hundreds of feet below. At the bottom lie a pack of fur seals—like their brethren on my side of the Pacific, they're hopelessly adorable, living stuffed animals. Rick warns us they can be ornery, but there's little chance of that unless one of us wants to do a cannonball ten stories down.

I'm happy I evaded the "bus hostels"—the two or three establishments with ties to Magic, the operating company—as I arrive at Duke Backpackers in Greymouth, a stucco building ludicrously painted mauve with flourishes of orange and neon green. Inside, I'm greeted with a familiar accent: the guy who runs the joint is Israeli. Bronwyn, a husky Australian girl who was on my bus, also chose this spot.

"I wanted a private room for a change."

Me too...like, all the time. Meanwhile, activities beckon: a bunch of folks are going on a brewery tour—perhaps the only real attraction in this fairly drab industrial town. It's not my thing—I'm not much of a beer drinker—but it does include dinner. There's peer pressure too:

I'm teased mercilessly by some of my cohorts when they learn I visited Dublin and skipped the Guinness brewery.

Beer manufacturing is surprisingly complex: it involves yeast fermentation, malted barley—I had to ask what "malted" was—and a battery of heating and cooling processes. The ruddy middle-aged guide walks us through spotless silver vats and mechanical bottling lines before finishing off the tour—where else?—in a wood-lined tasting room. A stuffed deer's head on the wall completes the effect. I get buzzed on six taster-sized glasses while the Danish girls and a dark-haired Irish boy put away many more and chuckle: *lightweight*.

Shoulda stayed here, I muse the next morning while strolling around Hokitika, our first stop of the day. This little town's a funky beachside community, way cooler than Greymouth (though no brewery). Spindly sticks of driftwood are lashed together near the seafront to spell out the town's name, the Blair Witch developing a hankering for signage. Rick points out a snowcapped mountain, hazy in the distance: our destination for the afternoon.

But first, a filler stop, no doubt driven by commission to the bus line: a gold mining museum that looks as kitschy as it sounds. I choose to remain on the bus for the half-hour or so we're here…until, halfway in, my stomach has other plans. I hurry to the bathroom to take care of business and am almost done when I hear muffled horn honking. Everyone's back on board. The elderly lady who'd given others a tour points me to the bus.

"You almost got left behind."

As we head off I'm made to sing a song as penance. Clearly traveler's diarrhea is insufficient excuse for delaying our appointed rounds. *What is this, second grade?* Though a part of me is secretly—guiltily—gratified when other latecomers are made to suffer the same fate later in the day.

At last we arrive at our day's destination, one that's certainly not filler. We're given the whole afternoon to see it, though some choose to stay an extra day to do it greater justice. Looking up at the mountains, I see it: a river of ice pouring into a vast fold in the slope, a giant fall of water frozen in place. Franz Josef Glacier.

The usual reactions ensue: awed by its beauty, cowed by its magnificence...and for me, more than a little embarrassed.

I have no clue what a glacier is.

Some Canadian I am.

The orientation session at the hiking shop provides answers: a glacier is indeed a frozen counterpart to a waterfall, a flow of ice sliding down an incline at, well, glacial speed. Glaciers have gotten lots of attention of late as harbingers of global warming. Our orientator: "Glaciers don't actually 'retreat.' Ice can't travel uphill."

Of course. Instead, a glacier is kept in equilibrium by ice at the bottom, the moraine, melting at the same rate as the pour of fresh ice at the top. If the melt is accelerated by a warming climate, the glacier appears to be moving backward. Al Gore couldn't have said it better.

"I know, you've told me *three times* already."

The petite, athletic, dark-eyed brunette isn't talking about the briefing. Instead she's quibbling with the lady at the counter about the legality of a messenger bag—one strap—on the glacier hike. Her name's Naomi, same as one of my sisters, and she's Canadian too, with Israel in her lineage.

"I don't volunteer *that* information," she adds when I tell her about the acrobatics I had to pull to get to Dubai.

Our hike begins with a walk through a tunnel of greenery. Glaciers on New Zealand's West Coast terminate in temperate rainforest, rippling white set against fantastical green. We crunch toward the moraine, a rocky moonscape fronting a dirty fringe of ice. The patter of light drizzle augments the dull roar of lacy waterfalls on either side.

It's time to don crampons, spindly metal affairs that strap onto our shoes like old-style rollerskates—except these contraptions feature spiky metal protrusions on the bottom instead of polyurethane wheels. Our two guides—one a cheerful, darkly complected Chilean gal and the other a leathery, wiry, tough-looking New Zealand fellow—help us put them on. I think I have mine on right, until the tough guy swings by and thrusts a bony finger at my shoe.

"What're you doing!? You've got it too *loose*. You want to fall and break your eenkle?" he barks, then wanders off to ruin someone else's afternoon. Marietta, the Chilean, is more helpful, smilingly showing me how to tighten the straps. Bereft of agro intimidation I get it right immediately. I'm gratified when we're divided into two groups and I'm not in the one led by Grizzly Adams.

The glacier is stark and elemental. Marietta points out chasms and cracks of "blue ice," caused when the frozen substance is heavily compacted causing light to refract through it differently. Normally these are only visible to full-day hikers who head higher up the glacier, but this season's heavier-than-normal rainfall has opened up these fissures at lower elevations. I can't help but notice the vaginal resemblances. "Not like I'm an expert," I tell Naomi. Turns out she's more of one, having played around with girls in her past. She's also mentioned a boyfriend, so I have to ask.

"Are you bi?"

"No. I don't identify as that."

"Why not?"

"Too trendy," she replies. Ah, kids these days.

The town of Franz Josef is all of one block long but that doesn't stop it from seizing the crown previously held by Wellington and Moscow for Most Fabulous Hostel. This YHA's cheery orange double room comes with fridge, loveseat, and corner view of primordial forest. New Zealand was almost called Fernland; the bushes out my window may resemble palms but are in fact members of this oldest of plant species. The room is flooded with light even on this gloomy day. Downstairs, in a comfy lounge populated with plush sofas, a rocky fireplace, and relaxed backpackers, sleeps a fluffy, longhaired cat. I feel one should come standard-issue with every hostel.

There's a bar in town, appropriately named Blue Ice. I show up for pizza and drinks. Some bus-mates are out as well, including Rick the driver. I ask him where's home.

"Hee. Eeverywhee. The bus is where I live."

He's originally from a small town outside of Auckland, but right now he's a professional nomad, an owner-operator, a free agent. All his worldly possessions reside in that mobile cube of steel and glass, his bed only a bed for the night. I find this compelling: I've always assumed travel-industry operatives had a home base. But not this fellow. After we've all returned to our lives and our schooling and our work he'll still be out here, plying the back roads of the South Island, willfully, wantonly, and, as far as I can tell, happily homeless.

The next morning sees a slightly different blend of riders: behind me sit two teens from British Columbia. Hillary's a slightly shy, fair-haired girl-next-door type, and Joe, an even blonder round-faced boy wearing shorts and flip-flops on this chilly, rainy morning.

"I'm *miserable*," he complains in a lispy voice that makes my gaydar go three-alarm fire. I ask if they're together—they're not, though Joe claims a girlfriend back home. *Uh-huh.*

"Did you guys see the glacier?"

Joe rolls his eyes. "No. Ours are, like, way better."

As the day goes on they engage in noisy tomfoolery, making me grateful I charged up my iPod the night before. Unlike yesterday, today's a full day of driving. We turn away from the moody coast, soggy sponges of cloud hanging over green mountains, and head into the interior. We pass lacy Thunder Creek falls, tumbling ninety feet into a cobalt-colored river. Nearby lies a familiar-looking canyon.

"Where Frodo meets Gollum for the first time," Rick narrates, though he's never seen any of the *Lord of the Rings* films—and, to my consternation, neither have any of my seatmates. Passing a mossy, primordial tree, I can see why this country made a great Middle Earth: mostly empty (population four million or so, barely more than the metro area I grew up in) and geographically isolated, it has the feel of a Europe long gone; one almost expects mythical creatures to march out of the misty thicket. Instead, we witness a more modern but equally random arrival at our roadside eatery during lunch: out of the sky, a military helicopter touches down and hungry soldiers pour out, their dun-colored uniforms mingling with our colorful backpacker gear.

Another filler stop, this one on first glance the dumbest of all: Stuart Landsborough's Puzzling World. It's a brightly-colored kiddie-style mishmash of puzzles and brainteasers erected by the eponymous New Zealand businessman. And yet...the computer geek in me finds it compelling. Most interesting are a series of wall hangings chronicling Landsborough's forays into the world of skeptical inquiry: he's offered up a challenge to the self-described psychics out there to find artifacts hidden on the property whose location is known only to him. Five different psychics have tried and failed; to date no one has delivered the paranormal goods. New Zealanders may be the butt of jokes for country bumpkinry…but at least *their* theme parks aren't devoted to creationism with men riding dinosaurs in Edenic dioramas (one of these in fact exists in Kentucky).

The bus heads off to pick up travelers staying in nearby Wanaka, and when it returns it's chock-full, my seat is taken, and the compact travel umbrella I'd left on board is missing. The new crowd's a lot louder, a bunch of hard-partying thrill seekers readying for some serious bungee jumping. Loudest of all is John, a New York investment banker doing the same around-the-world thing I'm doing, though in typical Yankee fashion his stories seem bigger, bolder, wilder. Where I enjoyed an afternoon scootering in Goa, *he* drove a motorcycle all the way down the state and had a fling with a hot girl to boot. I'm not sure whether to be jealous or exasperated until he reveals more.

"A friend of mine said she'd house-sit my apartment. Two months ago my landlord called me. My friend was renting the place out by the night like a hotel."

He almost got thrown out and sued for breach of tenancy, and had to fly home for a week to remedy the situation. Then there's his story in Hong Kong.

"I left my backpack in the hostel and it got stolen. They took *everything*—even my passport."

Hmm. Suddenly staying in private rooms and playing things a bit safer isn't looking so bad.

We're almost at our destination for the day and many of us are yearning to be there already. But no such luck: we stop at the Kawarau River, a gorgeous swirl of blue slicing through a rocky, verdant canyon. But we're not here for the scenery. Instead, the girls-gone-wild Brits and their New Yorker pal squeal in anticipation at the steel truss bridge hanging over the river: the original A.J. Hackett bungee.

They say the idea came from South Pacific islanders hurling themselves off of trees tied to vines, but the whole thing just doesn't do it for me. Nor does the price tag: on the order of NZ$175 for a thirty-second thrill ride. But this doesn't faze one of the gals.

"If I see something crazy like this, I just *have* to do it!"

A number of us are ready to mutiny at the prospect of sitting here for hours, our destination fewer than ten miles away. I ask Rick how long we're going to be here.

"As long as people are jumping," he says, a bit irked. *This is how I make my living.*

Fortunately, the bungee fanatics have decided this 150-foot drop is too tame for them: they all book themselves onto a newer contraption further on involving a special trip out to a high wire 450 feet above a different river. I have just enough time to visit the bathroom—gents and ladies pictograms playfully inverted in bungee-jump pose—before we're off to my last New Zealand stop and the end of this bus tour.

Queenstown isn't the first spot on my world tour maligned for touristic excess. It's a resort town brimming with wallet-lightening activities: in addition to bungee jumping there's rafting, skydiving, jet-boating, scenic gondola rides up a nearby mountain, skiing in the winter, plus the usual gaggle of shopping and dining options in jewel-box-sized establishments. It evokes Colorado ski towns but with a broader clientele: I can't imagine uppity Aspenites welcoming back-packers with open arms.

The weak Kiwi dollar lets me stay in a bit more style: the Novotel offers a modern take on a rustic ski chalet, three stories backing onto a wooded glen near the lakefront. After settling in, I run into a couple of German ladies from my bus headed for dinner. We pass John, invest-ment banker guy, in his jogging gear. Without his coterie of wild ones he seems withdrawn, lost almost. As it gets dark we come upon a huge flightless bird turned to stone: it's a statue of a moa, one of many native New Zealand species hunted to extinction after the arrival of humans. Its smaller cousin, the kiwi, is the New Zealand national symbol.

"I thought it was the fruit," I say to the Germans. They laugh.

"No, those are from China!" Naming it kiwi was a marketing ploy.

Next morning by the lakefront town dock, a highlighter-yellow boat pulls up. A bunch of us climb into the craft—sleek, flat-bottomed, with carry-handle-style airfoil and big engines at the stern: a jetboat, one of several specially developed for navigating the shallow waters of New Zealand rivers at breakneck speed.

We zip along the lake, navigating a few shallow byways where trees angle out over the water forming a leafy tunnel. Then on to the river itself where our cheery boat captain shows off the boat's abilities: like teens of my youth doing doughnuts in a frozen parking lot, he spins the boat in a lurching 360-degree skid. It should be thrilling but for incipient motion sickness. Happily no one barfs. Not even me.

It's a two-activities combo, so after lunch back in town I don the life vest again for an aquatic adventure further up the Kawarau. To get there, I opt for the scenic route: my first-ever ride in a helicopter. As a boy crazy for flying machines (that is, before the days of weekly plane travel and multi-hour delays), I'd dreamed of riding in one of these—so much so that when one boy's father showed up in one during summer camp visiting day, I nearly wept in awe as the thing lifted off. At age twelve I was still blissfully unaware of the materialistic vulgarity of the spectacle: who brings a *helicopter* to summer camp?

It's only a seven-minute ride, but the swoops and turns through the narrow canyons make it feel a lot longer. So too does returning nausea: I'm a bit grateful as we touch down beside big green rafts piled high like bookshelves. Two beat-up military-style school buses pull up with the rest of the gang. As the rafts are hauled out, our guide gives us orientation instructions in a familiar—and decidedly non-Kiwi—accent.

"Don't worreh if you fall out of de raft."

He's a Quebecer too, giving me the first chance to practice my Canadian-accented lingo in some time. Our slangy French echoes off the canyon walls.

It's a spellbinding sight, foamy blue waters set against sheer knife-edged rock. As with all things natural in this country there are counterparts elsewhere, but none feel quite as gothic, primordial, elemental as here, forty-four degrees south of the Equator and a million miles from anywhere. The rapids are fun and the water is cool and fresh, but the scenery is the real star.

"Dey tried to drain de river to get to de gold," our guide explains. Queenstown's another former mining town turned tourist mecca. Apparently, there remains some gold in them thar hills.

"One couple, dey found a rock dat was worth $15,000."

I'm not sure if this is simply a good tall tale, but it does seem to sharpen everyone's gaze for a spell.

I get friendly with a couple of gals from L.A., and between them and my bus-mates there's no shortage of socializing to be had in this burg. But my mood is trending a bit differently—I'm a bit wiped out—so I give Ryan a try on Skype. New Zealand's proximity to the International Date Line means New Zealand is twenty-one hours ahead of California—but going the other way that's only three hours behind.

"One second," he says after answering, but I can hear his muffled voice.

"Can I have a grande iced coffee?"

I've grown keenly aware of his coffee-drinking habits as I always seem to catch him when he's at a Starbucks drive-thru.

"I went skiing," he says, when I tell him about Queenstown's wintertime claim to fame. One of his seemingly limitless pool of female friends helped him learn; in spite of a career as a professional swimmer he still insists, "I'm a klutz." His one line about the whole day heartens me, however.

"Karen said, 'You're just learning so you can go with *David.*'"

Only four weeks until I'm slated to go home, and the signs are promising. Less encouraging are a couple of e-mails from former employers: as of this moment, nobody's hiring; it's unlikely I'll have work upon my return. The occupational hazard of the long-term traveler.

It's an early morning as I meet Verena, one of my Germans from the night before, and board yet another bus for a daylong excursion to Milford Sound. Back on the West Coast, though further south than previous forays, it's a scant sixty or so miles as the crow flies but over four hours by road winding through rugged terrain.

Weather is one Heisenberg uncertainty: even for the West Coast Milford is unbelievably rainy—over 260 inches a year. As we leave Queenstown, some low-hanging puffs over the Remarkables—mountains that live up to the name—suggest what's to come. Or maybe not: as we head closer and closer, the skies clear. Our driver—another grandfatherly fellow, the chattiest I've had—points out a bit of geographic trivia.

"We just passed forty-five degrees south latitude."

Just like where I grew up. Though my hometown, at forty-five degrees north, was decidedly less remarkable. We roll through the Eglington Valley, a broad, grassy field abutted by mountains of coffee-tinted rock coated with evergreens. We then wait at the Homer Tunnel—slicing through the coastal mountains, it's not wide enough for vehicles in both directions—and emerge on the other side to hills that seem too steep for trees to flourish...but there they are anyway.

"The trees are attached to each other by their roots. That's how they grip the rock. Sometimes thee's so much rain you get a tree eevalanche."

Below us, Milford. It's actually a fjord, not a sound, and like its Norwegian kin it's monumental, steep, carved into the earth by glacial activity. And sunny. Brilliantly, brilliantly sunny. We board a pristine white vessel for a two-hour cruise along the Sound to the sea. The vistas are mind-blowing: featherlike waterfalls pour down blushing-green slopes. Five-thousand-foot peaks thrust out of the waters. In my movie mind's-eye I feel like Frodo heading to the Undying Lands—and happily find a fellow Tolkienist, Sjors from the Netherlands, *finally* the first person I've met out here who's seen the damn movies and can relate. He's a techie too, natch.

"People from Holland have trouble in job interviews in America," he says about career-hunting Stateside.

"Really?" I ask. They seem like such an easygoing lot.

"We're too modest. Even if we have all those degrees and credentials, we don't like to brag about them."

Unintentionally, Sjors reveals another clue in my psychic puzzle: *My damaged friends sure beat the alternative.*

It was true in my upwardly mobile community growing up and an order of magnitude more so in the bright lights of America's big cities: all those competitive, brash folk set my teeth on edge. While such personalities no doubt exist in other places, somehow the American imperium feels like their nexus. Alexis de Tocqueville, for the most part one of America's early boosters, termed it "the perpetual utterance of self-applause." My disdain for this trait saw me run far from it—too far—to the opposite extreme, to those beaten down by misfortune.

Meanwhile, back to splendor: for the trip back, we're offered an entrancing—and speedy—option: instead of the four-hour bus ride we can catch a prop-plane across the Sound, over the Southern Alps, and back to Queenstown in forty-five minutes. It's too good to pass up: our eight-seater buzzes skyward from Milford's airstrip and floats low between the verdant mountains, crayon-blue waters below. It's official: Cape Point, South Africa has just been bested on this trip for Greatest Scenic Wonder.

The next morning, a ride at the edge of town offers a picture-postcard denouement: from the summit of the Skyline Gondola peak, I see the town circling around the deep blue of Lake Wakatipu. The vintage steamer TSS Earnslaw chugs away for a lunchtime cruise while paragliders sail below on mountain updrafts. Distant shouts from a mountainside bungee echo in the air. The far-off roar of a jet holds more significance: my flight away from here is leaving soon, away from this country, this hemisphere, this Middle Earth.

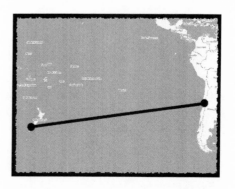

South American Way
Santiago & Valparaíso

O kay, now *I want to go home.*

In spite of all the personal breakthroughs—or perhaps because of them—I'm actually homesick for the first time in six months.

This sensation creeps into my brain as I board a long-tubed four-engine LAN Chile Airbus A340 for a flight across the Pacific. I've given myself a couple of weeks in South America as a coda to my journeys…though part of me is resistant, a kid after a long day at the fair being made to go on *one more ride.*

As rides go this one's the longest yet, across Earth's biggest ocean. The Pacific could swallow all the planet's landmasses and still have room for another Africa. One nice surprise: LAN catapults to the top of my economy-class airline ranking. Wide-screen TVs, friendly flight attendants, and surprisingly roomy, well-engineered seats. After eleven hours, much of it spent asleep, my seatmates open their window shades. The cabin floods with brilliant sunshine. Massive brown peaks hurry past the window—the Andes. I'm back in my native hemisphere once more. Thanks to the International Date Line, it's now midday on the same March date I left Oceania.

Santiago's as good a place as any to crash and recover: a safe, welcoming—if not especially interesting—capital city. Fast-food joints are omnipresent. So too is a clean and efficient metro and a visitor center around the corner from my little hotel; inside, a mustachioed fellow plies me in near-fluent English with info on how to get to

Valparaíso on the coast. Between the palm trees, the mild weather—this makes the fifth Mediterranean climate I've visited, every one on Earth—and the Spanish signs, it feels almost as much like home as did Sydney. About the only drawback is the gently rundown hotel, where my toilet detaches from the wall after a vigorous flushing.

Twelve hours of sleep cancels out jetlag, and the next day it's time to check out Santiago's offerings. Walking the streets of Providencia, it suddenly hits me.

I know fuck-all about South America.

Somehow this seems a greater sin than ignorance of glaciers.

First off, the mystery of this country's odd shape—thousands of miles in length, only a few dozen miles deep. Geography's the cause of that: the Andes, the ocean, and two deserts laid out these frontiers before the arrival of humans. As for history, Chile's is consistent with its South American brethren: *conquistadores* brutally wiping out the natives; independence from Spain in the nineteenth century; periodic wars with its neighbors. Sadly, though, Chile is best remembered in modern times for Augusto Pinochet, the brutal dictator from a generation ago. His secret police "disappeared" and tortured many, and artists took notice: both the 1987 Sting song "They Dance Alone"—big in my youth—and the play (and subsequent film) *Death and the Maiden* were based upon those times.

Less controversial was Pinochet's break with Latin American economic dysfunction: adopting free-market reforms of the Milton Friedman Chicago school granted Chile the distinction of being Latin America's wealthiest country in GDP per capita. This is apparent not only in upmarket Providencia where I'm staying but also in the city's downtown. There are dodgy spots, to be sure, but nothing like the *favelas* of Brazil or the slums of Perú. Crime too is negligible compared with, say, São Paolo or Caracas.

It's not an *entirely* forgettable city either: a rocky hillock, Cerro Santa Lucia, marks where the city was formed in 1541. It's now a handsomely landscaped park: tufts of bush, spiny cacti, and worn stone stairways that seem to lead nowhere. Nearby lies the Plaza de Armas—the gotta-have monumental central square for a Spanish colonial city, hugged by ornate European-style political and religious edifices evoking Madrid or Rome. Farther on is a concrete channel—

L.A. River-style—bearing the Rio Mapocho, muddy snowmelt from the mountains that surround the city. On clear days the huge peaks are easily visible—but like Pasadena or San Bernardino, Santiago isn't exactly known for its clear days.

Nevertheless, a sprawling city view feels right just about now: passing funky-painted homes in barrio Bellavista, I reach the funicular up Cerro San Cristóbal, which climbs the mountain over 1,000 feet above the sprawling city. It's an open-air conveyance with stairstep-like sections. I pick one that houses a youngish couple—a stocky blonde fellow and a darker-haired female holding hands—and, next to them, a heinously cute guy with styled, wavy hair, a Hurley shirt, and flip-flops out of which protrude perfect, pink feet.

Turns out they're Mormons from Salt Lake City. Joel came out here some time ago and ended up marrying a local; Paulina aids us with linguistic nuance. The tragically fetching boy is Joel's twenty-two-year-old friend, Doug, visiting from back home. He's gregarious and chatty and, as we reach the top, out of the more conservative couple's earshot, he lets me in on a secret.

"I'm a recovering heroin addict."

"Aha," I reply. "So does your family know?" This is, after all, a sect that doesn't even condone *coffee*.

"Yeah, they're cool."

His dad's a well-to-do businessman who was good enough to send him to rehab. He's recently kicked Methadone and says he's a bit out of sorts, though his easygoing manner and billion-watt smile belie that.

"Do you know where I can get some weed?" he asks. *Am I that obviously a pothead?* I laugh.

"I don't exactly have a hookup in Chile."

He goes on to regale me with stories of his gay drug dealer, who'd ply him with substances in the hope of a little something extra. *I wish.* But Doug doesn't swing that way—though he seems fine that I do. That generational shift again.

"So tell me," I ask, "does Salt Lake have a, uhm, big underground scene?" I try to frame it without coming out and asking *so how'd you score heroin in Mormon-land?*

"Oh totally." No surprise, that.

No party favors for us but the scenery offers compensation enough: killer views of the hazy skyline, a small stone church, and a sixty-foot statue of the Virgin Mary that distantly echoes the mammoth Christ the Redeemer in Rio de Janeiro. A gondola runs down the other side of the mountain, depositing us right back in Providencia where I started my day's wanderings. We emerge in a park filled with oddball contemporary sculptures—neon-blue clawlike shapes, concrete in the form of squared-off tree trunks—before I bid the Utah folks farewell.

That was weird. Not merely the incongruity of druggie Mormons in Chile, but the fact that even here I seem to attract the same element as who made up my friends and lovers back home: down-to-earth, sometimes well-to-do, always in some sort of jeopardy.

At least now I can see the signs.

There are those moments in long-distance travel when something familiar connects with the view out the window. In this case, Chilean wines, rapidly making a name for themselves along with the South African varietals I sampled all those months ago. My bus to the coast rolls past clumps of vineyards—tidy rows of green crops blossoming against rolling mountainscapes. As we descend toward the ocean another familiar sight floats into view: low-lying clouds, the "marine layer" as they call it back in Santa Monica. We pull into Valparaíso's humdrum old bus station—and almost immediately, a tout greets me.

"Do you need a taxi?"

Not again. Ignoring him, I proceed outside—only to discover that touting in these parts isn't like in Asia: the taxi driver outside quotes the same price, reasonable in either case.

As in SoCal, the marine layer burns off by midday as the taxi pulls up to the hilltop guesthouse where I'm staying. It's a simple white-washed old home with mustard-colored window frames and forest-green shutters.

A cheery "Welcome to Valparaíso!" from husband-and-wife inn-keepers as they unlock the gate and lead me upstairs. The high-ceilinged corner room overlooks the harbor where containers in all colors of the rainbow are loaded and unloaded via hulking blue cranes. Offshore lie a couple of gray military ships.

"You can take the *ascensore* to the downtown," my innkeeper says. In case I hadn't seen enough inclined railways already, Valpo (as the town is known) sports almost a dozen of them. They are, in fact, the city's original public transit system, almost a century old: the one running down Artileria, the hill on which my guesthouse is located, creaks its way down the mountain, pulled by tramway-style cables on an inclined track. An old turnstile inside a Victorian hilltop shed leads to the vehicle, a rusting metallic bit of canary yellow with an interior of rustic wood panels.

Valpo is slightly rundown and sometimes dangerous ("Don't walk around at night," I am advised), but wasn't always so: in the days before the Panama Canal it was a key port city in Atlantic-Pacific trade, the Singapore of the 1850s. Waves of immigration made it cosmopolitan. The downtown streets near the waterfront are lined with columned stone commercial structures, telltale signs of a Victorian-era power center. The city helped supply the California Gold Rush, and with its climate and hills it was once dubbed "Little San Francisco." Nowadays, an uptick in Chilean trade—hence the busy harbor and its containers—seems to be sparking a revival. I'm guessing it's only a matter of time before the forces of gentrification return. For now, however, the commingling of workaday port and micro-urban center gives it an authenticity sometimes lacking in the gentrified cities of the First World—Big San Francisco included.

It's my birthday. A herald that my thirties will be ending soon—though not just yet. It's a quiet, contemplative one, though in the Internet age no one is totally alone: both my e-mail and Facebook page are cluttered with wishes from folks far and near. I look up other people who've shared March 12 with me and two seem to fit: Liza Minnelli and Jack Kerouac.

One note comes as a surprise: it's from Steve, whose birthday is a scant week after mine. The year before we celebrated with a joint party; now that feels like a lifetime ago. The missive is polite and cordial, bearing none of the hostility of six months back. *He's reaching out.* I've been around long enough to read the temperature of a fight blowing over, where no one apologizes and things slowly return to normal, a movie running in reverse. But not this time. Not after my past six months of wander-soaked introspection. I respond politely, but in my head I know there's no going back. *I already said goodbye.*

Later in the day a different sort of message arrives, this one from my mother: my oldest nephew, Jackson, just turned seven—his birthday is a day before mine. That night, he was rushed to the hospital with pains in his side, and far younger than I endured his first surgery, an appendectomy. *Is he okay?* I toy with the notion of flying back early; such is my intensity of feeling for the little ones. Happily, no need: I reach my family on Skype to learn he's doing fine, the surgery was hitch-free, and like any seven-year-old he's far more fascinated with the hospital equipment in his room than he is in any pain.

On top of the funiculars, my train-obsessed nephews would appreciate this city's brand-new metro, running along the seafront to the neighboring town of Viña del Mar. Blessed with proper beaches, Viña has become the premiere Chilean holiday spot—though I find it to be a bland, high-rise sort of town, a Monaco to Valpo's Nice. Still, it offers its pleasures: at a balcony terrace eatery I order a burger and fries while listening to ABBA's "Chiquitita" playing over loudspeakers; later, I enjoy a stroll past the town's floral clock, then up a nearby hilltop of winding streets and incongruous mock-Tudor homes. An auburn Labrador retriever snoozes in the sun. I head back down the hill to the seafront, rocks, sand, and sighing waves. Six thousand miles to the west, I see myself from weeks ago staring back: Macau, Koh Phangan, Byron Bay, Manly. I now see the allure of the crumbly Pacific Rim, one reason why I chose to make it my home: the notion of living on a part of the Earth that's not fully baked, a place where so much seems possible.

I reach Castillo Wulff, one of Viña's seafront mansions literally perched halfway into the water. It's a bizarre combination of mock-Tudor on one end and stucco medieval castle on the other. This one comes courtesy of a Chilean industrialist—a transplant from Germany early in the twentieth century. It's being remodeled and, as I wander its walkways, a surveyor on a break says hello and offers some advice.

"Be careful in Valparaíso at night."

Okay, thanks. Never have a people been more mindful of a visitor's safety than the Chileans on my visit.

Fortunately, it's easy to abide and eat well at the same time: a stellar seafood restaurant sits perched on the hilltop in a gingerbread-blue Victorian, kitty-corner to my guesthouse. Overlooking the arc of city lights from Valpo's hills I order too much food—courtesy of a language barrier with the Spanish-only waiter—and then it hits me.

I'm not afraid to be alone anymore.

Okay, big surprise: I've been on my own for six months. But this is bigger than it sounds. On the one hand, headstrong folk like myself seem the paragon of rugged individualism: I've never had room-mates—not even on this trip; the longest I ever lived with a spouse was three months almost a decade ago. And yet…as far back as I can remember my mind has rung with a throbbing ache: *I don't have enough friends. I have nothing to do on a Saturday night.* Even if I had plenty of friends and loads to do any night of the week.

It's often said of gay men that they live a protracted adolescence to compensate for the loss of a real one: clubs, parties, drinking, drugs, sex…the sort of existence married couples fantasize about and profess to envy. Seldom discussed is that other adolescent hang-up: the need to feel included, in the club, part of the "A" crowd. I've seen this urge, this need, this desire expressed again and again in my contemporaries and peers…and in spite of my independent-minded ways have oft-fallen prey to this sentiment as well. I expressed it a bit differently than most: instead of a large circle, I devoted blazing intensity at just a few people. But as with any incandescence, burnout inevitably ensued. *Hopefully not again,* I muse, as I gaze out at Valpo's twinkle, alone at my table, a year older, and at peace.

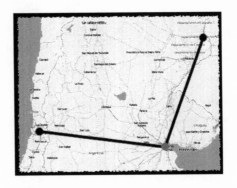

Porteños y Cataratas
Buenos Aires & Iguazú

I cross from Pacific to Atlantic, though the bombast that implies is diminished this side of the Equator: long and skinny, shaped like a rib-eye, South America is barely a third the width of its northern counterpart. My transcontinental flight lasts barely two hours.

Nevertheless, familiar tropes from home persist: the Palermo district of Buenos Aires on a Friday night has the feel of a bustling American northeastern city, cafés and discos filling up and nattily attired urbanites out and about. The weather matches too: Chile's dry Pacific lightness has been replaced by thicker warmth and humidity, Atlanta-like on an autumn's eve.

It's late when I arrive—I'm not quite sure how late since it's Daylight Saving Time switchover weekend, and the spring-ahead/fall-back rule applies to some South American countries and not to others; I almost need a spreadsheet to reconcile with opposite changes back home. But not now: *porteños*, as residents of Buenos Aires are known, fancy themselves European and start their evening when many back home are ending theirs. It's one o'clock: time for a party.

The city is also reputed to be the gay mecca of Latin America, though my first nightspot stop belies that: Bulnes Class is yet another glitzy gay lounge bar, walls spotlit in red and modern plushy chairs. But it's practically empty—even though this should be prime-time before the town's night owls skip off to dancier and prancier locales. What gives?

Maybe that trio of English-speaking guys can help: Greg's a tall blonde Australian with slightly weathered face and something of a cantankerous attitude. Tim and Sup ("like 'wassup,'" he says) are an Asian couple from Atlanta. Tim's the more Americanized one, with broad, square face and fluid voice honed by public speaking.

"I'm in politics," he explains. It sounds promising, until he delivers the next line.

"I work for a Republican."

Groan. He qualifies that local candidates in his neck of the woods offer a different political-spectrum pastiche than the national scene. Besides, they're both quite nice and kind of cute, so my attention is retained.

"This place is dead," Greg offers. *No shit, Sherlock.* He offers up another place to go. We hop in a cab and alight at Rheo, a dance venue with huge outdoor terrace. It's newly opened and hopping—*porteños* are a fickle lot, always on the hunt for the newest and freshest. Apparently, the previous spot was oh-so two years ago.

Greg snorts in disapproval. "It's *nothing* like Brazil." This in spite of the establishment's play-on-words name.

"How so?" I'd decided to skip Brazil on this trip, partly over concerns about crime in its biggest cities.

"Look at how they're dancing." I look, and it's a fairly typical spectacle of boys bopping and generally tying one on. So?

"If we were in Rio, they'd be grinding, sweaty, and half-naked. Half these guys'd be making out."

Okay, he's got a point: there's a bit of a high-school-dance feeling to this crowd. I'm not sure if it's just early, or if this says something about Buenos Aires mores and attitudes.

"So! You gonna hook up tonight?" asks Sup. He's a newbie to the scene; the question reminds me of something I would ask years ago. *Like it's that easy.* Right now the vibe I'm getting is a resounding *no.* As we walk around the terrace, clumps of Argentines gaze at us in apparent disdain. I think I even catch a couple snickering like schoolboys. Finally, I strike up a chat with a friendlier cluster who sport yet another blonde Australian—we seem to have lost ours. This Aussie offers an explanation.

"They really don't like Americans."

"But I'm Canadian!"

He smiles. "Like they can tell the difference."

Maybe he's right and maybe he isn't, but at least his chums seem to like me just fine. Most of the gang is from abroad: a bunch of French exchange students. Their token local, however, is the fairest one of all: square-jawed face, pale skin, jet-black eyes—and not a word of English. Oh, and he's nineteen.

I do a lot of listening, since my Spanish is weak and Mariano the Argentine is the least frisky of the bunch. The rest of the gang gets into a protracted exchange about the role of Muslims in France and Australia. Normally I'd care, but I've been up for as many hours as Mariano is young, and the drinks aren't helping. Finally, the gang offers to get some food. Mehdi, the most social of the bunch, gives me the signals: flirty talk, arm draped around my shoulders…but I get the sense his heart is set on the Argentine teen. A threesome isn't in the offing. The night ends late but strictly PG rated.

As I stroll around Palermo, one thing is clear: this city's an aesthetic treasure—though I knew that already from, of all things, the film version of the musical *Evita*. Within minutes of my bed & breakfast lie towering churches, rows of old stone townhomes hiding shyly behind spindly trees, and town squares bearing gelaterias and pizzerias. There's a reason for those: a hefty proportion of the city's immigrants were Italian.

The *subte*, the city's rumbling old subway, likewise gifts the place with a Grand Old City feel. It's not the cleanest—but then, neither is the city overall, dirtier than Rome but cleaner than Cairo—but it's extensive and efficient and drops me off outside a large white obelisk sitting smack in the middle of Plaza de la República. The Plaza is merely a small swelling of Avenida Nueve de Julio, an obscenely broad thoroughfare wide as a city block. It's one of many avenues in coup-prone Latin America named for a date of political transition—though I later learn this one's not so frivolous: Argentine independence in 1816.

One date deserves another. Nueve de Julio is bisected by Avenida de Mayo, Argentina's Pennsylvania Avenue, though comparisons with the Champs-Élysées might be more fitting: two unbroken lines of neoclassical and Art Nouveau structures, all pomp and gray stone and Paris-style mansard rooflines. A polished brass plaque on one building marks my first—though by no means my last—Evita sighting.

No, certainly not the last. At one end of Avenida de Mayo lies the Casa Rosada, "The Pink House," which like its white-hued counterpart in the U.S.A. houses the executive branch of government. I recognize it from the movie, the showstopper that immortalized the campy refrain, "Don't cry for me, Argentina." I wonder how reputedly uppity *porteños* feel about the Andrew Lloyd Webberization of their past.

Inside, I stumble upon a guided tour—though in Spanish only. Still, it affords a peek into white-columned courtyards filled with sun and palms running into elegant halls of white and gold leaf. If Argentines truly yearn to click their heels and pretend their country is part of the Old World, this place pulls it off.

It's not quite the same story on the other side of the avenue: a broad plaza fronts on Congreso de la Nacion, the Argentine legislative hub. An original cast of Rodin's "The Thinker" looks away broodingly from the white Beaux-Arts beast with the slender green-copper dome. Oh, the building is grand and appropriately imposing, but it's dirty and apparently has been vandalized repeatedly. We may protest our government back home, but nothing in the U.S. or Canada quite compares to the epic coups, failures, and revolutions of Latin America. I grow dizzy just reading my guidebook pages on it, trying to glean a little background.

I batter-up again on the socializing front, this time online. A couple of promising chats with one or two guys end with them disconnecting mid-convo. This isn't entirely unusual in Internet-land, but it's a bit brusquer than the reception I've had to date. An in-person night is called for, then. But first, more pragmatic matters.

A sprawling city ensconced between a great waterway—the Rio de la Plata—and the *pampas*—the verdant Argentine prairie—Buenos Aires is akin to Chicago transplanted to the Southern Hemisphere. It was the pampas that made Argentina one of the richest nations in the world early in the last century, a legacy that spawned Buenos Aires' elegant buildings and attitudey citizenry. One other feature of the city's prairie past is a penchant for carnivorous cooking; the place is positively crawling with *parilla*, eateries offering a range of grilled meats. This merits a try, so I walk a hefty part of the way across sprawling Palermo for one of these. The late dining thing is for real: it's 10:30 p.m. and every place is packed.

From here, on to the *real* meat market: Amerika, the city's biggest gay disco. It's a stunning, multilevel space with second-story dance floor walled in by soundproof glass. Whirling spotlights blast revelers with flashes of color. I start off dancing with one fetching fellow, wavy dark hair, midnight-blue V-neck—and again, doesn't speak a word of English. But his straight couple friends do; the woman, a slender type a bit like a young Sonia Braga, tries to hook us up but boyo isn't biting. I move on. Wandering up the stairs, someone tugs at my arm. It's Mariano, the cute nineteen-year-old from the night before.

"Oh, hi!" I exclaim, forgetting that his English approaches non-existent. His other gaggle of friends soon shows up, bringing with them another fetching local—older than nineteen, happily, and moderately bilingual. Now *he* seems to be flirting with me. We all move on to the dance floor, and since flirty boy is dancing next to me, I casually put my arms on his hips.

Wham! He slams them off with a flourish. Clearly not that kind of girl. He then moves away, dancing behind his other friends. You'd think I'd just spat on him. I've been rebuffed in the past, but not this way, not in a long time. Buenos Aires begins to carve out a new list-topper for this trip: Most Fabulous Place to Repeatedly Strike Out.

The sightseeing trail offers more distractions: south of downtown lies San Telmo, the original high-tone district before yellow fever outbreaks forced residents to higher ground up north. Like older parts of Paris untouched by Haussmann's boulevardization, San Telmo is old-school urban: narrow cobbled streets, red-brick sidewalks, restored ornate façades. Plaza Dorrego, its leafy central square, is quiet on this weekday afternoon—its busy time is on weekends. Numerous café umbrellas cast octagonal pools of shade. Sipping a latte out of a tall glass mug, I see my waiter angrily shooing away pigeons as he clears the remains of lunch from a neighboring table.

Back in Microcentro, the city's core, I happen upon Calle Florida, this city's entrant in the Pedestrian Malls of the World contest. It wouldn't win: it's dirty and downmarket, though some grandeur of yore persists: Gallerias Pacifico, this city's version of the Grand Arcaded Mall in the manner of Moscow's GUM or Sydney's QVB. The faux-frescos adorning the central dome, bearing pastoral and native *mestizo* scenes done up in Renaissance style, feel like yet another voice in this city crying out, "We're *European*, goddammit!"

Back toward the water lies the city moniker's *raison d'être:* the term *porteño* is a bit misleading since this town—unlike New York or San Francisco—didn't possess much of a natural harbor to begin with. It languished through much of Spanish colonial history as a result. Only later, in the nineteenth century, did engineering come to the rescue, dredging up a region fronting the Rio de la Plata to create Puerte Madero. The burgeoning demands of later years, however, rendered the place obsolete; as with London's Docklands or Montréal's Old Port, the district languished until urban renewal worked its magic. Now it's a yuppified paradise of sandblasted red-brick warehouses housing condos and shops; primary-color-painted old harbor cranes; and, completing the effect, a swooping cable-stayed pedestrian bridge courtesy of the master of architectural swoopdom, Santiago Calatrava. Another of the city's European bona fides: a similar structure was built by Calatrava in the early 1990s in Seville.

Lorena, one-half of a lesbian couple who runs the bed & breakfast where I'm staying, helps me with laundry logistics. She's the chattiest person I've met here outside the student Parisians from the other night. She hears my stories of nightlife adventures and laughs.

"*Si,*" she offers. "In Buenos Aires, they laugh at me too."

"Really?" I'd taken her for a local.

"Oh, no. Not from here," she replies. "From Mexico."

I finally luck out online: a waifish blonde, sparkles in his hair and a screen name "mysilverstar," offers to meet me the next day at—of all places—a Starbucks in a nearby mall. I show up at the appointed time—it's in Recoleta, the yet-more upscale district adjacent Palermo. I wait—ten, fifteen, twenty, thirty minutes…luckily I brought my netbook with me and the place offers free Wi-Fi. Sure enough, an e-mail from mysilverstar is waiting, telling me he had to go meet some designers for his school program as a fashion student. *Typical.* Well, at least he bothered to inform me, though I can't help but wonder if this is all part of a pattern.

So much for that. I sit in a nearby park and eat a sandwich, watched closely by a herd of errant cats. Then it's off to the Evita Museum, housed in a former women's shelter the former Spiritual Leader of the Nation placed here partly to annoy the neighboring gentry. Evita, Argentina's most famous fag-hag (yes, really) had a flair for the vindictive, and made every attempt to screw the middle classes—in Andrew Lloyd Webber parlance—who rejected her as an illegitimate child. The museum is more reverential, pointing out Evita's aid to the poor and her penchant for high fashion. It also serves as a reminder that, like most wealthy nations of a century ago—America and England included—"middle class" was shorthand for "only a handful of servants."

I still have some time for one final Evita landmark: her grave, part of the Duarte family's mausoleum in Recoleta Cemetery. This place is utterly unlike the grassy rows of headstones I think of when the word "cemetery" is uttered: it's a clutter of ornate above-ground structures, miniature versions of the townhomes and apartment blocks just outside its walls. Through the dirty glass doors of some of these lie coffins, stacked in rows like berths on a sleeper train. The Duarte family's edifice is well kept, however, and of course surrounded by flocks of visitors. Even in death this dame pulls in a crowd.

The words "bus" and "South America" don't sound like a great combination; I have visions of Kathleen Turner in *Romancing the Stone* riding a filthy clunker into the Colombian highlands, packed to the gills with chickens and old ladies before the vehicle tumbles into a ravine or is hijacked by *banditos*. Fortunately, I overlook the clichés and follow the advice of fellow travelers who tell me Argentine buses are among the finest in the world. In a continent with still-pricey airfares and weakly maintained rail links, buses fill the gap. I book a *super-cama*, a vehicle with airline-style sleeper seats, to get me to my next Argentine destination, Puerto Iguazú some 600 miles to the northeast.

A blend of Argentines young and old huddles around the double-decker green-and-white coach as dusk deepens over crowded Retiro station. Inside, it's as fab as promised: a thick plushy seat that reclines to virtually flat, an echo of my mileage-award flying of prior months. Tinny Latin pop gives way to a movie on the bus's overhead screens. A steward comes by with edible but unspectacular meals. A long, sleepy night and, by late morning the next day, arrival into Iguazú's small, sunny bus terminal.

A couple of taxis—my less-than-helpful hotel fails to point out a much cheaper bus service—land me on the doorstep of Iguazú National Park. It's relatively uncrowded in the subtropical noonday heat, and feels like the most fastidiously done-up heritage site to date: groomed paths, a tidy quadrangle of shops, a cutesy open-air train winding its way to the park's main attraction; later I learn it's almost faster to walk.

A meander down the *posada inferior*, the lower path, leads to a small cascade, but it's just a preview of what's to come: Iguazú Falls is the second-largest series of waterfalls in the world, and a lot more accessible than the largest, Victoria Falls on the Zambezi River between Zimbabwe and Zambia—is it me or did they just use up every "Z" in the Scrabble playbook? This one also straddles an international frontier: Brazil is on the other side and Paraguay is nearby.

"Breathtaking" is a word heinously overused, but here, as in a few other places on this trip, the shoe fits. The walking track winds past views of the cascades, scores of lacy white tendrils rushing over brown rocks infested with rich greenery. It feels familiar thanks to its cinematic bona fides: both the Indiana Jones and James Bond franchises have used it as a backdrop.

A short boat ride carries me to Isla San Martín, the island that divides the main cascades. Through a square-shaped opening in a large rock the falls peek through, perfectly framed. Back on the mainland, a wander through the paths brings me to a large grassy lawn. Tucked away at its end, hugging the jungle, is one of those low-rise tropical resort hotels from the 1970s. Its rooms are garlanded by balconies and look as if someone slid them into the building like dresser drawers. It evokes the age of heavy investment in Latin America a generation or two ago, one I remember from schoolboy texts.

A trio of young ladies chats with me on the short train trip back. They snort disapprovingly.

"This place is like Disneyland."

"Kind of ironic," I remark. "I didn't think they were too crazy about Americans." I recount tales of my Buenos Aires woes.

"Oh, yeah. You need to speak Spanish," one of them says, pointing to the Latina in the group who does. The few phrases gleaned from my iPod didn't cut it; we compare with Paris, where they claim to have endured a frosty reception. They weren't too fond of Buenos Aires either, though.

"Everybody kept saying it was so beautiful. Where?"

I offer them a few suggestions. There's the rub about travel: experiences are necessarily subjective. The potential exists for diametrically opposite experiences—even in the same place at the same time.

This gets me thinking about home and my now-I-want-to-go-back-now-I-don't seesaw of emotions: Argentina's arrogance toward its continental brethren evokes America's haughty disposition. Its largest city and capital is redolent with history and culture, the home of Borges and Guevara just as the de facto U.S. capital, New York, spawned the likes of Whitman and Gershwin. And while I revel in the grandeur of these lands and their achievements, I find the attitude of the citizenry sometimes hard to take.

Riding the bus back to town, I pass a sprawling complex with gangs of youths sitting by the crowded pool: the Iguazú hostel looks pretty fabulous. *Shoulda stayed there.* I got a good deal on my spot, though, and its pool is huge, empty, and home to a small cascade of its own under which to soak. But then, on checkout the next morning, a harangue about credit card hiccups—how is that *my* fault?—and about checking out late. Their checkout time is 10 a.m. I look at the clock hanging over the front desk: it reads 10:13.

Back at the park, the high-level *posada superior* offers suitable palliative: a long set of wooden paths straddle the tops of the falls. It all seems rather quiet but for the jet-engine-like roar coming from behind a stand of trees. A ruined catwalk creaks nearby, victim of hard rains a few years back. Finally I reach it. Iguazú's grand dame, the *garganta del diablo*, the Devil's Throat.

The other *cataratas* (waterfalls) are broad and scenic, but this one's a plume of liquid foam blasting down a narrow gorge. Ionized spray fills the air for hundreds of feet, perking up everyone like a triple espresso. Eleanor Roosevelt's comment upon encountering this monster seems apt: "Poor Niagara!"

This one merits an up-close-and-personal boat ride: down at the bottom, a chunky motorized raft ferries life-jacketed passengers into the heart of it all. *Espíritu santo* is the boat's name, the Holy Spirit. We ride closer, closer, closer to the cascades, then—*splash!*—we're soaked to the skin as we buzz underneath. Not the Garganta itself, fortunately.

In spite of these pick-me-ups, anxiety creeps in as I head away from the falls and consider what's ahead. Will Steve's unpredictable nature spark a reprise of hostility? Will Bradley find a way to hurt me some more? It shouldn't preoccupy me but sometimes it does; old habits die hard. I have hopes for something restarting with Ryan…but that too remains a wildcard; I haven't heard from him since New Zealand. To say nothing of more humdrum stuff, as I head home to unemployment in what many are calling the worst recession in modern memory. Just as I've never undertaken a journey like this before, I've also never come home from a journey like this before.

Clambering through the jungly trails I see a number of children giggle and point: a cluster of coati roam the path, cousins of the aard-vark and the raccoon in both lineage and appearance. Monkeys swing through the trees, again evading my attempts to snag a photo. And the falls, glimmering through the thicket, sigh reassuringly. Nature seems indifferent to our worries…or perhaps, with its intricate marvels, underscores that life has a penchant for working itself out.

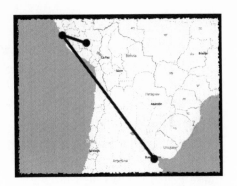

Old Mountain
Lima, Cusco & Machu Picchu

T he vagaries of geography make Perú my final stop, though its relative proximity to North America conceals a reality I'd never considered: the closer to the equator, the poorer the countries become. Colombia and Venezuela are particularly troubled, but Perú has its problems as well; Lima is no Buenos Aires. Stay in Miraflores, I was advised, an upscale beachfront suburb.

Not that I need much incentive to park myself in a beach town. Miraflores is also the city's gay district—though I'm also warned that Perú's gay scene is paltry compared with Argentina's. We'll see.

Lima's detractors were right: on arrival it's a sorry place, the first spot I see shantytowns since Cambodia.

"It's nice hotel," offers the driver as he drops me off at a diminutive yellow structure on a quiet side street. I'm hopeful, as it has the feel of many small, homey spots I've frequented on this journey. Then I'm shown the room—a dark, dank, moldy closet of a space for which I've paid a twenty percent premium for booking online—I later learn Perú is the first country in my travels where this is the norm. Maybe I'm just growing weary of all the months of vagabonding, but I actually find myself complaining to the front desk, the first time I've done so.

"Is it because no satellite TV?" They offer. *Oh, geez. They think I'm one of* those *people.* I haven't watched a lick of television in half a year. So, a first on this trip—and in my last country of call—I check myself out and roam the streets in search of new lodging.

Score another win for serendipity, because just down the road I find a glitzier high-rise hotel that's not full; they warmly offer me a rate not a whole lot higher than at the last place.

"Do you want to look at the room first?" they ask. *Sure.* This is the old-school way, the manner in which accommodation was secured in the days before TripAdvisor and Hostelworld. Though here there's hardly any need: it's a rockstar-ready room, with Jacuzzi tub, king bed, and floor-to-ceiling views of the ocean three blocks away. *Yes, please.* Interestingly, a subsequent browse through TripAdvisor shows this hotel, the Miraflores Colón, ranks significantly lower than my original booking. One man's treasure.

Miraflores is predictably a delight, a Latin Laguna Beach or Manly tucked away in another dramatic corner of the Pacific. Parched brown cliffs rise 200 feet above the water and adjacent coastal highway; blue and white Victorian structures straddle a rocky pier; perched on a clifftop is an outdoor mall, Larcomar, flashy but predictable with an array of American chain restaurants. There's no escape.

The grassy park overlooking the cliffs is better. Mosaic-tiled balustrades of salmon, white and blue curl around the precipice surrounding the sculpture that gives Parque del Amor its name: a cartoonishly modern depiction of a couple lying in passionate embrace. Decidedly Latin in flavor; I begin conjuring the protests that would no doubt accompany it if it were ever unveiled in a public park Stateside.

"You must try *chifa*," says my amiable hotel concierge when I ask about places to eat.

Chinese food isn't something I associate with Perú, but apparently the country has its own locally infused variant. I'm directed to an eatery down the street, and sure enough, it's a savory blend of local spices and ingredients infusing Chinese favorites such as won tons and glass noodles. Most of humanity's agricultural staples come from Eurasia, but of those that stem from the Western Hemisphere, a disproportionate number come from Perú.

I return sated to find my online profile brimming with messages from some earlier missives I sent out; looks like Lima boys are a lot more approachable than Argentines. I set a tentative meetup with the cutest one, a day-spa worker named Jhonattan, for tomorrow night.

"Fanny Lú," the hotel staff says when I ask who that pop singer is dancing her way through a catchy tune on the breakfast room's TV. "Like Christina Aguilera." Indeed, Fanny's got the slender build, blonde hair, and pop-sultriness. "Tú No Eres para Mí," becomes my anthem of this place, even though Fanny's Colombian. Close enough.

"Talk to him, he'll take you," says the doorman, motioning to a nearby cabdriver. The fare seems reasonable and he's mine for the afternoon for a roundtrip to Lima's downtown—the city's historic sights are concentrated in the old center. Most of the neighborhoods between Miraflores and downtown are a shambles. It's unfortunate: once this was the capital of colonial Spain when Buenos Aires was but a village.

The city's Historic Center remains impressive. At its heart is yet another Plaza de Armas, a quadrangle of pastel-yellow colonial buildings bearing ornately carved wooden-enclosed balconies. I feel a twinge: here's one bit of South American history I know well, care of a careful reading of UCLA professor Jared Diamond's *Guns, Germs & Steel*. Spanish *conquistador* Francisco Pizarro took down the Inca empire with a handful of soldiers care of the eponymous arsenal. A few years later, he founded the new Peruvian capital on this spot. It may seem like a banal plaza of touristic horse-and-buggy rides and stately monuments, but the chill of brutal conquest reverberates.

Pizarro's other grand creation, the thoroughfare of Jirón de la Unión, has gone the way of many a historic narrow street: yup, yet another pedestrian mall. Its colorful buildings now hawk equally chromatic bits of latter-day commerce. Perhaps it's fitting: the *conquistadores* were, after all, in it for the buck.

Why Miraflores has a park named after John F. Kennedy—complete with commemorative bust—is beyond me, but it's one of the more pleasant spots to people watch and eat *ceviche*—another Peruvian specialty—at a sidewalk café. It's a perfect afternoon: a heavenly plate of brine-soaked calamari, an Israeli couple burbling amiably behind me, children running and playing in the playground across the street, locals and tourists rummaging through goods at the weekly flea market, the sun slowly turning orange in the west. I finish my meal, then chase the solar orb to the seafront at Parque del Amor, where it sinks into the sea and paints the sky purple and blue and orange and red against silhouettes of bushy palms and whitewashed stucco homes. A perfect beach-town end of day.

It's time to meet Jhonattan and his friends, who've invited me for a birthday celebration at a local Miraflores pub. I wait for him with that familiar trepidation, and...

He's cute. Lean, angular face, high cheekbones, and soft, flowing hair. Something of a Latin American Shaun White, a vaguely dorky look I dig. He's nice too, with a welcoming coterie of friends all hailing from Piura, a beach town up north. We head to a nearby Brazilian bar where some provocative ladies dance us up. A few drinks, then around the corner to Downtown, Lima's gay disco.

"Who tells you Lima has no gay nightlife?" he says.

He's right: this place is no different than in any other big gay city, for better or worse. I feel it's for better as we get to dancing and begin to move closer and closer.

"You're hot," he whispers in my ear. We start making out. We close down the place with his friends, then he comes back with me for a stellar night in the rockstar room, my first and likely last hookup in South America. I couldn't imagine a nicer fellow to share it with. Take that, *porteños*.

This elicits a realization: I've never been as successful meeting guys in gay mega-centers—the New Yorks, the Londons, the Buenos Aires. I've always been luckiest in the "tier two" locales—the Dublins, the Cape Towns, the Singapores, the Limas. Logical, perhaps: I grew up in a such a town; even now, with many thousands of miles under my belt, the tween-sized places still feel right.

The Inca came from the mountains. Cusco, their capital, lies scrunched between bare, crinkly peaks at 11,000 feet. Although I come ready with altitude-sickness pills, I'm not sure if they make things better or worse: no headaches or dizziness, but on arrival I feel woozy, spaced-out. And zero stamina: stepping off the bus at the main town square, I hike up the hilly street to my hostel. It's steep, with staircase-style sidewalks, but nothing beyond the abilities of a San Franciscan who's spent the last six months hauling a backpack. Nevertheless, after barely a hundred yards I'm panting like I've run a marathon. The pair of sofas just inside the hostel entryway make for a perfect place to collapse. I'm guessing that's what they're for.

The Loki Hostel doesn't quite snatch the award for nicest budget accommodations from those in New Zealand, but it wins hands-down for setting: a 450-year-old courtyard building, Inca-style stone base, heavy plastered walls, red-tiled roof. It's intimate and local-feeling, though like many such spots all over the world it's run by foreigners, former backpackers who fell in love with the Peruvian highlands. Such is the mixed blessing of travel: it brings tourist dollars, but all too often the beneficiaries are others from abroad, enterprising folk with just as keen a sense of backpacker needs as Starwood and Hilton have of their better-heeled clientele.

To wit: a weekly dinner of roast beef. Waiting in line for it I encounter my second-ever gay backpacker to date, a twenty-six-year-old attorney from Sydney fleeing his life. *Sounds familiar.*

"It all got so catty, me and my friends. We'd get together every weekend and put people down. All 'girl' this and 'bitch' that."

We park ourselves at a table with a newfound friend of his, a gal with dark, stringy hair, Ashley from New York. Julian aims to move to the Big Apple, so the pair have become inseparable following a recent river-rafting trip.

"We're a rare breed, us gay backpackers," I offer. This provokes a scowl from New York.

"I don't know *what* you're talking about. There's a guy here who's always on Manhunt," Ashley snaps, referring to the gay hookup site.

Alrighty then. We go on to compare travel tales…and, inevitably, travel romances. Julian's taking a break from all that in his time away. Ashley's had none. *What a surprise.* I recount mine.

"Wow, aren't *you* focused on age," she says, noting that I often include a guy's age in my stories and, yes, they're mostly younger than me.

"It's my curse," I joke. "I'm not fixated on the number—it's just what I end up finding." I motion to my face with a comic flourish, "Might as well while I can still get away with it." Rumor has it I don't look my age.

"What makes you say *that*," Julian retorts—then immediately apologizes. "See," he says, "that's what I'd say if my Sydney mates were around."

I want to tell him he's replaced one set of bitches with another. As the conversation continues, Ashley proceeds to pick apart everything I say, ruthless dissection on our dinner table.

Later I lie awake in bed. *Another American I can't stand.* It's the flipside to all that salesy self-applause: the intimidating, combative know-it-all. It's that TV-producer fellow in Goa all over again. *Now I don't want to go home.* I recall my conversation with Sjors, the Dutch fellow, on that boat ride back in New Zealand. One point he made especially stuck: we see the flaws of our own country more deeply than do outsiders. Our own dirty laundry sets us off the most. Indeed, I find my homeland's stereotypes echo loudly overseas—more loudly, it seems, than those of other places. Perhaps this is part of travel's purpose: to grant an astronaut-like perspective on your origin point, see it reflected back from a distance.

Only now I'm not liking the view, and Earth's getting mighty close in the window.

Altitude wooziness eases the next morning and I set out on explorations. Skies have cleared to crystalline high-elevation blue. At the bottom of the hilly street sits an old woman wearing a white stovepipe hat and blue overcoat, surrounded by piles of clothing. The main town square, filled as only a tourist town can be with moneychangers and

Internet cafés, is—yes—also a Plaza de Armas. But this one's a bit different: it saw life before the Spaniards, an Inca gathering place going back nine centuries. It's fronted by Spanish colonial structures—more glorious enclosed wooden balconies—but side streets offer a blend of the two civilizations: the Spaniards built atop the Inca ruins, those ancient foundations of carefully fitted stones. A crowd of tourists huddles around a guide who points out the intricacies of a famous one, a massive twelve-sided slab. Where the Romans and Egyptians made blocks of equal size, the Inca molded existing shapes to fit into each other, the world's largest jigsaw puzzle.

The touristic vibe is not oppressive: an Irish pub bills itself as the highest on the planet at 11,156 feet. A small girl in sandals and patterned red poncho poses with her alpaca. Street vendors hawk their wares, but gently, gently. For me, that's a more inviting environment in which to shop than prior experiences in haggle-land, and given that this country is my last stop, I begin loading up on gifts for my nieces and nephews. For the first time on this journey, my luggage begins to grow.

"Rio's not any worse than Cape Town," says a British teen at dinner back at the hostel. "You just need to keep your wits."

That settles it: I should have done Brazil. I don't regret having gone where I did, but these high schoolers' stories of samba and all-night parties sound appealing. The one offering this advice is South African by birth, with he and his three mates doing the gap-year thing from London. After the previous night's display of Yankee combativeness, this company is refreshing.

"Byron Bay's great," I tell them when I hear their Australia plans. "And be sure to make a stop in Nimbin." They're headed the other way than I, just starting their journey. Now *this* is why I like hanging with the young: at its best, their optimism is infectious. Plus after months of soliciting info from others, it's nice to pay it forward.

The Inca Railway runs from just outside Cusco to Agues Calientes. As in New Zealand, sixty miles as the crow flies translates into a three-plus-hour journey, in this case winding through the Andean highlands.

There are three classes of train: the no-frills Backpacker, the somewhat-pricier Vistadome with windows carved into the ceiling, and the super-luxurious Hiram Bingham at $300-plus each way. Option two strikes my fancy and budget, and it proves a good choice: crisp blue train cars with plushy gray seats and tablecloths. The crowd is older than the hostel gang. A thirtysomething woman and her parents enter, prattling away in Spanish. They introduce themselves: Americans from Mexico originally, now living in L.A. Gloria sits next to me and whispers a confession.

"I love my parents, but they're driving me *crazy*."

The scenery offers distractions as the early-morning rain clears: mountains shrouded in mist, more green than brown, moisture-laden now at the end of the rainy season. Although the Inca highlands are thousands of feet above sea level—same as the Colorado Rockies or the Swiss Alps—the equatorial latitude gifts this place with a mild, if soggy, climate. We pass the starting point of the Inca Trail at Ollantaytambo. From here, it's a four-day hike to Machu Picchu for the hardy, which we are not. We stay on the train until Aguas Calientes, where buses ply the thousand-foot switchback to the ultimate mountaintop aerie.

No one is quite sure of the purpose for Machu Picchu—Quechua for "old mountain." It wasn't the Inca capital—Cusco had that distinction. But a site so striking, so intricately built, must have been important. The *conquistadores* never found it; abandoned by the collapsing empire after the Spanish arrived, it lay forgotten, known only to local farmers until a modern-day Indiana Jones, a Yale professor named Hiram Bingham—hence the train—rediscovered it in 1911. Now it's on the front cover of seemingly every Perú guidebook, mine included. And yet…as with countless other well-visited spots on my journey, this one, my last, is popular for good reason.

I don't mind the crowds: they're no different than in any urban space, and Machu Picchu, for all its lonely isolation and jaw-dropping vistas, was once a city. Passing from guided group to guided group, I glean bits of info like a kid with ADD flipping channels.

"Why did the Inca live in the mountains, so high up, so far away? Because of the soil," one guide explains. "Rich, black, and volcanic. Anything will grow in it."

Another, at the *Templo de las tres ventanas*: "What are the three windows for?" he asks a group of bored middle-aged tourists, fanny packs and chunky cameras at the ready. "In the winter solstice, the sun enters these exactly." He reminds us that winter solstice here is in June.

Terraces, terraces, and more terraces. It may have been a smallish settlement—only a few thousands souls, a fraction of Angkor or even Petra—but hierarchy persisted: agriculture at the lowest level, on the smooth grassy terraces; smallish houses of rough-hewn stone on one side; and more elegant homes—now merely stone outlines—dramatically overlooking the sheer cliffs. The Inca knew good real estate when they saw it.

Back in Aguas Calientes, the power's gone out: a mudslide outside town is the cause. Apparently, this happens a lot. It doesn't hamper my appreciation for my cute little inn, however; my room fronts the Urubamba River, its roar the ultimate white noise. There's a faint smell in the air—I begin to worry, until looking around I discover it's the aroma of fresh flowers on the nightstand. *Nice touch.*

Emerging for a bit of dinner, I bump into a middle-aged fellow in a bathrobe exiting an adjacent room. His face is as white as the foamy river outside.

"Be careful what you eat," he says. "I'm barely hanging on."

"What happened?"

The hotel breakfast, he suspects. I figure now's probably not the time to begin grilling him on his water-drinking habits, though I've been playing it safe with that here as I did in India and Thailand.

"It's these crappy little tourist towns," he adds. "Most people are only here for a night, so they don't care what's in your food."

So much for seeking out culinary adventure. I was almost ready to brave it and try *cuy*, a Peruvian dish of roasted guinea pig. Instead, I play it safe, heading to one of the more upscale spots in town and ordering spaghetti Bolognese. The place is busy, typically a good sign. I've gone seven months without food-borne illness and I'm determined to keep it that way for two more nights.

A band starts to play a familiar tune: it's maybe the dozenth time in Perú I've heard the melody for the Simon & Garfunkel song "I'd Rather Be a Hammer Than a Nail." A small group from Arkansas laughs when I ask about it.

"It's a traditional Peruvian melody, El Cóndor Pasa."
Okay, *now* who's the dumb American?

These "national patrimony" spots are all the same: a small tourist-centered town adjacent the national park, and one—but only one—exclusive hotel right at the site itself. The Sanctuary Lodge has a fabulous terrace where I figure breakfast will be safe. Plus, it's aswarm with friendly college students, also from Arkansas—Harding University, to be exact.

"We're on an exchange program in Viña del Mar," says one of them. Weston's a computer science student and a *Lord of the Rings* fan, so we instantly have far too much to talk about.

"I've never seen mountains this sheer," he remarks. I agree: they give their counterparts in New Zealand a run for their money. They could have filmed the fantasy epic here.

"So are you hiking Wayna Picchu?" they ask.

"Uhm…sure, why not?" I'm game.

Turns out it's not so easy: the peak is on the far end of the complex and affords yet-more heartstopping views…but it's navigable only via a narrow path and is limited to 400 people per day.

"We got here at five in the morning to get tickets."

So that's out. The Harding boys—and one girl—suggest I try the Sun Gate, a more leisurely climb in the other direction. I walk with them a ways, basking in the aura of the warmest, friendliest Americans so far. A little investigation later on reveals that Harding's a Christian college—for once, these kids offer a positive representation of that ideal. *It's an omen*, I decide. I instantly feel better about going home, and it comes not a moment too soon: today's my last day abroad.

I pass the Temple of the Sun, the central sacred space for the Inca. They believed their emperor was a deity, literally descended from the solar orb. The temple is the only structure with rounded walls, its stones engineered to be earthquake-resistant and hewn as smooth as modern-day brick. Nearby, another masterful feat of Inca engineering: a cascading series of fountains, their water emanating from a mountain spring for which the Inca built an aqueduct. Another tour guide: "The fountains were made exactly the same size as the Inca water jugs."

Passing grazing alpaca I head upward toward Intipunku, the Sun Gate, entryway to this complex from the Inca Trail. Colorful floral bushes protrude onto the path. The guitar licks of "All Along the Watchtower" wail on my iPod in a true movie moment: the approach to the Sun Gate is punctuated by a guard post. Down in the valley 1,000 feet below a blue strand of railcars winds into Aguas Calientes. Journey's end.

It's after dark by the time I arrive back in Cusco. My altitude sickness is vanquished—I climb the hill to Loki Hostel like a champ. None of my previous dinner-mates are around so I wander into town for a final meal. In Plaza de Armas, the buildings are brilliantly lit in golden phosphorescence. Reminds me of another town square, in Bruges, my first stop in Europe, seven months and 60,000 miles ago.

I did it. I've drunk deep from the well of the traveling life; it feels as second nature to me now as commuting to a software-coding job once did. The world and its multifaceted people have offered answers and solace, a grander perspective on things that all those hurly-burly years of career, love, life, and pain never quite could.

I'm ready to go home. For real this time.

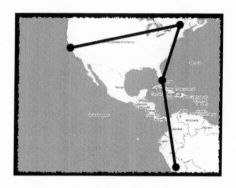

Home
Miami & Montréal

"I t's over," I say to Julian, the gay Sydney attorney, whom I spot just as I'm getting into a taxi on a sunny Cusco morning. He bids me a farewell that feels almost mournful: he would have been an interesting guy to know unsullied by his dour compatriot. Such is the way of travel: all those ships passing in the night sometimes miss each other.

From Cusco to Lima and northward. It's a full day of plane rides, yet even on the ground in Perú I feel North America drawing closer: TACA, the Central American airline that brings me Stateside, bears familiar Caribbean destinations on its route map along with a smattering of U.S. gateways.

Finally, after midnight, landing in Miami. My first time using my U.S. passport to re-enter my adopted homeland. The immigration official flips, flips, flips through the stamp-cluttered pages, but asks few questions and soon sends me on my way. I pick up a rental car and drive to a small motel in Surfside—it's Winter Music Conference, and finding midrange lodging was tricky. Inside the small, carpeted lobby a baritone African-American gentleman hands me my key. ESPN is on the tube behind. It's two-thirty in the morning and I feel like Rip Van Winkle.

I rouse my old life from its slumber over the next two days. I reactivate my mobile phone account. I sample a latte from Starbucks. I arrange for return of my storage container back home. I feast on French toast on Ocean Drive. I buy one or two final kiddie gifts at

Toys R Us. Ryan calls me on my mobile—the first time he's been able to do that since September.

"I've got a swim meet in San Francisco on Saturday," he says. We make plans to meet up as it's two days after I arrive. *That's a good sign.* I order pizza and catch *Real Time with Bill Maher* on HBO and have no idea what his guests are talking about: Goldman Sachs bailout? The Octomom?

It's springtime in Eastern Canada: the snow's mostly gone but the chill lingers. The home my sister Naomi and her husband Jon were in the process of acquiring is now theirs. I'm familiar with talk of floor finishes and bathroom tiles, but right now it feels alien, another life.

So too the sprouting of the children: my oldest nephew has short hair; his younger brother speaks in rambling paragraphs; the littlest one, not even two, now walks and talks. I put together a video for them of all the trains and beasts I've ridden. It runs almost two hours but they watch it all and still want more. Uncle David just got more interesting.

Just then my phone rings. The area code's familiar but the number isn't.

"Hi David. It's Bradley."

Whoa.

He's made the move with his parents into central Boston—hence the new number. His voice quavers slightly—this call is no doubt just as big for him as it is for me—but it's congenial. He's doing well, seeing another new guy (hearing *that* bit of info rankles me some), and has even begun training to run a marathon down in Florida, a feat he'd tried and failed before getting sick.

But the biggest surprise is what he says next.

"It's been three years since the surgery. Happy anniversary!"

Shit, I forgot. I'm not sure if my lapse is simply a byproduct of being otherwise preoccupied, or if it signifies something deeper about moving on. We end the call on a cordial note. Although our lives have diverged, it feels like Bradley and I are back in respectful balance. For now, that seems enough.

Final flights home. The Red Hot Chili Peppers song "Californication" plays on my iPod; amber digital lettering above my departure gate reads "SAN FRANCISCO." On the most humdrum of levels, the trip was a breeze: never lost my luggage or got robbed; never got food poisoning. But no shortage of adventures and insights nonetheless. This is the truest expression of globalization, world travel, practiced not by corporations but by inveterately curious people.

But it's the inner journey, the real reason we go, one whose dimensions may not yet seem apparent on return. For my part, maybe, just maybe, this experience will spur me to seek connections stabler and longer-lasting than those before. Just maybe I'll find a job again soon. Just maybe, having exorcised the wanderlust bug, used it to understand myself, my roots, my yearnings, I'll stay for longer in one place; settle in, give it a chance, allow disappointment and frustration to boil off. Just maybe now I'll express nomadism not through angry rootlessness and transience, but through further growthful journeys to places faraway and wondrous.

Just maybe.

Made in the USA
Lexington, KY
11 July 2010